The Prodigal Daughter

The Prodigal Daughter

A Biography of Sherwood Bonner

Hubert Horton McAlexander
With a New Introduction

The University of Tennessee Press / Knoxville

Originally published by
Louisiana University Press in 1981.

The paper in this book meets
the minimum requirements of
ANSI/NISO A39.48–1992 (R 1997)
(Permanence of Paper).
The binding materials have been
chosen for strength and durability.
Frontispiece courtesy of Bessie Craft Driver.

LIBRARY OF CONGRESS CATALOGING-IN-PUBLICATION DATA

McAlexander, Hubert Horton.
  The prodigal daughter : a biography of Sherwood Bonner / Hubert
Horton McAlexander. — Paperback ed.
        p. cm.
Originally published: Baton Rouge : Louisiana State University Press, c1981.
  "The works of Katharine Sherwood Bonner McDowell": p.
  Includes index.
  ISBN 1-57233-049-X (alk. paper)
  1. McDowell, Katherine Sherwood Bonner, 1849–1883. 2. Women and
literature—Southern States—History—19th century.—3. Women
authors, American—19th century—Biography. [   ] I. Title.
PS2358 .M37 1999
813'.4—dc21
[b]   98-40283

For Pat
With love and
gratitude

Contents

Illustrations

Introduction to the Paperback Edition

ALMOST TWENTY YEARS after *The Prodigal Daughter* first appeared, I find great pleasure in seeing this biography of Sherwood Bonner reprinted. The occasion brings with it a flood of memories, a chance to make corrections and place some matters in context, and a need to review the work done on her in these ensuing decades—as well as an opportunity to put into the record another portrait of my subject sketched by a contemporary friend, which came to light only after my book had been published.

What I remember most vividly is the exhilaration of being able to draw upon both my literary training and my lifelong interest in local history for this book. Many others knew well the literary period, but only I among them knew also the milieu that had shaped Sherwood Bonner. The people of that place (Holly Springs, Mississippi) and the Bonner kin responded generously to my requests for aid. Attics were searched, boxes of rat-chewed papers produced, interviews freely granted, and confidences shared. Today I realize anew just how fortunate I was, for virtually everyone who helped me is dead, their households disassembled, and the whereabouts of some documents now unknown. Quite possibly my photocopies are the only evidence remaining of some of the Sherwood Bonner papers. In order to make my materials available to other scholars, I have now placed them in Special Collections at the University of Georgia Library.

The thrill of the detective work and the resulting discoveries sustained me throughout the project. With only meager travel support and limited research assistance, I was elated when so many of my hunches paid off. In the bowels of the Boston Public Library at the very nadir of its financial history, when the surly staff worker expressed disbelief that I would stay until he could unearth the

1869 issues of the *Massachusetts Ploughman*, I burst out, "Listen here, I've traveled a thousand miles. Just get the damned journal!" After what seemed like hours, he retrieved the volume, and there it was—Sherwood Bonner's first story. I had been right. No one had been able to find the story because she had misrepresented her precocity: it appeared when she was twenty, rather than fifteen. Other breakthroughs followed. Helen Craft Anderson's annotations of her copy of *Like Unto Like* showed me that James Redpath, mentioned only in passing in a couple of earlier Bonner studies, had played an important role in Sherwood Bonner's life. Then came the day I realized that several of her protagonists bore the same initials as the mysterious General Colton Greene, and I began to investigate him. Other bits were harder won. I ground through microfilms of the *Memphis Avalanche* covering ten whole years, but how rewarding that labor was.

As far as corrections go, I must begin by cautioning the reader that, in the use of grammatical constructions and ethnic designations, my study reflects accepted usage at the time of composition. In that regard, the book is perhaps closer to Sherwood Bonner's time than to the present, so rapid have been the changes in such matters in recent years. I hardly need point out (as one reviewer gleefully did) that, as every school child should know, General Colton Greene could not have died on September 31, but on September 30. Other errors are more significant. In the bibliography, I followed earlier sources in assigning the pamphlet *A Chapter in the History of the Epidemic of 1878* to Bonner, when I should have been able to deduce (as I now have) that it was the work of Mrs. John Newton Craig, wife of the Holly Springs Presbyterian minister. I told Anne Gowdy of my mistake, and she made the correction in her recent dissertation, as well as discovering two stories and two articles by Bonner that I had not found. A final word of caution must be given about two sources used by many Bonner scholars. Both Jean Nosser Biglane's 1972 master's thesis, "An Annotated and Indexed Edition of the Letters of Sherwood Bonner" (Mississippi State University), and William L. Frank's transcription of Sherwood Bonner's 1869 diary, published in *Notes on Mississippi Writers* (Winter 1971, Spring 1971, Fall 1971), contain errors because of failure at deciphering the handwriting and misidentification of persons mentioned.

Since *The Prodigal Daughter* appeared, a number of people have done excellent work on Sherwood Bonner. I will focus on those studies, rather than noting merely cursory treatment or pieces that repeat old errors. The first category is academic criticism not yet in print. Kathryn Burgess McKee's "Writing in a Different Direction: Women Authors and the Tradition of Southwestern Humor, 1875–1910" (dissertation, University of North Carolina, 1997) examines Bonner in an interesting context, as does Darlene Pajo's "The Woman Question in the Life and Fiction of Sherwood Bonner" (master's thesis, University of Louisville, 1989). The most helpful study in regard to biographical issues is Charles Steven Palmer's master's thesis, "'Our Most Noble Stranger': The Mystery, Gallantry, and Civicism of Colton Greene" (University of Oklahoma, 1995), which may reveal as much about this figure as we will ever know.

Published studies of Bonner have also added to our understanding. Historian Donald E. Sutherland, using the discoveries in *The Prodigal Daughter*, speculates further about Bonner's relationship with James Redpath in "Some Thoughts Concerning the Love Life of Sherwood Bonner," *Southern Studies* 26 (Summer, 1987), 115–27. He incorporates some of this material in his treatment of Bonner in his *The Confederate Carpetbaggers* (Louisiana State University Press, 1988). Lisa Pater Faranda's essay, "A Social Necessity: The Friendship of Sherwood Bonner and Henry Wadsworth Longfellow," in *Patrons and Protegees: Gender, Friendship, and Writing in Nineteenth-Century America*, edited by Shirley Marchalonis (Rutgers University Press, 1988), argues convincingly that Bonner's "strong, though sorely tested, sense of self resisted not only the notion of mentorship but the obligation to acquiesce to established order."

More of Sherwood Bonner's work is in print today than has been since the 1880s. In 1990 NCUP, Inc., brought out *Dialect Tales and Other Stories* in its Masterworks of Literature series, with an introduction by William L. Frank. The volume includes the contents of both of Bonner's published collections, *Dialect Tales* (1883) and *Suwanee River Tales* (1884), as well as three uncollected works. The Frank introduction is a reprise of material in his 1976 Twayne book. In 1997 the University of South Carolina Press reprinted Sherwood Bonner's *Like unto Like*, with a splendid introduction by Jane Turner Censer. In 2000, the University of Tennessee Press will publish *A Sherwood Bonner Sampler, 1869–1883*, edited by Anne Gowdy. In addition to making important Bonner texts once again accessible,

Censer and Gowdy display in their introductions an impressive knowledge of cultural and literary contexts, both those that produced the works and those in which the literature of the nineteenth century is currently being evaluated. The Gowdy dissertation, which includes the most extensive bibliographies of both primary and secondary works, reflects the breadth of the author's career, supporting her contention that Bonner has been "too lightly estimated and too narrowly classified."

Obviously the final verdict on both Sherwood Bonner's life and her career has yet to be delivered. Scraps of evidence are still emerging even from the nineteenth century. Five years after this biography was published, Sherwood Bonner's grand-nephew David McDowell III discovered, in an album that had belonged to his aunt Lilly McDowell, a sketch of Bonner published in an unidentified newspaper on March 10, 1886, and unnoted in all subsequent scholarship. Though I searched microfilms of a number of likely newspapers, I have not been able to establish the source. The writer, a woman, is identified only as "Our Regular Correspondent"; the column was sent from Holly Springs. After some remarks on the season and "the grand old mouldering house wherein Sherwood Bonner first opened her baby eyes," the correspondent begins her reminiscence:

> She was a kind friend to me in my early life of sorrow, and was my friend, faithful to the end. We all are her friends now. The dead have more friends than the living. A proud, ambitious, self-willed woman, she was much condemned by some for her perseverance in her literary course. With an eye of contempt she looked upon those who spoke ill of her course. Had the world hissed at her she would quietly have pursued the course she took. She abhorred the word fail, and if she had lived long enough, would have conquered all things and reached. . . .

Here the clipping is torn, leaving a gap. "Whatever her faults may have been," the next fragment begins,

> we all do acknowledge that hers was the brightest, and most powerful intellect of any woman ever raised in Holly Springs, and today we are proud that she was one of us.
>
> Sherwood Bonner was a strange, eccentric woman, apparently heartless, yet with a heart, and though I love even her memory, I was not blind to her faults. The unhappiness of

her married life, I always thought she brought upon herself. A nobler, better husband no woman ever had than Edward McDowell, and his love for her was as intense, tender and as pure as mortal's love could be, and he would have made her a good husband had she allowed, but her vocation was to be an authoress and she loved her profession better than her husband. She never loved him at all I think. She always loved to say odd, queer things, something that would shock her friends, within her heart scarcely meaning what she did say, and when asked if she really was going to be married, said, "Why yes. Betsy, Cary, Ada, and all of my friends are married; do you suppose I am going to allow them to do more than I do?" I always believed the secret of her marriage was that she might gain a point with her father, that of going to Boston to study for her profession. She had long tried, but in vain, to gain his consent to let her go, but he violently opposed her wishes. She knew that her marriage with Mr. McDowell would only give her freedom to act as she pleased, which it did. She left him and her child and went.

Again here the column is torn, but one can piece together the next sentence:

I never knew much of her after then, though often heard of her troubles as well as the few pleasures that fill such a life. But I remember many, many things of her when I was a child, of how beautiful she was with her soft blue eyes and golden hair, and how I loved to hear her talk, how smart I thought she was; child-like I believed everything she said, even in jest. I remember once I went to her with my arithmetic, the first day I had ever studied it, and I asked her to learn me my lesson. She tried for awhile to make me add— I could not add. Quietly she handed me the book, and with a look of sympathy said: "You are a fool." I firmly believed it before I ever learned the multiplication table. Hers was such a quick mind that it absorbed readily at a glance what others could not learn in an hour.

"Enough," the correspondent concludes abruptly, "'Let the dead and beautiful rest.'" But, in fulfillment of her own dreams, Sherwood Bonner is still the subject of scrutiny, and whatever one makes of this long-lost sketch, there she is, as if alive!

Hubert H. McAlexander
Athens, Georgia

Preface

SHERWOOD BONNER, when she is remembered at all today, is recalled hazily by a few literary specialists as a nineteenth-century American writer of the local color school. She has not been given her due. As a person and as a writer, she was caught amid dramatically changing values; and both her life and her works provide an interesting reflection of conflicts in American life and literature during the two decades following the Civil War.

Born in 1849 into the luxurious life of the southern planter aristocracy in one of the richest cotton-producing areas in the country, she later came to know enough of deprivation to abandon the traditional domestic role of the southern lady; and she had enough courage to assume the role of breadwinner. She was to prove such an unconventional woman that by 1873, after marrying and bearing a child, she left both husband and child and struck out on her own for the literary capital of Boston. There she became a highly visible and controversial figure. In the remaining decade of her short life, she established connections with many of the leaders of that capital and became a well-known writer whose career was aided by one of the great publishing empires. Hints of scandal followed her to the end, the rumors centering around a series of public men—the country's best loved poet, a radical reformer and fellow conspirator of John Brown, and a fashionable and mysterious Confederate general.

The southern lady who spent her productive years in the center of anti-southern sentiment, the loving mother who had abandoned her infant, the feminist who was still a coquette and expected gallantry always, the writer capable of great originality who modeled many works on those of financially successful contemporaries, the emerging realist who could never quite shake the hold that romantic periodical fiction had early exerted upon her—Sherwood Bonner presents a mass of cultural and literary contradictions. Whether celebrated or shunned by various contemporaries, she remained a mystery to most. Misunderstood by her own age, she should be better understood by ours.

Acknowledgments

A BIOGRAPHER'S DEBTS are always great and often complex. Mine begin with two grand-nephews of Sherwood Bonner—David Mc-Dowell III, and the Reverend Dr. George Royster Stephenson. They gave unlimited access to their splendid collections, undertook searches in my behalf, and put themselves generally to a good deal of trouble in the interest of this book. I also profited from their intelligent and lively impressions of family history. Obviously, without their interest and their aid, I could never have written the biography.

My next obligations were incurred in Holly Springs, Mississippi, Sherwood Bonner's native town and mine. Everyone whom I called on there responded generously. Their names are found throughout the footnotes, but I wish to single out a few here whose full services could never be explained in a mere note: Mrs. Bessie Craft Driver, Mrs. L. A. Smith, Mrs. R. L. Wyatt, Vadah Cochran, Charles N. Dean, Mrs. Glenn Fant, Mrs. H. H. McAlexander, the late Mrs. Netty Fant Thompson, and Mrs. Fred Belk.

I owe a special debt to Professor Andrew Hilen of the University of Washington, editor of the *Letters of Henry Wadsworth Longfellow*, four volumes of which have already been published by Harvard University Press. Professor Hilen not only kindly allowed me access to manuscript pages of the final two volumes, but he also shared with me his unparalleled knowledge of the Longfellow papers. Professor Thomas K. McCraw of Harvard University proved most helpful at various stages of this book. Lloyd D. Alexander and George E. Pesely provided valuable genealogical and historical materials, and Patty Povall Lewis aided in the gathering of the illustrations. Of the many people with whom I had contact at various libraries and archives, I am particularly grateful to

Norman Chronister of the Mississippi Department of Archives and History and Marte Shaw of Houghton Library, Harvard University.

I gratefully acknowledge the many courtesies extended to me by several institutions and libraries, including the permission to use letters, manuscripts, and other materials specifically designated in the notes: the Marshall County Historical Society, the Marshall County Public Library, Memphis/Shelby County Library, the John Davis Williams Library of the University of Mississippi, the Mississippi Department of Archives and History, the University of Georgia Library, the William R. Perkins Library of Duke University, the Butler Library of Columbia University, the New York Historical Society, the Massachusetts Historical Society, the Longfellow National Historic Site, and the Houghton Library of Harvard University. I also appreciate the permission of the editors of the *Southern Literary Journal*, who had previously published a part of Chapter Five.

I wish to thank Professors James B. Colvert, John Algeo, and Coburn Freer, who, as heads of the English Department at the University of Georgia, arranged that I receive support for the writing of this biography. I also benefited from the counsel of Rayburn S. Moore of the department. Sylvia Shurbutt aided me as an efficient research assistant for one quarter.

Professor Louis D. Rubin, Jr., the editor of this series, has earned my deep gratitude for his dispatch, his encouragement, and his strong support. I am also happy to thank here the various editors at the Louisiana State University Press through whose hands my manuscript has passed: Beverly Jarrett, Martha L. Hall, and Marie J. Blanchard.

Finally, my most profound obligations are to two colleagues— Jon Spence, and Patricia Jewell McAlexander. Dr. Spence served as an astute, imaginative, sympathetic, but rigorous critic of the working manuscript. Dr. McAlexander's contributions are all-encompassing. I could not possibly list them.

The Prodigal Daughter

Chapter One

Kate Bonner of Holly Springs

ON THE TITLE page of her copy of Sherwood Bonner's 1878 novel
Like unto Like, Helen Craft of Holly Springs, Mississippi, identified the author as "the playmate of my childhood, the rival of my
school days, the friend and confidant of my young ladyhood, the
puzzle of my maturer years!" By the age of thirty, the child of privilege, the precocious schoolgirl, the romantic young lady had become the often shocking woman—an enigma to many who had
known her longest. And, in great part, their bewilderment must
have sprung from the fact that both the background and the rearing of this woman who delivered so many blows to convention
had been so highly conventional.[1]

On the maternal side, her background lay squarely within patterns common to many in the Deep South's cotton-supported gentry. Her maternal grandmother was of the Martins—a family of
wealth and social prominence, who had been leaders in the settlement of both west Tennessee and northern Mississippi. The Martins had arrived in Tennessee from South Carolina in the 1820s,
married well, and prospered. Particularly notable there was a
great-uncle, Major Andrew Lesper Martin, a lawyer, who was
elected for several terms to the state house of representatives and
who built a mansion in the town of Jackson that later became the
central building at West Tennessee College.[2]

It was his brother, however, who led the family during its golden

1. The extensive annotations of Helen Craft (later Mrs. W. A. Anderson) in her copy of
Sherwood Bonner's *Like unto Like* (New York: Harper & Brothers, 1878) have been of
great value in this study. I am indebted to two members of the Craft connection in Holly
Springs for this source: Mrs. L. A. Smith, who alerted me to its existence, and Mrs. Fort
Daniel, who graciously allowed me to use it.

2. Samuel Cole Williams, *Beginnings of West Tennessee: In the Land of the Chickasaws,
1541–1841* (Johnson City, Tenn.: Watagua Press, 1930), 220, 236; Richard Ward, "Union
University and Its Predecessors: Historical Highlights," *West Tennessee Historical Society
Papers*, XIX (1975), 59.

epoch in Mississippi. By the 1832 Treaty of Pontotoc, the Chick-asaws ceded to the United States the whole of north Mississippi, the northernmost reaches of this acreage lying only sixty miles from Jackson, Tennessee. Married to the daughter of Samuel Dick-ens—one of the men who had prospered most in the opening of west Tennessee—Colonel John Davidson Martin had seen the op-portunities possible when the government sold new lands; and he acted quickly, buying vast tracts in the Chickasaw Cession and playing a key role in the settlement of the area. One of the organiz-ers of Desoto County, Mississippi, he also donated land for the county seat of Oxford in Lafayette County, where among his other holdings was the site of the University of Mississippi. His largest block of land, however, was along the Tallahatchie River in Mar-shall County; and this last county, bounded on the south by the Tallahatchie and on the north by the state of Tennessee, was to be-come the new home of the whole Martin connection.[3]

Following his brother's example, Andrew Martin too bought a plantation there on the river; and he chose for his home site a tract two miles to the west and north of the new county seat, Holly Springs. Accompanying her brothers to Mississippi was Ruth Martin, who in 1820 had married Samuel D. Wilson, son of one of the organizers and early legislators of Obion County, Tennessee. Samuel Wilson had himself served as a county trustee in Madison County, and he was already a prosperous planter when he pur-chased his Tallahatchie tract. By the 1840s, the entire Martin con-nection were firmly established near Holly Springs, and the broth-ers had built impressive houses. To the southwest of the village, John Davidson Martin was living in a large frame plantation house, and northward the Andrew Martins had erected an elegant brick house of eight rooms on Martin's Hill, from which, Sher-wood Bonner was to observe, "the town could be seen like a pic-ture in smoke." Though the Martins had been successful in west Tennessee, here in northern Mississippi they reached the height of their influence, power, and wealth.[4]

3. Robert Lowry and William H. McCardle, *A History of Mississippi* (Jackson: R. H. Henry & Co., 1891), 473, 425; C. John Sobotka, Jr., *A History of Lafayette County, Mis-sissippi* (Oxford, Miss.: Rebel Press, Inc., 1976), 25, 28; a survey of Martin and Wilson deeds in the Chancery Clerk's Office, Holly Springs, Mississippi.

4. All important family dates are taken from the family Bible belonging to Samuel D. Wilson and Ruth C. Martin, which has been passed down through five generations, now in

Sherwood Bonner's father's background was less typical of the antebellum southern ruling class, but of great dignity and propriety. His grandfather was the Rector Hamilton of Treutaugh, Strabane, County Derry, Ireland. Of the three Hamilton daughters, known as the "Three Graces of Strabane," one had married a Mr. Sherwood; another, a Mr. Gault; and the third, Catherine, Charles Bonner, a dour and intellectual Presbyterian. The Bonners had emigrated to America in 1820 and settled in Susquehanna County, Pennsylvania. Among their several children was a son Charles, who after completing his medical training went south, first to Huntsville, Alabama, and finally to Holly Springs, where he formed a partnership with Dr. Willis Lea about 1845.[5]

At the Lea plantation home, Wildwood, Dr. Charles Bonner met seventeen-year-old Mary Wilson, whose parents had recently died, leaving her under the guardianship of Dr. Lea. The young couple were married on October 20, 1846, by Dr. Page, the rector of Christ Church in Holly Springs. Here the two strains were joined that produced the controversial literary lady Sherwood Bonner. By all accounts both beautiful and charming, Mary Wilson was a careful product of her southern upper-class nurturing—graceful, accomplished in the feminine arts, domestic. On the other hand, Dr. Bonner, like the Hamiltons and Bonners before him, was intellectual and literary. Even more than his wife, however, the doctor was a highly conventional person.[6]

Upon his marriage, Charles Bonner inherited through Mary Wilson the life of a southern planter and became, like his professional associate, a planter-physician. The Bonners and her sister, young Sallie Wilson, settled to a pleasant, comfortable life on a

---

the possession of James R. McDowell of Batesville, Mississippi. Williams, *Beginnings of West Tennessee*, 153, 236. Descriptions of the Martin houses were furnished by Charles N. Dean of Holly Springs.

5. Hamilton genealogical chart in the collection of David McDowell III, of Batesville, Mississippi (hereinafter cited as McDowell Collection). Letter to the author from Miss Lepearl Bonner of Stewartville, Minnesota, April 9, 1969. The character of the first Charles Bonner is reflected well in his volume of lectures—*Addresses to Youth* (N.p. [1836?])—copy in the collection of the Reverend Dr. George Royster Stephenson of Jackson, Mississippi (hereinafter cited as Stephenson Collection). George Royster Stephenson, "Sherwood Bonner" (a 1932 typescript in the Stephenson Collection), 2.

6. Dorothy Gilligan, "Life and Works of Sherwood Bonner" (M.A. thesis, George Washington University, 1930), 2; Alexander L. Bondurant, "Sherwood Bonner," *Publications of the Mississippi Historical Society*, II (June, 1898), 44–45.

plantation that Dr. Bonner purchased near Holly Springs. The next September was born a son Charles, who lived only a day. Then on February 26, 1849, the daughter was born who was to shock all of Holly Springs, become one of the town's best-known citizens, and die an enigma to many old friends. Catherine Sherwood she was named in honor of two of the Hamilton sisters, but Katharine she signed herself, and Kate she would be to all who knew her well.[7]

Though Kate Bonner was born on a plantation and lived there until she was eight, she was to make little use of plantation life in her later writings; the setting for the majority of her works instead would be Holly Springs. Established in the midst of prosperous plantations with quaint names—Wildwood, Hedge Farm, Strawberry Plains, Snowdoun—the village of Holly Springs was the hub of this north Mississippi cotton country, and the place for which she would always feel her deepest attachment. At Kate's birth in 1849, the county had been officially opened for white settlement for only thirteen years; but Holly Springs was not the raw frontier village that it might have been in other areas. Surrounded by settlements a decade or two older, north Mississippi was the last pocket of land in the area ceded by the Indians. Of course some adventurers and ruffians did pour in with the other settlers, but the case of the Martin and Wilson families—people already well established who sought even greater opportunity—was fairly representative. Many of the settlers had come from nearby places—like Jackson or Paris in Tennessee; Florence or Huntsville in Alabama—bringing their slaves and moving intact large establishments. Others, including many professional people like Dr. Bonner, had come from the older seaboard states. Even though in May of 1836, when town lots were first put up for sale, an observer noted that the settlement consisted of "only a few log cabins in the woods," the place developed rapidly. By 1839, one citizen could boast:

Holly Springs four years ago was a cotton plantation; now we number a population of 2,500. Marshall County at the same time was little

7. Confusion and error in the spelling of Katharine Sherwood Bonner McDowell's name have continued even after Professor George W. Polhemus' clarification of the matter some years ago—"The Correct Spelling of Sherwood Bonner's Name," *Notes and Queries,* VII (July, 1960), 265.

better than a wilderness, now one of the most populous counties in the state. Our population consists not of adventurers who came to the South for the purpose of regaining a lost fortune, but of substantial men, who brought their fortunes, and better still, their intelligence with them, who believed they could enjoy in substantial degree the advantages of cultivating the great staple commodity of the South and at the same time breathe a pure, healthful, invigorating atmosphere, and they were not mistaken.

In his chauvinism, the writer overestimated the population, which was only 1,117 two full years later; but his statements in general were accurate, and the chauvinism itself remained very much a mark of the town.[8]

The citizenry, in truth, had much to be chauvinistic about. By 1850 the county led the state in cotton production. References now abounded to it as the "Empire County" and to Holly Springs as the "Capital of North Mississippi." As a result of this prosperity, Kate Bonner was born not into a settlement of a few cabins in the woods but into a village of white cottages. And the flush times were only beginning. By 1861 leaders claimed that Marshall County was producing more cotton than any similar division of land in the country. One of the results was that in the short twenty-five years from the initial settlement to the Civil War a remarkable architectural record was left. Added in the 1850s to the log dwellings and the many white cottages were a host of brick mansions, including, in 1857, that of Dr. Charles Bonner. On suburban Salem Road, where other planters, lawyers, doctors, and merchants were erecting their mansions, he built Bonner House, a structure recognized today as a notable example of Gothic Revival architecture. Here the Bonner children—Kate, Ruth Martin (born 1851), Samuel Wilson (born 1854), and Anne Lea (born 1858)—grew up amid other families of this cotton-supported aristocracy.[9]

A picturesque gate hung between two ancient bois d'arc trees

8. An 1838 letter quoted by Nash K. Burger, "An Overlooked Source for Mississippi Local History: The Spirit of Missions, 1836–1854," *Journal of Mississippi History*, VIII (1945), 173; *Marshall County Republican*, June 1, 1839, p. 1.

9. James H. Stone, "Economic Development of Holly Springs During the 1840s," *Journal of Mississippi History*, XXXII (November, 1970), 356; William Baskerville Hamilton, "Holly Springs, Mississippi, to the Year 1878" (M.A. thesis, University of Mississippi, 1931), 38–40; Wayne Andrews, *American Gothic, Its Origins, Its Trials, Its Triumphs* (New York: Vintage Books, 1975), 98.

formed the entrance to the Bonner estate, an expanse of land on the highest ground in Holly Springs. Set well back from the road at the end of a broad brick walk stood the two-story house. Piercing its brick mass were long gothic windows, and across the front facade ran a delicately filagreed porch of cast iron, which gave to the whole the appearance of a delicate and fanciful valentine. Within, one entered the first of two halls, a wide entry with huge sliding doors on each side. Behind the right set was the parlor, furnished in the fashionable "French antique" mode; behind the left lay Dr. Bonner's library. For entertaining, both sets of doors were opened, and the front of the house thrown into one grand room. The rest of the house contained a long dining room, various halls, a dressing room, and five bedrooms. To the rear of the building, amid the gardens and orchards planted by Dr. Bonner, were several brick dependencies, including what Sherwood Bonner would recall as "the pleasantest place in the world," the "great wide kitchen, with its roomy fireplace, where the backlog glowed and the black kettle swung." This was the domain of her beloved Negro "Gran'mammy," who had reared Mary Wilson Bonner and was now cook and nurse to the Bonner children. In infancy Kate and the other children would "clutch at the great gold hoops in her ears, or cling to her ample skirts like little burrs"; and throughout childhood they listened spellbound to the old nurse's countless tales. Years later, it would be by using these tales that the oldest of the Bonner children was to begin making a name for herself as a writer.[10]

Kate had already absorbed a great deal of Gran'mammy's lore before she began her formal education under the tutelage of her mother. Throughout her life she saved one quaint document attesting to her schooling before the age of five:

REWARD OF MERRIT

This testimonial is given to Miss Kate S. Bonner in consideration of her having given satisfactory evidence of progress in her studies during the past week.

Given under the hand
and Seal of precipship
December 9th 1853   Mary Bonner

10. Sherwood Bonner, *Suwanee River Tales* (Boston: Roberts Brothers, 1884), 4, 3.

By the time that she reached school age, Holly Springs, in the midst of an agricultural region and in a state of small towns, had become an educational center with between four and five hundred students annually enrolled in four schools—for boys, St. Thomas Hall (a school of the Episcopal diocese) and Chalmers Institute, and, for girls, Franklin Female College and Holly Springs Female Institute. It was to the last of these, where Dr. Bonner had served since 1849 as lecturer in chemistry, that Kate was sent. The school had been established by prominent citizens at the town's settlement, and in 1840 a handsome building of the Tuscan order, two stories and basement, large enough to accommodate 140 pupils and to board 60, had been erected amid a park laid out in promenades of native trees. During its first decade the Institute was usually headed by the Episcopal rector, and its object, as set forth by an early president, was "to impart a sound, substantial, liberal education, not masculine, but approximating as near to it as the peculiarities of the female intelligence will permit." The curriculum included ancient languages, higher mathematics, natural science, vocal and instrumental music, German, French, chemistry, Christian evidences, English literature and poetry, physiology, and hygiene.[11]

In the year 1859, when she was ten, Kate had progressed to McGuffey's Fifth Reader, and she had begun the study of French and piano. The precocious child was already given to self-dramatization, and she had begun her juvenile compositions. After one incident in which she had fought with a playmate and gotten her pinafore torn, she responded to her mother's inquiry about her appearance by producing a paper and tragically exclaiming—"Read this. It will tell you all!" The earliest bills from the Institute list charges for "extra stationery for writing," and one of her schoolmates later observed that even Kate's first schoolgirl essays seemed to the rest of the group "marvels of rhythm and rhetoric." By 1861, Kate had entered the collegiate department of the Institute, where she continued French and music and where she wrote an allegory that, again, seemed remarkable for one of her years.[12]

11. "Reward of Merit [sic]," in McDowell Collection; Debow's Review, XXVII (July, 1859), 117; Marshall County Republican, June 1, 1839, p. 1.

12. Tuition bills from the Holly Springs Female Institute, Stephenson Collection; Bondurant, "Sherwood Bonner," 46; [Helen Craft Anderson], "In Memoriam," Holly Springs Reporter, August 16, 1883, p. 2.

The precocious twelve-year-old, involved in her play and her compositions, probably failed to realize, however, that forces were at work now that would alter her life and the lives of all she knew and change radically the social and economic system of her region. Holly Springs, at the height of its prosperity in 1861, reflected in a particularly interesting way an entire era. With its not infrequent juxtaposition of log dwelling (often now covered with clapboard) and columned mansion, the prosperous country village represented, within its short twenty-five-year span, the history and culture of the cotton-rich Deep South in microcosm. The writer Sherwood Bonner remembered it from those days as a "sleepy, prosperous little town—so pretty that the country papers called it the 'City of Flowers,' and never tired of extolling its exquisite gardens, spacious handsome houses, and dainty park where the young folks walked on summer evenings and fed tame squirrels or made love to each other on the 'swinging seats' under the linden trees." It was a place where to her young eyes, "mothers and grandmothers gossiped placidly at 'early teas' or solemn dinner parties. Daughters went to church, rode horseback, and read Richardson and Scott, with occasional longing glances toward Fielding and Smollett on the high shelves—sealed books to them until they were married." The men, on the other hand, were devoted to politics: "The planter and the merchant, as the one ordered and the other measured jeans and linsey for the hands; the young men in broadbrimmed hats and negligent neckties, who lounged at the street corners and arranged the details of fox-hunts and game suppers; the village great man and the village loafer— had all the same common interest." And for the young, to vary the monotony, came often "the wild excitement of a tournament" or "at election times much dissipation in the way of barbeques and torchlight processions." But none—not even a girl of twelve— could finally ignore what was happening at the fort in Charleston's harbor.[13]

To Kate Bonner, however, with her love of drama, the war proved often a time of high romance. And even later when the mature woman recalled the war years, she saw them with the eyes of

13. Sherwood Bonner, "From '60 to '65," *Lippincott's*, XVIII (October, 1876), 500–501.

the romantic young girl. "Years of peril and disaster, of hardship and suffering," she called them. "Yet they held all the fascination of romance, the splendid excitement of passionate tragedy." It all began for her amid the fervor and hope of those early days of 1861 with a ceremony attending the conversion of the local iron foundry into a small arms factory, a ceremony that for the young Kate marked the beginning of the war:

> Crowds of people were outside the building, and as many as were al-lowed to enter were within. Standing there amid the din and whir of machinery, while the sooty-faced workmen hurried hither and thither and the great furnace roared and reddened, [we found] the hour preg-nant with significance. As the melted ore poured forth, a woman's hand held under it the great iron ladle and emptied it into the mold with the solemnity of a priestess assisting at a holy rite. Every woman and child followed in turn. It was our consecration to the cause—an hour that I cannot remember now without a thrill of emotion akin to that which thrilled me to the very centre of my being as I clasped my hands around the iron handle and felt that in that moment I sealed my devotion to the South.

The next martial occasion, the presentation of a flag to the town's first regiment, brought an equal measure of excitement with its blend of pageantry and idealism. In the grove to the east of Holly Springs, Kate watched "the ranks of soldiers in their spotless gray uniforms, the platform gay with ribbons and vases, the colonel with his plumed hat and scarlet sash, the gorgeous banner whose silken folds fluttered around the slight figure of a dark-eyed girl . . . the heroine of the day [who] had been chosen to present the flag." But after the ceremonies, the troops marched off for the front, the foundry began its monotonous work, and the town was left as peaceful as it had been earlier.[14]

The war was not to touch Holly Springs directly for over a year, and young Kate Bonner was again an ordinary schoolgirl under the care of Professor Hackleton at the Female Institute. Long be-fore she ever saw a Federal soldier, however, the war made itself felt by disrupting her education. The Institute was closed in March of 1862, the same month that Dr. Charles Bonner received an ex-

14. These and all other quotations describing Kate Bonner's experiences during the Civil War are taken from "From '60 to '65."

ecutive order from the governor of Mississippi to establish a hospital in the town. Battle sites were daily moving closer to Holly Springs, and the doctor began preparing the Female Institute building to receive casualties. The first were brought a month later after the bloody battle of Shiloh. In early October the hospital was filled again with the wounded after the terrible Confederate rout at Corinth.[15]

During the autumn, despite the casualties, despite the sight of the army, poorly equipped and in disarray, Holly Springs was gay. General Sterling Price made the town his headquarters for two months, his second in command being the gallant, ill-fated General Earl Van Dorn. All the houses of the town were thrown open, and the balls and reviews that the young girl watched filled the weeks with golden days. But these passed quickly, for in late November Price received word that the Federal cavalry was only twenty-five miles away and that Grant's army was advancing on the town. Between midnight and dawn the Confederate force marched through on its retreat south, and by morning the town lay within the Federal lines. This was the end of general gaiety for Holly Springs for the next three years. "It was a sad day when the army left," Sherwood Bonner later wrote, "for we bade friends good-bye to prepare for foes. Boxes of silver were buried at night under flowerbeds or ash heaps; gold pieces were secured in leather belts; doors were locked and windows barred. Then we waited until one bright morning in December, when frightened Negroes came flying in from the country round with the dread news, 'The Yankees are coming!'" The war had finally come to Holly Springs and it came "with the sound of music and the beating of drums, into a silent town. From behind closed blinds we listened to the tread of their advancing feet or peeped timidly at the blue ranks marching by. Before sundown the pleasant groves of [the town] were dotted with white tents, the stars and stripes fluttered from a high flag-pole, and from the park the inspiring strains of 'Yankee Doodle' seemed to mock our impotent anger and bitter humiliation."[16]

15. Helen Craft Anderson scrapbook, now in the collection of Mrs. John Craft and Mrs. James Driver of Holly Springs (hereinafter cited as Craft Collection); Executive order from Governor John J. Pettus, March 4, 1862, in Stephenson Collection.

16. In addition to using Sherwood Bonner's own account of the early war years in Holly Springs, I have drawn on Mrs. Carrington Mason's "Van Dorn's Raid into Holly Springs or

The humiliation deepened when the town discovered that General Grant had determined to make Holly Springs his headquarters. He began accumulating a huge depot of supplies, and he commandeered public buildings for offices and the best houses to lodge his staff. Included was Bonner House. The town's impotent rage was well reflected in the response of the Bonner children, who refused to pass under the American flag which hung over the porch of their house during its Federal occupation.[17]

Just as the townspeople had become used to their situation—to alien soldiers; to the hundreds of sutlers; to the spectacle of freed slaves drunkenly celebrating their liberation; to the fact that many officers' wives, among them Mrs. Grant, had settled themselves for the winter in the homes of the citizens—the Confederate cavalry executed one of the daring tactical maneuvers for which it became famous. "The *Glorious*, GLORIOUS Twentieth," Kate Bonner termed the date in her diary, the date in December of 1862 when General Van Dorn's troops surprised the sleeping Federal garrison at dawn, gained a surrender without a fight, and burned a million dollars worth of ammunition and supplies. For the girl Kate, the incident provided the peak of the war's excitement, and the writer Sherwood Bonner was to return to it almost every time that she wrote of the war.[18]

But the town's great wartime moment was short lived. The Confederates were gone before nightfall; and Holly Springs, explosions still echoing through it, was left with 2,500 Yankee soldiers—defeated, hungry, and threatening the town with the torch. Within a few days Grant and the rest of his army returned, these soldiers too seeking vengeance. On this night the citizens had their trunks packed for instant flight, and at one time fourteen fires glowed in the skies over the countryside.

As soon as the situation had stabilized, Dr. Bonner sent his old-

Why General Grant's Flank Movement on Vicksburg Failed" (Typescript in Marshall County Historical Society, Holly Springs) and Cora Harris Watson Carey's "Rambling Recollections: Between the Lines" (MS in Cora Carey Collection, Mississippi Department of Archives and History, Jackson, Mississippi).

17. William L. Frank, *Sherwood Bonner (Catherine McDowell)* (Boston: Twayne Publishers, 1976), 32.

18. A more famous Mississippi writer was equally fascinated by the Van Dorn raid. William Faulkner found uses for it in several works, most notably in *Light in August*, where it serves as one of the central images.

est daughter away. After the closing of the Holly Springs Female Institute, Kate had been enrolled at Miss Lucilla Read's hastily devised Beauregard Institute. Deciding that Miss Lucilla's failed to provide the proper stimulus for a bright young mind and that chaotic Holly Springs was no place for a thirteen-year-old girl, Dr. Bonner sent Kate to Montgomery, Alabama, still a Confederate stronghold and the site of Hamner Hall, a fashionable girls' boarding school of the Episcopal diocese of Alabama.

In January of 1863, Kate Bonner and a friend named Eliza enrolled at Hamner Hall. Shortly after her arrival Kate wrote her earliest letter now extant to Cary Freeman, a Holly Springs classmate back at the Beauregard Institute. It reveals a spirited and rather undisciplined young girl, who had probably listened often to her father's lecture on the Parable of the Talents:

> *At last* I have reached that long desired haven of Montgomery—*at last* my mind is at rest upon that *all* important subject an *education.* I now have *every* advantage, and it will be my own fault if I do not improve . . . I am not at all disposed to slight this opportunity for receiving a good education, but study with all *possible diligence.* You can hardly credit this can you . . . that Kate should study so very well. But it is even so. Kate is transformed, and is *determined* not to disappoint family and friends when I return.

The letter then—after commenting on the "'Italian'" climate of Montgomery, as opposed to the "'Northern'" winters of Holly Springs and bemoaning the situation of being one of three Mississippians among the Alabamians—shows a bit of Kate's schoolgirl pretension and more than a little homesickness:

> I have not time to dwell . . . as it is badly "comme il faut" to write so long a letter. I can only charge you as my parting request to be sure to *write soon* to your loving friend.
>
> Kate
>
> Love to all. Eliza sends her love. Give my love to Miss Lucilla
> Kate Bonner

The homesickness was to dissipate, and being thrown among so many Alabama girls proved not to be a problem at all. Because of her precocity, her highly developed sense of pride, and her too ready wit, the tall young girl had never been a general favorite; but she managed here, as in Holly Springs, to attract a small but devoted band. And though she proved again to be a bright but un-disciplined student, still she made the most of her exposure to new people and ideas and to the city so "delightfully gay" while General Joe Johnston made his headquarters there.[19]

In the summer, at the end of the term, Kate left Montgomery, itself no longer the citadel it had been six months earlier, to travel through a ruined countryside back to Holly Springs. The last part of the journey she made on the only vehicle left on the Mississippi Central Railroad, a handcar run by a blind man, a cripple, and two former slaves. The Van Dorn raid was only the first of sixty separate raids made on Holly Springs during the course of the war, as the town found itself in the line of one army or another, or, worse, stragglers from the armies. Consequently, even the six months that Kate had been away had wrought devastating change. "I should never have recognized in the dreary village the once prosperous, comfortable little town," she wrote.

> Rank weeds grew everywhere, and desolation hung over all things like a funeral pall. Where the town-hall had stood was now a shapeless heap of brick and mortar overgrown with nettles and dog-fennel. The door of [our] church . . . had been torn away, and, looking in, I saw the organ bereft of its pipes, the pulpit of its cushions. The seats were broken up, and not a pane of glass was left in the windows. Even in the graveyard the destroyer had been at work: the gravestones were top-pled over, and upon the white columns yet standing were scrawled rude jests and caricatures. . . . The school-house was leveled to the ground, but its red chimneys stood, like faithful sentinels, over the ruined pile. . . . The square was deserted, except by a company of small boys, who were marching round it in soldier-fashion, and a few old men with long white hair, who were dozing in the sun.

The desolation which the young girl found was only to worsen during the next two years. Many a night now the townspeople slept with their clothes on and their trunks packed, ready to flee. They lived always with the fear of incendiaries, a fear kept alive by the burning of the courthouse and several business houses in August of 1864. And constantly the names of men and boys of the town were being added to the lists of those taken prisoner,

19. Kate Bonner to Cary Freeman, January 20, 1863, in Walthall-Freeman Collection, Department of Archives and Special Collections, University Library, University of Mis-sissippi; Bondurant, "Sherwood Bonner," 47.

wounded, or killed. For the Bonner family there was also another grief, the death of the youngest child, Anne Lea, a little girl of five, in November of 1863.[20]

So the long months stretched on, and by the late winter of 1864–1865 the last great body of Union troops had left Holly Springs. The citizens had now merely to wait, receiving mixed reports of distant battles with alternations of hope and despair. When the final news came, however, they were unprepared. On an April evening, the Bonners had just received two young women collecting money and plate to be sent to Richmond for the depleted Confederate treasury; and Kate and her sister had walked with them to the brow of the hill beyond, when they saw an aged neighbor coming up the hill almost at a run. The girl was never to forget the next moments: "In the wild white face that he turned toward us there was such agony as I have never seen. . . . He looked at us a moment in silence, then in a hollow, harsh voice *struck* us with the words, 'General Lee has surrendered!' and passed on into the falling darkness." The girls, the town were stunned. It was over, and eleven years later Sherwood Bonner was to express the town's state and her own feeling well: "Of the suffering of that after-time I have even now no words to speak. Its very memory is so terrible that I do not know how we endured it then. You, who have lost much, suffered much, for a cause that you have gained, cannot measure the suffering of those who gave their all and lost."

As the soldiers began straggling back home, the defeated began to attempt to pick up their old lives. The county had suffered greatly during the four years. Fences were gone, many barns and houses had been destroyed, most of the stock had been confiscated by the Union Army, and the neglected land had become badly eroded. In the town three-fifths of the large central square lay in ruins. Increasing the sense of oppression was the appearance of an army of occupation less than a month after Appomattox. Many citizens talked of leaving, of new opportunities in Texas or Brazil;

20. Good accounts of Holly Springs during the last years of the war are provided by Cary Johnson, "Life Within the Confederate Lines as Depicted in the War-Time Journal of a Mississippi Girl (M.A. thesis, Louisiana State University, 1929), and the Belle Strickland Diary (Typescript in possession of Miss Josephine Wyatt, Holly Springs).

but most remained and began the work of salvaging what they could and earning a livelihood.[21]

Again, Bonner House was filled with a great sense of loss. In the autumn came the death of Mary Wilson Bonner, the gentle mother whose life, in her daughter's view, "had been set to such sweet music that her spirit broke in the discords of dreadful war." Still the work of rebuilding and reconciling had to go on, and Dr. Bonner, who had been a town leader during the war as director of the hospital, now proved a leader in other areas. On the May Sunday after the occupation troops had arrived, he and another citizen surprised the village by riding out to the Federal camp and escorting the colonel and other officers to church. Following the death of his wife, Dr. Bonner had sent for his unmarried sister Martha, a teacher in Penn Yan, New York, to help manage his household and mother his children. A year after his first gesture of reconciliation, with a stable home again established, he agreed to rent a part of the upper floor of his house to General Ord of the occupying army. The two men had become close friends by the time that the general left to assume command of the Fourth Military District, comprising all of Mississippi and Arkansas, one of five districts into which the old Confederacy had been divided.[22]

Other work was also left to be done. The education of Holly Springs children had virtually ceased during the last years of the war. The Holly Springs Female Institute had been burned by local citizens after its use as a hospital for infectious diseases. St. Thomas Hall, likewise, was now only a pile of rubble; and the two schools whose buildings remained had closed three years earlier. Thus it was with a great interest that the town learned in August of 1865 of a "Select School for Young Ladies" to be conducted at the residence of J. W. C. Watson. Mr. Watson, a graduate of the University of Virginia, a successful lawyer and a former member of the Confederate senate, was one of the town's leading citizens. His daughter, Miss Lizzie, who was to head the school, had been the person most vitally interested in education during the war years,

21. Ruth Watkins, "Reconstruction in Marshall County," *Publications of the Mississippi Historical Society*, XII (1912), 155–213.

22. Bonner, *Suwanee River Tales*, 5; Stephenson, "Sherwood Bonner," 4; Johnson, "Life Within the Confederate Lines," 71; John Mickle, "Name 'Bonner House' Stirs Old Memories," Holly Springs *South Reporter*, November 20, 1930, p. 1.

undertaking the schooling of a number of younger children of the town. The response to the "Select School" was immediately enthusiastic, and the two daughters of Dr. Charles Bonner were among the first to be enrolled.[23]

Though the time Kate Bonner spent at school in the great white house surrounded by Tuscan columns was brief, only a year, the influences encountered there were among the most important of her life. Miss Lizzie Watson herself, then in her middle thirties, had been described fifteen years earlier by a young Princeton student as "the most intellectual girl of her age that I have ever known," adding to "fine natural abilities considerable information attained by reading" and "conversing with the ease and at the same time with the force and elegance of a well educated gentleman." Here, for the first time, Kate Bonner fell under the influence of a truly intellectual woman. But Miss Lizzie's mind and example were not all that was provided in the Watson house, for here, in the years immediately following the war, was formed a definite coterie, of which Kate was to be one of the lights. Here was formed her own Holly Springs circle.[24]

At the center of that circle was the Watson family itself. A Presbyterian household known for both rectitude and cultivation, it received a necessary counterbalance to the tone of high seriousness from its younger members—the sons Jimmy and Eddie, Kate's contemporaries, who would eventually finish their educations at the University of Virginia; and the daughter-in-law Cora Harris Watson, at twenty-two a charming dark-eyed war widow, who assisted Miss Lizzie in the school.

Linked closely with the Watsons in Presbyterian probity were the Crafts, a family living across town in a similar columned residence. The patriarch, Hugh Craft, had come to Holly Springs in 1839 as a land agent and remained to prosper. Those qualities that stamped the household, however, had been provided not so much by him as by his seven children, especially three of the youngest—Heber, a graduate of Centre College, who ran a popular Holly

23. Johnson, "Life Within the Confederate Lines," 73; Hamilton, "Holly Springs," 206–209; Helen Craft Anderson, "A Chapter in the Yellow Fever Epidemic of 1878," *Publications of the Mississippi Historical Society*, X (1909), Footnote 1, 223–24.
24. Henry Craft Diary (MS in possession of Mrs. L. A. Smith, Holly Springs), April 5, 1849.

Springs bookstore both before and after the war; Addison, who
not only graduated from Centre but also married Frances Breckinridge Young, the daughter of the college's distinguished president
and the niece of John C. Breckinridge; and Helen, intelligent and
literary, one of Kate's schoolmates at the Watsons' and long her
closest friend.[25]

Bound inextricably to the other two families, but interfusing at
least a muted note of greater Episcopalian license was the Walthall-Freeman connection. Again, here, the family's founder, who
was of distinguished Tidewater Virginia origin, was not nearly so
important to the group as were his descendants. One son was the
Confederate general Edward Cary Walthall, a successful lawyer
and the partner of L. Q. C. Lamar, the figure who would soon be
ranked among the nation's most conspicuous southern public
men. More important for Kate Bonner, however, was the daughter, Mrs. Kate Walthall Freeman, whom the young woman found
"nearer to perfection than any woman I ever knew," a person of
"manifold perfections." Endowed with intelligence and great
charm, Mrs. Freeman became the social and cultural leader of the
town, giving to it a full measure of her time and energies. She was
captured well by Sherwood Bonner in her novel *Like unto Like* as
the thrifty, clever widow Mrs. Oglethorpe, who "timed the music
of the [town] orchestra." Mrs. Freeman's daughter Cary, though
she had been Kate's friend since infancy, presented quite a different
case. Without intellectual qualities but with a fresh blond beauty,
Cary was now a belle and, for Kate, a strange mixture of friend
and rival. She was what Kate both disdained and halfway desired
to be.[26]

These families formed a definite circle, one that cohered even
more strongly because of the bond of wartime suffering and postwar confusion. The members of this group mutually sustained
each other, and in their insistence on preserving an intellectual and
cultural life amid a land in ruins, they probably succeeded in creating a far more stimulating environment than the one that had ex-
isted before the war.

25. W. Henry Grant, *Ancestors and Descendants* (n.p., 1929).
26. Hamilton, "Holly Springs," 204–206; Kate S. Bonner Diary (MS in McDowell Collection), July 12, 1869; Sherwood Bonner, *Like unto Like* (New York: Harper & Brothers,
1878), 23.

One of the group's earliest ventures was the founding of a musical society, the Philharmonic. Canvassing a poor populace, they were able to raise sufficient funds to buy a fine Knabe piano, and they worked diligently on their first effort, Schiller's "Song of the Bell," given in the auditorium of the Presbyterian church, begun in 1860 and kept unfinished by the war, to an appreciative packed house. Mrs. Freeman, organist and director of the choir at Christ Church, was the guiding spirit of the Philharmonic and lent them her home for meetings. Ruth Bonner, a fine musician, sang lead parts; and Kate was featured less conspicuously, often in comic duets.[27]

The first organization to be founded after the war, however, and the most significant to Kate Bonner's development was the Philomathesian Society, the first literary club in the town's history to include women among its members. Its founding was engineered in 1866 by Miss Lizzie Watson and Mrs. Cora Watson as a means of providing further stimulation for the young women, Kate Bonner among them, who were concluding their study in the Watson home. Some local distinction was gained by having the name, denoting lovers of knowledge, suggested to Mrs. Freeman by L. Q. C. Lamar; and the officers were always male. No rigid course of study was attempted, but programs were arranged for each meeting that included original essays and poems. Kate became one of the stars—taking part in the reading of plays (ranging from *Macbeth* and *Midsummer Night's Dream* to *The Honeymoon*), proving herself a leader in discussions, and reading her own works. And during the course of the club's two-year existence, she joined a group within the group, a small circle of the young. This coterie included A. Stewart Marye and Henry M. Anderson, two professors in the Holly Springs schools which were now reopening; Howard Falconer and Henry Paine, lawyers; Cora Watson; Helen Craft; Cary Freeman; and Kate. A lively group, its quality was captured by Mr. Marye when he afterward wrote Mrs. Watson, bemoaning the cultural barrenness of Little Rock and wishing for "your aesthetic analysis, Mr. Anderson's urbanity,

27. John Mickle, "Roster Is Found of Philharmonic Club," Holly Springs *South Reporter*, December 15, 1932, p. 7.

Mr. Paine's force, Howard's smartness, Miss Kate's speculative sprightliness."[28]

The "Philo," in addition to providing both a forum and a stage for Kate, also led to her first romantic attachment of any seriousness. That romantic interest emerged in the person of Henry Martin Paine, a university-educated man in his mid-twenties, cultivated and as much a rake as minister's sons are so often disposed to be. Large, athletic, and handsome, he projected strong physical appeal and a carefully cultivated Byronic image. Before Henry Paine had completely cast his Byronic spell over her, however, another young man appeared to complicate the situation.

Edward McDowell, just a year older than Kate, had paid visits to relatives in Holly Springs since he was a child; but Kate saw him with new eyes in the summer of 1867. The mutual attraction was immediate. On her part, she must have found him the most cosmopolitan man of her age that she had ever encountered, and in a sense he was. His father James R. McDowell, who had died on the eve of the war, was a member of a wealthy Belfast family and had come to America in the late 1820s and established himself on the Mississippi River at Vicksburg. There with family backing he soon became an important merchant and planter, his plantations lying across the river in Louisiana. In 1834, he married Jane Mills, a lady of another moneyed Vicksburg connection; and in 1850 he formed a partnership with her brothers in a commission firm, Mills, McDowell, and Company, with offices in New Orleans and New York. This firm bought cotton in the wide area from Vicksburg to Galveston, and in their own vessels shipped it to English ports. Their interests grew to include banks, over a hundred thousand acres of land—much of it on the Brazos—and hundreds of slaves. Edward, the sixth of the nine McDowell children, grew up in the midst of the empire building; and by the time of the war he had experienced the life of privilege which the empire afforded. The family's seat, after they moved from Vicksburg, was Sparta Plantation in Madison Parish, Louisiana; but they retained the old Mills home in Kentucky, and they also had houses in New Orleans

28. John Mickle, "First Literary Club the Philomathesian," Holly Springs *South Reporter*, December 10, 1931, p. 16; Philomathesian notes and A. Stewart Marye to Cora Watson, March 4, 1868, both in Cora Carey Collection.

and on Forty-Second Street in New York, the two places where most of the English trade was carried on. The family also traveled widely, and Edward and the other children were exposed to high circles of American society both North and South. At the beginning of the war, with the oldest son in the Confederate army, the second son had gone to Germany for his medical education; and later Edward, the third son, had been sent to an English public school. Kate Bonner had never met a young man with the experience and exposure of this slender, tall boy of nineteen now visiting his uncle William Mills in Holly Springs.[29]

Edward McDowell was also literary and highly romantic, just the person to appreciate Kate Bonner as she was and as she imagined herself to be. She was, at eighteen, a tall girl; but she had developed from the gangling adolescent into a young woman of what the period considered "heroic type." Her well proportioned figure was enhanced by decided grace of carriage and manner, and the features that all noted were her abundant copper-colored hair and her penetrating grey-blue eyes. Adding to her striking appearance were other very real assets—intelligence, liveliness, and charm. But there were also poses. One absent friend's inquiry seems to cover the range. "Is Miss Kate," he wrote, "Mystic, Transcendental or Poetical at present and how is she?" Unlike that writer, Edward McDowell could appreciate, and even worship, all the images, real or affected, as an early description in his hand tells us. That description, written by one "so unworthy," is a sketch of "St. Katherine":

> When you looked at her face, in its aureole of Guinea-golden hair, the first feature noticed was nose; a peculiar one; not large, yet very forcible, and indicative of ability to the advancement of its fair owner in any direction toward which her asperations [sic] tended. A nose, it was too, of active self-defense.
>
> Next you would observe the mouth; being most-like to find there either a kind, sweet smile or a bright, playful half-laugh; but were these absent the sweet lips fell into a melancholy drooping (sweeter, if

29. Obituary of Jane Mills McDowell and Mills-McDowell genealogical chart, both in McDowell Collection; Jesse A. Ziegler, "Ziegler Writes of Early Texas Merchant Princes," Galveston *Daily News*, March 12, 1933, p. 11; biographical sketch of Robert Mills in Walter Prescott Webb (ed.), *The Handbook of Texas* (Austin: The Texas State Historical Association, 1952), II, 200.

possible than either smile or laugh). This drooping expression, by the way, I finally ascertained to be habitual when she was alone. In looking for her eyes, one must first ever have remarked the forehead, with its slight retreat, and heavy base which overhung the eyes—eyes like the sky of a Northern sunrise, making the saddened soul of weakly ones to glow, even as the grey-blue light of morning freshens the erstwhile darkened earth. Such was her gaze of love, but were her righteous anger roused, those eyes would give one quick look—that one look all sufficient, and then deigning no more she would turn with a scornful lifting of her expressive lip and leave the object of her contempt in mingled wonder and humiliation. She never relied on words for the expression of her anger. Her general bearing was stately as a queen's; but when joyed at the meeting of some dear friend or lover she would glide as swiftly to meet them, as I have seen an Autumn-tinted maple leaf wander gracefully in mid-air, seemingly independent of common law until catching sight of the clear lake, it would dart toward it with a quick flutter at thought of union with its love.

Her soul was all Truth, Honor, Charity, & filled with saint-like love; and the music of good deeds had made a full high harmony of her life but that the chord of hope was loosened and sent forth a melancholy sound, which, though it sweetened that harmony, made it the less cheering.

This tribute, despite its youthful excesses, reveals a great deal about both parties. It shows clearly Kate's magnetism and her pride, which displayed itself so often as hauteur; and it suggests that, given even the fact of her posturing, there was a very real vein of deep melancholy in her nature. Of Edward's condition, the manuscript is even more revealing. Here was a very young man, an innocent despite his cosmopolitan exposure, both reveling in playing to the hilt the role of romantic lover, and in addition, feeling himself very much in love.[30]

As the summer days passed into autumn, the two saw more and more of each other. Despite warnings that she was in love with Mr. Paine, that Kate Bonner was a coquette who would break his heart, Edward's feelings were only strengthened. Finally came Saturday, November 30, 1867, a day that both would always remember. Edward had paid a call on Helen Craft, and by mid-afternoon the two had dispatched a note to Kate asking her to join them.

30. A. Stewart Marye to Cora Watson, February 13, 1868, Cora Carey Collection; unsigned "St. Katherine" MS, a draft heavily revised, in Stephenson Collection.

Other company came and went, but the two young people stayed to supper, Kate, saying that she was unwell, moody until after the meal. Helen had then settled herself at the piano in the back parlor, and the two left in the front parlor began exchanging notes. After a considerable amount of paper was consumed, they reached a point where, in Edward's words, "the die was cast." He observed later that he had seen stars for the rest of the evening, and both were to refer to the date as the "day of our understanding each other." No formal engagement took place then, and marriage was deferred for over three years, but on that night Kate Bonner took a step that would lead her to a complex fate.[31]

31. Edward McDowell to Cora Watson, December 1, 1867, and December 15, 1869, in Cora Carey Collection.

Chapter Two

The Road to Boston

THE NEXT SIX YEARS were a time when the early influences upon Kate Bonner and the forces within her own nature led to choices and actions. She found herself first confused, then entrapped, and she finally embarked on a course that flouted family and convention. She viewed herself at the end of this period, she told Ralph Waldo Emerson, as one whose life had been a failure, "because, perhaps, I did not recognize its possibilities." Her daring decision, however, was based not only upon a recognition of her illusions and mistakes, but also upon a strong faith in herself bred by an early success.[1]

A little more than a year after her secret engagement to Edward McDowell came a great triumph for Kate—her entry on the printed page. After the night of November 30, Edward was constant in his attentions; but suddenly Christmas was over, and he was gone, not to return until the next summer. In a social climate as marriage-dominated as that of Jane Austen's novels, Kate was left with plenty of time to dream and to brood; but Edward's departure released her from some of the old concerns about romance and courtship. She turned more serious attention to writing, and her first story appeared in print just a few days before her twentieth birthday. Her success did not completely surprise the friends who remembered the precocious child explaining her torn pinafore by way of an essay, or the schoolmates from the Institute who recalled her compositions, so unlike theirs. From an early age she had seemed innately literary, but there were factors that had propelled her and that gave a particular shape to what she wrote.

A primary influence was the literary atmosphere at Bonner

1. Katharine McDowell to Ralph Waldo Emerson, March 23, 1874, in Emerson Collection, Houghton Library, Harvard University.

House itself. Literature was valued by no one in Holly Springs more than by Dr. Charles Bonner, and his collection of books was among the best in town. An interesting view of the probable contents of his library is provided by Sherwood Bonner in her novel *Like unto Like*, where she observes of the Holly Springs gentry's reading tastes:

> Their reading was of a good solid sort. They were brought up, as it were, on Walter Scott. They read Richardson, Fielding, and Smollett. . . . They liked Thackeray pretty well, Bulwer very well, Dickens they read under protest—they thought him low. They felt an easy sense of superiority in being "quite English in our tastes, you know," and knew little of the literature of their own country, as it came chiefly from the North. Of its lesser lights they had never heard, and as for the greater, they would have pitted an ounce of Poe against a pound of any one of them.

Many of Kate's childhood hours were spent in the Bonner House library, her father encouraging and directing her reading. And the father's love of books was early and strongly imparted to his oldest child.[2]

Further strengthening the child's literary bent was surely Kate's exposure at an impressionable age to a much revered literary man. The village of Holly Springs, so dominated by politics and so far removed from the literary centers, had been the home of one of the country's most prolific and financially successful writers. Joseph Holt Ingraham, after having produced dozens of sensational adventure novels, had entered the Episcopal clergy and written biblical novels that were as successful as the lurid works of his youth. He arrived in Holly Springs in 1858 to serve as rector of both Christ Church and St. Thomas Hall, the diocesan school for boys. Here, before his death in late 1860, he wrote two more best sellers, *Pillar of Fire* and *Throne of David*. Kate Bonner had known him rather well. He was rector at a time when she was quite religious, his youngest daughter had been one of her playmates, and his intimacy with her kin was so strong that Ingraham was buried on the

2. Alexander L. Bondurant, "Sherwood Bonner," *Publications of the Mississippi Historical Society*, II (June, 1898), 44, 46; George R. Stephenson, "Sherwood Bonner" (a 1932 typescript in the collection of the Reverend Dr. George Royster Stephenson of Jackson, Mississippi), 3; Sherwood Bonner, *Like unto Like* (New York: Harper & Brothers, 1878), 17.

Martin lot in the Holly Springs cemetery. Perhaps even more significant than her own direct contact with the novelist, however, was his being ranked among the town's great figures. Holly Springs did have among its roster of heroes, primarily military and political, one who was literary.[3]

Under such influences, the strongly individual young girl early began to write her own stories and poems. Kate's first surviving juvenilia dates from 1863, an elegy for "Verna," a girl of sixteen. The poem, written in seven stanzas, is a direct reflection of Kate Bonner's reading in the English romantic poets. To the same year, when Kate was fourteen, probably belongs the uncompleted manuscript of a short story, set on the gloomy wedding day of the beautiful maid Ella Montroy. The last known item among her juvenilia offers the only early literary evidence of the ironic humor that later helped to make Sherwood Bonner a successful writer. This piece, entitled "A Peep Behind the Scenes," was written in collaboration with Helen Craft shortly after Kate's school days. It satirized Holly Springs society through several detailed portraits. Obviously the satire hit the mark. Among the subjects of the sketches was Cary Freeman, once Kate's closest friend, but now not only one of the belles of the town, but also Kate's rival for Henry Paine. When the anonymous work came into Cary's hands, she immediately destroyed it.[4]

Over the years, as Kate Bonner was trying her hand at various kinds of writing, she continued to read everything in sight. By the time that she had graduated from Miss Lizzie's school, she had read all the books in her father's library, even *Tom Jones* and the plays of Ben Jonson, kept on the highest shelf and forbidden to

3. Warren Graham French, "A Sketch of the Life of Joseph Holt Ingraham," *Journal of Mississippi History*, XI (July, 1949), 155–71. The earliest historical sketch of Holly Springs (an unidentified 1874 clipping in Helen Craft Anderson's scrapbook in the collection of Mrs. John Craft and Mrs. James Driver of Holly Springs; hereinafter referred to as Craft Collection) notes Ingraham's place among the town's illustrious citizens, and Sherwood Bonner gratuitously includes a reference to Ingraham's memorial tablet in Christ Church in *Like unto Like*, 162.

4. "Verna" MS in the Kate Freeman Clark Collection, Marshall County Historical Society, Holly Springs; "Ella Montroy" MS in Walthall-Freeman Collection, Department of Archives and Special Collections, University Library, University of Mississippi. Information on "A Peep Behind the Scenes" comes from Nash Kerr Burger, Jr., "Katherine Sherwood Bonner: A Study in the Development of a Southern Literature" (M.A. thesis, University of Virginia, 1935), 33; and from Charles N. Dean of Holly Springs.

her. And she had encountered still another influence, and a quite pervasive one. She had read not only most of the novels in town, but also "thousands of old magazines." In fact, two of her three earliest extant notes and letters contain requests to borrow "Frank Leslie's" and "Appleton's" and the notes mention the return of other such journals.[5]

By the late winter of 1867–1868, after years of absorption in other writers, Kate was struggling to find the right fictional mode for herself. She began work on a piece entitled "Seven Nights at Edgewood" and tried the old device of isolating a diverse group of people and having each tell a tale to pass the time. The result of her labor is a terrible hodgepodge, but the manuscript offers a revealing view of the influences upon her and certain cross-tendencies within her, the counter attractions of which took years to resolve. She fills Edgewood with people whom she knew and whom she disguised very little—the vivacious widow Mrs. Withers (Cora Watson), the mild lawyer Heber Forrester (Howard Falconer), the charming rector Dr. Percival (the Reverend Dr. Pickett), among others. She also gives space to a rendering of conversations that she had probably heard at the Philo—for example, an argument about poetry, centering on Whitman, Byron, Pope, and Poe. In short, she seems to have wanted to convey the life that she had seen and known. But a counter tendency is more pronounced: she is even more strongly drawn to the exotic. Edgewood, instead of being the Leggett plantation house from which she took the name, becomes an English country house; and, of the two tales recounted in the surviving manuscript, one is set in New Zealand, a story of shipwreck, cannibalism, and a love affair with a native princess; while the other details a long series of heroic exploits, including entrapment in a burning building, as a noble young man repeatedly defends and rescues his fallen sister. The Edgewood manuscript may contain allusions to Shakespeare, to Samuel Johnson, and to Byron, but it owes its major influence neither to life as Kate Bonner had seen it, nor to the great writers of the past, but to

5. Bonner, *Like unto Like*, 66, 38; Kate Bonner to Cary Freeman [1865–1866], in Walthall-Freeman Collection, Department of Archives and Special Collections, University of Mississippi; Kate Bonner to Cora Watson, December 10, [1869], Cora Carey Collection, Mississippi Department of Archives and History, Jackson.

hundreds of stories in American periodicals. For the past twenty years these magazines had been dominated by the melodramatic, the sentimental, the contrived. Kate Bonner, after devouring a great many of these tales, was trying to produce one of her own.[6]

Before the year was out, she had; and with "Laura Capello" she entered what Louisa May Alcott called the "frothy sea of sensational literature." Earlier that year, after seeing a letter from Nahum Capen giving literary advice, Kate Bonner had begun a correspondence with the Boston literary man, then an advisor to the "Ladies Department" of the *Massachusetts Ploughman and New England Journal of Agriculture*. On the twenty-first of January, 1869, she mailed him what she referred to as "my Italian story"; and on February twentieth appeared "Laura Capello, A Leaf from a Traveller's Notebook," written for the *Massachusetts Ploughman* by Clayton Vaughn. Her selection of a male pseudonym was still a not uncommon practice among some American female writers, but Kate Bonner probably felt in it a link with the British writers Charlotte Bronte and Mary Ann Evans, whom she was often to hold before herself as models of the literary woman. The meaning of the names themselves is more difficult to explain. Clayton was the surname of a friend since her days at Miss Lizzie's, Clara Clayton; and Vaughn, the maiden name of her favorite maternal aunt, Anne Martin. Perhaps she merely liked the ring of the two. If the pseudonym defies a completely satisfactory analysis, the story itself does not. The week before Clayton Vaughn's offering, the *Ploughman* gave its readers "Buried Alive—A Night in Greenmount Cemetery," and, a week after, "Frozen In," with a Rhine setting. Kate Bonner outdid them both with her Italian thriller.[7]

"Laura Capello" is as contrived and as melodramatic as the stories preceding and following it, and it is far more sensational. But, given its formula, it is also a much superior piece of work, displaying overall an ease of style and real storytelling power. The narra-

6. "Seven Nights at Edgewood" (MS in the Stephenson Collection). Beneath the title, Kate Bonner wrote "by Clayton Vaughn." This is evidently the first use of that pseudonym.

7. Louisa May Alcott, *Little Women* (New York: Macmillan, 1966), 406; Nahum Capen to Dr. Charles Bonner, October 12, 1873, in Stephenson Collection; Kate Bonner Diary (MS in the collection of David McDowell III, of Batesville, Mississippi), January 21, 1869 (hereinafter cited as Diary).

tor is a male artist wholly dependent upon his "slender earnings," who in his travels with a friend stops at a village in southern Italy. A gossipy innkeeper recounts for the pair the history of the village and its two most revered citizens: Lady Hervey, a universally beloved Englishwoman who, with her daughter and her late husband, had taken possession of the nearby castle some twenty years earlier; and the village priest Father Eustace, "one of God's own saints" and "the one person who is loved more than my lady." The artist is curious about another figure—a young man who stands out from the mass of villagers both because of his obvious superiority and because the others seem to shun him. The innkeeper identifies the youth as Lorenzo Caspa, whom both Lady Hervey and the priest have encouraged to pay court to her ladyship's daughter. As a result, his old companions have ostracized him, not only because he seems to have stepped out of his class, but also because he seems to have played false with Laura Capello, a girl left as a foundling in the village and reared by Mother Capello, a peasant woman.

Later the narrator accidentally gains an even closer view of Lorenzo's situation. After the artist has climbed to the top of a tree to gain the proper vantage point from which to sketch the village in moonlight, the rotten limbs break, and the man crashes to the ground. His companion leaves to search for help, and now, after considerable contrivance, the perfect situation for a voyeur narrator has been created. Hidden in the shadows, the artist spies upon a chance meeting between Lorenzo and Laura and learns that both are being manipulated by others. Lorenzo cannot ignore his summonses to the castle, which remove him from Laura; and Laura has been instructed by the priest that her parents' sin can be expiated only by her giving herself to God and entering a nunnery. As Lorenzo protests, a Gothic figure, his form shrouded in the folds

No one studying Sherwood Bonner had read "Laura Capello" since 1898, when Professor Alexander Bondurant saw the copy she had pasted in her scrapbook. The scrapbook has since vanished, but Bondurant quoted this notation in the author's hand: "First story ever published, aged fifteen, *Boston Ploughman*, twenty dollars" (Bondurant, "Sherwood Bonner," 47). The age that the author assigned herself was clearly misleading, but wholly consistent with her lifelong tendency to change ages slightly for heightened effect. Her 1869 diary, however, should have led all researchers to both "Laura Capello" and the two subsequent *Ploughman* stories.

of his cloak, appears and pronounces the words: "The bride of Heaven must never know aught of earthly passion." When Lorenzo demands to know who has the authority to speak so, the figure replies, "Her father"; pushes his cloak aside; and reveals a countenance, "cold, haughty and severe," the "index to a heart filled with the most baleful passions of humanity," the face of a man "whose whole life had been a weary struggle against the power of overmastering evil." Threatened with exposure by Lorenzo, the satanic figure draws a dagger and stabs the youth "to the heart." At this moment, the narrator conveniently loses consciousness, and thus ends part one.

The artist regains his faculties several days later to find that Laura is on trial for Lorenzo's murder. He hurries to the courtroom and gives his testimony to the attentive judge, who is completely satisfied, wanting only a priest before whom the artist can give his oath. Father Eustace is summoned, and the narrator immediately recognizes the demon-murderer. Amid the commotion caused by this revelation and by Father Eustace's denial, the priest uses his power over Laura and forces her to confess to the crime. The judge immediately imposes a sentence of death, at which Lady Hervey shrieks and delivers her own confession. She reveals that Laura is her own child by Father Eustace and that her husband's shock at discovering the fact had caused his death. She and the priest had subsequently placed the child on the Capello doorstep, consecrated her life to the church in expiation for their own sin, and sought to distract Lorenzo, who had recently threatened to foil their plan. Now Lady Hervey cries passionately—"Eustace! Eustace! You may kill me if you will, but ah! God, I cannot see my child die!" At this, the priest walks from the room as the villagers sit stunned.

Following is a coda in which the artist returns to the village after several years to find that Lady Hervey had died soon after the courtroom scene "without any known disease," a mere pining unto death, and that Laura and Mother Capello go about, blessed, doing good. Then Kate Bonner disposes of her villain-priest in a crescendo:

> As for Father Eustace, the man who had blighted so many lives, nothing more was ever heard of him after the day of the trial. Whether

he plunged into the world's vortex for forgetfulness, or tried through prayer and penitence to make his peace with an outraged God I cannot say. But I often think that, hide himself as he may from the eye of the world, the day will come when all disguise must be swept away and side by side with his victims he will be judged before the awful tribunal of God.

Despite the sanctimony of this final pronouncement, neither the shock expressed by the mother of one of the author's friends nor that woman's forbidding any discussion of religion between Kate and her daughter is particularly surprising. Here, indeed, the young author had created a man of the cloth worthy of Monk Lewis. And the story had appeared on the same page with recipes for raisin cake and ginger snaps and an advertisement for Wilcox and Gibbs's Sewing Machine. How Kate Bonner's rebellious soul must have relished it all.[8]

Probably she did not realize, however, that her entry into the literary world was similar to that of many other established writers of her time, particularly female ones. Louisa May Alcott stands out as a notable example, and it is interesting that she too had made her debut with an Italian story, "The Rival Painters: A Tale of Rome," also under a pseudonym, though a female one. Through the 1860s, Miss Alcott was helping to keep her family afloat by means of thrillers, or what she called "romantic rubbish"; and her editor became quite frank in his requests that she furnish him with "a sensational story." The two women shared another bond: both understood the formulas of this sort of fiction completely. They could observe the conventions; they showed skill at handling the props and machinery. In short, they could deliver. Kate had shown this well in "Laura Capello."[9]

She continued to reveal her competence in the two other stories that appeared in the *Massachusetts Ploughman* later that year. The next, "The Heir of Delmont," owes something not only to other periodical stories, but also to Walter Scott. It presents another deep-dyed villain in the person of the aged Earl of Delmont

8. Diary, January 19, 1869.
9. Alcott's sensational stories are reprinted and discussed intelligently in Madeleine Stern (ed.), *Behind a Mask: The Unknown Thrillers of Louisa May Alcott* (New York: William Morrow & Co., 1976). Both Alcott's remarks and her editor's are quoted in Stern's introduction, xxvi and xxiii.

and plenty of melodrama as the result of his treachery, but it also contains faithful retainers, the triumph of youthful love despite family obstacles, and more than one character motivated by the highest dictates of chivalry. Kate Bonner's third offering is in no way a thriller, but it too follows a definite convention. The story "Saved" is much closer to the tale following it in the *Ploughman*, "Love in a Saw Mill," than it is to Kate's two earlier works. It is her attempt at the tale inculcating the domestic virtues and arguing for the marriage of true love. The main character Marion, beautiful but poor, is in love with the stalwart young John, but she is also being courted by rich old Squire Dermon. Pondering the choice between the two men—a choice between baking, mending, washing, cleaning, or leading a life of luxury—she falls asleep, and she dreams. In her dream she chooses to marry for money and she subsequently creates a life of misery for both herself and the old squire. With relief she wakes, saved by the dream from an awful mistake. She accepts John immediately, and the story closes with a mellow picture of true love in a cottage. In its contrasting of the world's vanities with true domestic bliss, "Saved" lies in easy juxtaposition with the surrounding recipes.[10]

Though she had now demonstrated her talent for producing different sorts of marketable fiction, her success did not bring Kate Bonner complete happiness. She had published three stories in the year 1869, but many facets of her life were clearly not under control. Much of her confusion sprang from the question of marrying Edward. But the causes of her recurrent bouts of melancholy were even more deeply seated, and she was not to understand them well until years later. Now she spoke of herself often as a "rudderless ship," and she noted in her diary many intense depressions, like the experience on a coach bound for Holly Springs, after which she wrote: "Last night spent the night on the chaise in weeping— the wherefore I know not." Nine years later, however, in creating

10. "The Heir of Delmont," which Kate Bonner referred to when she sent it off as the "exciting story without a name—all about a modern Quixote called Henry White" (Diary, May 12, 1869), is a long piece which the *Massachusetts Ploughman* presented in two installments, August 28 and September 4, 1869. "Saved," published on October 9, had been originally titled "Marion's Mistake" by its author (Diary, May 23, 1869). These two stories appeared without the pseudonym Clayton Vaughn; they are designated as simply "written for the *Massachusetts Ploughman*."

for her novel a twenty-year-old heroine, Sherwood Bonner located the basic conflict, responsible for so many forms of unhappiness, in herself at the same age. At the core of the character Blythe Herndon, a battle between indolence and ambition is being waged. Blythe admits that she is basically lazy. "But," she comments, "I have an intellectual consciousness that laziness is contemptible. So my two selves are constantly at war; I am torn by conflicting desires." Clearly Blythe Herndon here is the young Kate Bonner. Again and again, Kate made her resolutions—such as renouncing society for the winter and devoting herself to the study of French, German, and music. She was haunted by guilt for the opportunities that she had let pass and by the consciousness of her wasted talents. "Every one tells me I could make of myself what I would," she wrote in her diary, "and I am determined to make one last effort." Again and again, she broke the resolutions; for, on the one hand, she enjoyed companionship and society's many attractions, and, on the other, she was drawn to passive literary pursuits, like reading "trashy novels" while drinking "much lemonade"—perhaps her favorite occupation. She was pleased with her literary success, but dimly she knew that she must work harder to develop her talents. She wanted to be Emerson's active soul, but she also wanted to indulge herself, and she could not enjoy her indulgences thoroughly because of the resulting guilt. One effect of the conflict was an extreme sensitivity to the whole issue, as evidenced by her reaction to the rector's "scathing sermon," entitled "Why stand ye here idle"; and her subsequent distaste for "bullying denunciations from the pulpit." The more pervasive response, however, was simply an often ill-defined sense of unhappiness and discontent.[11]

Her discontent was aggravated by the fact that she was a woman in a highly traditional society, but this problem was another that Kate Bonner recognized only vaguely. She had stirrings of feminist resentment as evidenced by her comment after enjoying an evening at Mobile's St. James's Club, "What a grand privilege it is to be a man!" or her feeling during the election of 1869, "Regret more than ever that women are denied the privilege of voting." But her rebellion against woman's commonly accepted role was expressed,

11. Diary, February 26, May 11, June 4, 1869; Bonner, *Like unto Like*, 76; Diary, September 13, September 26, October 10, July 11, September 11, 1869.

for the most part, simply through a desire to do and say the unconventional. After Henry Dancy's wedding at "*the* party of the season," she found particular pleasure in the many compliments paid her by gentlemen because all the ladies were aware that she was wearing the shortest dress in the room, her feet showing "so plainly!" When her family failed to meet a train on which Kate and Helen Craft arrived in Holly Springs, the two asserted "our woman's independence by walking alone from the depot"; and Kate found great satisfaction in her belief that "scarcely any other two girls in the world would have been so brave and so imprudent." She also enjoyed the shock at her fiction registered by people like Sophie Shepard's mother. Indeed, both her diary for the year 1869 and her letters for the rest of her life abound in references to Mrs. Grundy. Kate was always quite aware of the public's expectations and judgments and often far too ready to fly in the teeth of them. Even at this early period, however, her rebellion did express itself in less juvenile forms. The foremost instance is provided by her defense of a teacher at Franklin Female College dismissed because the woman was judged "fallen." [12]

Paradoxically, both her rebellion against propriety and her fundamental acceptance of her societally imposed role can be attributed, in great part, to her own family's rigid conventionality. Aunt Martha Bonner had tried hard to become a mother to the Bonner children, and both her definite role and that of Dr. Bonner are reflected in Kate's diary entry recording their parting words to her as she left on a trip south: "Aunty says God bless me, & Papa asks if I have left any bills unpaid." Dr. Bonner was, to use Edward McDowell's designation, "her stern parent." Kate was probably his favorite child; certainly she was the most like him in her intellectual interests. He expected a great deal from her, and he held the reins tight. Being rather puritanical, he forbade some pleasures, like a particular masquerade ball, which the girl felt was one of life's moments of real color. At the least, even when events did not bring out the puritan streak, he was guided by abstract standards. Sherwood Bonner was later to treat this side of her father humorously when she had Blythe Herndon comment, "Papa never

12. Diary, April 9, November 15, September 1, November 22, January 19, November 23, 1869.

willingly gives gossip any food. I believe he would like for us all to be drowned at sea to avoid the sensation of a funeral in the family." At twenty, however, Kate Bonner lacked the distance for a humorous response, and she found herself not only forbidden "trivial" pleasures, but also lectured on matters like taking part in politics. Again, only later did she realize the depth of her family's feelings on woman's role. She captured that feeling in her novel with an incident from her childhood. During the war a little French boy new to town had formed a company of girls and taught them to drill. Dr. Bonner judged the business "unladylike," and he had forbidden Kate to join the group. After days of her daughter's tears, Mrs. Bonner made something acceptable to cheer the girl—an apron decorated with the stars and bars. At twenty, despite her various sorts of rebellion, Kate Bonner, whether she knew it or not, felt the apron her only choice. One diary entry is particularly revealing. On the first of December, 1869, she wrote: "I have thought much of my future & am determined *unless I marry* to carve out my own fortune." The italics are mine, for the qualification is indeed strange. Earlier in the same entry she had written of Edward that she "never loved him better." She was actually viewing what she would later think of as "self-definition" as something outside of marriage, and at the same time she knew that marriage was to be her fate.[13]

She could hardly have come to any other conclusion, given her milieu, her rearing, and her own deep romanticism. Before the war, when just a child, she had cherished a "secret passion" for a "knightly being" whom she had seen riding at a tournament under the name of Glendower. As a young woman, she still craved a knight, someone to carry her away, though she was finding it more difficult to sustain her illusions. "I wish I could find a hero," she wrote in her diary. "Are they all dead? or do they only live in the novelist's brain?" Still she tried, wavering back and forth among other candidates during Edward's absence. Henry Paine still held some of his Byronic appeal for her. "Surely," she felt, "God never made a nobler-looking man." But he had now shocked and es-

13. Diary, January 6, 1869; Edward McDowell to Cora Watson, May 29, 1868, in Cora Carey Collection; Bonner, *Like unto Like*, 76; Diary, November 10, 1869; Bonner, *Like unto Like*, 80.

tranged many of his friends by turning Republican and getting elected county attorney on the "Radical" ticket; and he was becoming increasingly dissipated. Even the dissipation, however, was not totally lacking in appeal, as one description reveals. One night as Kate and her party passed a local saloon, the Can-Can, "Looking in, I saw a sight that is stamped upon my brain—Mr. Paine, with his coat off, & a glass raised to his lips. He turned his face almost as I did mine and its expression—wild, defiant, glaring, he flushed, and with blood-shot eyes—I shuddered as though I saw some wild animal." But he proved to be not even a somewhat debauched and sensual knight, when Kate learned that he had sworn love not only to her and Cary, but also to Ida Topp, to whom he had denigrated the other two. Gradually it became clear that Edward McDowell was the most likely candidate for knighthood.[14]

Edward, she wrote at the end of 1869, is "my one hope." But she had chosen a weak reed on which to lean. Obviously the young man was charming; he had won all of the Holly Springs circle. Among his foremost qualities in Kate's view must have been the fact that he seemed preeminently cultivated. In a single letter to Mrs. Cora Watson, he mentions Charles Reade, Dion Boucicault, Dickens, Swinburne, Arnold, and George Eliot, as well as *Lucille*, *Abelard and Eloise*, and *Don Juan*. He subscribed to *Every Saturday*, a fashionable literary journal devoted to English and Continental works. Deeming himself "a lover of the *Beaux Arts*," he had assembled a collection of prints. He was also interested in scientific developments and the latest inventions. Despite his apparently wide range of interests, he was actually not a Renaissance man, but a dilettante. Working as secretary to his uncle Robert Mills in a commission house in Galveston, he was bored; and not being consistently occupied with his duties, he roamed the Galveston bookstores and, as he put it, "carried on a business of my own." His dilemma was not an uncommon one for young southern men of his class after the war. He had been reared in the luxury provided by a social and economic system that was now gone. As a result, he was lost. "Isn't it hard to make one's self a martyr to circumstance?!" he wrote. "At least so I have found it—in doing

14. Helen Craft's annotations of *Like unto Like* (in possession of Mrs. Fort Daniel, Holly Springs), 80; Diary, December 15, August 7, September 25, 1869.

commission business. I was brought up latterly among young men whose objects in life were—what?—That's the question. *Nothing*, I should say; for they were all wealthy, and indeed so was I *then*—but the times are changed, alas!" He was later to vow to Kate that he was "going to work with an iron will" in order to be able to support her, but the strong will turned out to be hers. Edward was always to be the same cultivated, attractive man, ever dreaming of future wealth, always fundamentally unwilling to work to get it.[15]

Kate was not to come to grips with the fact of Edward's weakness and instability for some years. In the meantime she was left with recurrent feelings of discontent about her own wasted talents, her lack of purpose, her uncertain future, and her ambivalence toward the idea of marrying him. Despite her melancholy streak, however, her life was not all gloom. Many people were struck most, in fact, by her wit, her capacity for gaiety, and her coquetry. That wit, which others sometimes dreaded, could also be turned upon herself. In her diary she could indulge in self-pity by noting of Bronte's *Villette*, one of her favorite books: "Oh! the inexpressible pathos of the book! How exactly it suits the wild spirit that weary of its useless rebellings against fate rests at last in the calm of despair." But she could then ridicule her own pose in the very next entry: "Miss Mixsell's new dresses arrived from Philadelphia & were so pretty that they suggested to me something to live for." The active Holly Springs social scene often engaged her interest thoroughly, and on many occasions she bloomed in it—as on the night of Colonel Walter's ball, when she noted with some humor at her own vanity that she had been a great success, flirting, teasing, and looking "'radiant'—in a mermaid dress of sea green tarleton & many 'golden curls.'" So the time passed with a round of picnics, suppers, serenades, balls, and wedding parties, a trip to New Orleans and Mobile, and pleasant sojourns at nearby plantation houses, Martin's Hill, the seat of her mother's relatives, or Edgewood, the beautiful home of her old school friend Corrine Leggett. There was a great deal of light to compensate for the periods of shade in her life.[16]

15. Edward McDowell to Cora Watson, January 26, February 16, December 31, May 29, 1868, in Cora Carey Collection; Diary, July 8, 1869.
16. Diary, June 29, June 30, 1869.

Edward had come to Holly Springs for summer visits in 1868 and 1869. The second time he did not return to his uncle's commission house in Galveston. He had decided, instead, to go to California and make his fortune there. His letters were fascinating, his purpose seemed firm, but the California plan did not work out. By the summer of 1870, he was back in Holly Springs living in the home of his Mills uncle and working as a clerk in that uncle's store on the square.[17]

Obviously Edward's circumstances were not promising ones for marriage. Still, many people were in reduced circumstances. Dr. Bonner himself had been renting out part of the upper floor of Bonner House for the last four years. More even than upon economic factors, however, Kate Bonner's scrutiny should have been focused on her own ambivalence toward the young man. "I do feel that I love him very thoroughly indeed," she wrote in her diary; and then she followed the sentence with—"I suppose one never meets his ideal." Later, pressed down by feelings of despair, she wrote, "My one hope is in Edward—but he would not understand these feelings." Withal, she was a confused young woman. At the end of the year in which she had published the three stories in the *Ploughman*, she could write, incredibly enough: "I have decided to be an actress—after hesitating for a long time in favor of a literary life." At twenty, at twenty-one, she was still very, very young.[18]

In her youth, with her so basically romantic soul, amid the marriages going on about her, she took Edward's ring and they set the date. If she was going to marry, she was going to do it with flair. She chose Valentine's Day, and she had a host of bridesmaids: Holly Springs would not forget her wedding. On that February night in 1871, the wedding and reception over, the young couple having departed for their wedding trip, one of the bridesmaids, Kate's sister Ruth, recorded in her diary: "Kate was married tonight. I wonder what her future will be." That young maid, so sweet, so gentle, so thoroughly proper, could never have guessed.[19]

Kate's future began in an ordinary enough way, however. With her low threshold of tolerance for what she always considered

17. 1870 Census, Marshall County, Mississippi, Holly Springs, Ward One, p. 16.
18. Diary, August 20, December 14, December 1, 1869.
19. Ruth Bonner Diary (MS in Stephenson Collection), February 14, 1871.

household drudgery, she took the advice of a friend already married for several years—"If you . . . take the responsibilities of matron . . . just make up your mind to board, and I can from experience suggest the house of Dr. Charles Bonner." So, after their return from the wedding trip, she and Edward moved into the upper floor of Bonner House. The choice spared Kate domestic exertion; it was also almost necessary given Edward's financial state. She had hardly settled into the social routine of receiving and returning wedding calls when she discovered that she was pregnant. She passed the rest of the year preparing for the birth, and on December 10, a daughter, Lilian, was born to her at Bonner House.[20]

The last months of 1871 also brought pressing financial worries. Edward's uncle William Mills, old and in poor health, had decided to sell his house and his store in Holly Springs and to join his brothers and his sons in Galveston. Thus, Edward found himself without employment. He was saved for the moment from resolving the issue of his livelihood by his mother's decision to move to Holly Springs. First her oldest daughter and now Edward had married into families of the village, and she herself had long used her brother's house there as a retreat from her plantation in the malarial season. With the once great McDowell fortune now gone and only the land remaining, she had to simplify her mode of living. The healthful location and the relative cheapness of life in Holly Springs seemed to provide the answer. During the early months of 1872, Edward was involved in purchasing a large frame cottage on Salem Street for her and in helping with other details of her move from Louisiana. On June 20, Edward, Kate, and Lilian left Bonner House and moved down the street to his mother's cottage to live with her, her daughters Lilly and Mary, and her youngest son David. This change accomplished, Edward was forced to look at his own problem, and by fall he had determined to attach himself once again to the Mills's interests in Galveston. When he departed for Texas, he left his wife and child behind.[21]

A year and a half of marriage had brought Kate face to face with

20. Laura Pickett Thomas Robinson to Kate S. Bonner, April 15, 1869, in Stephenson Collection.
21. Obituary of William Mills, Holly Springs *Reporter*, October 10, 1872, p. 3; undated obituary of Jane Mills McDowell (McDowell Collection); *McDowell* v. *Craft and*

many of Edward's weaknesses. During the long months at Bonner House, he had contributed nothing toward the household expenses. Now he had simply transferred the financial responsibility for his wife and daughter from her family to his own, and he was off to make his fortune again, espousing the same sorts of plans as when he had left for California. Kate could no longer find much consolation in the fact that their financial situation was not unusual, that many others who had also once been rich were now rather poor. She was to comment with some bitterness, in fact, even five years later on the postwar social scene's being "mixed in a dreadful way," citing particularly that "some of our best people are clerks for petty shopkeepers." Marshall County, like much of the South, had been devastated. In 1860, the assessed value of real estate had been fourteen million dollars; in 1870, four million. The total personal property, moreover, had gone from twenty-five million in 1860 to less than two million a decade later. But the full story was more complex. Despite depressed conditions, rebuilding was going on; many were repairing their fortunes. The Holly Springs *Reporter* could boast in the Fourth of July issue for 1872 that "there is not a town in the great state of Mississippi which has made such steady and substantial strides in improvement since the close of the war as our own," mentioning particularly the physical structures rising "on the ground where but a few years ago the crumbling walls and moldering debris told the sad story of how fiercely the fiery flame had done its work in times of war." Some of those responsible for and profiting from this rebuilding were, indeed, not considered "the best people." Kate was galled by one James House, who had run a livery stable before the war, had made a fortune during the war running the blockade, and had recently built the only mansion to compare with the prewar structures. But the postwar economic situation presented more than the simple case of the bottom rail now being on top. Addison Craft, Helen's brother, had just built a large and elegant house; and Jimmy Watson, Kate's and Edward's old friend, was establishing himself well as a young lawyer. That was the complete picture

---

Bonner (Custody Suit over Lilian K. McDowell), No. 1657 in Chancery Docket, Chancery Clerk's Office, Marshall County Courthouse, Holly Springs (hereinafter cited as Custody Suit).

against which she began to view Edward's circumstances and his character.[22]

In addition to her new, clearer view of her husband, there were other factors to contend with. She had been forced to accommodate herself quickly to many changes. Within ten months, she had become wife and mother. Her earlier feeling about babies ("unmitigated pests & nuisances") had changed, and she loved little Lilian deeply. But she was not notably adept at caring for the child. Domestic duties in general were not very congenial to her. Before her marriage, she had vowed: "Marriage is not to sink *me* into a drudge or nonentity, whatever it may do for the weaker sisters." That—she now began to feel—was exactly what marriage had done. Dependent on Edward's family for food and shelter and with almost no money of her own for anything, she cared for Lilian, tried to aid in the running of the McDowell household, and brooded over her fate. After the publication of her three *Massachusetts Ploughman* stories, she had published a poem in a musical journal and sent a story to one of the Frank Leslie publications; but after Edward's return from California, she had given herself over to romance and to the charm of his dilettantism. Now she turned to the matter of a literary career again, but, worried and confused, she found writing harder—when she could snatch the moments for it—and she feared that she was losing what ground she had once gained.[23]

22. Custody Suit; Sherwood Bonner, "From '60 to '65," *Lippincott's*, XVIII (October, 1876), 500; Ruth Watkins, "Reconstruction in Marshall County," *Publications of the Mississippi Historical Society*, XII (1912), 213.

23. Diary, October 13, September 4, 1869. Using Sherwood Bonner's scrapbook as his source, Professor Bondurant wrote these ambiguous sentences: "'Laura Capello' was followed by 'A Flower of the South,' published in a musical journal. Somewhat later a piece called 'An Exposition on One of the Commandments' was sent to *Frank Leslie's Journal*" (Bondurant, "Sherwood Bonner," 47). One assumes from Bondurant's ambiguity that the works themselves were not pasted in the scrapbook, that they were merely noted there. A survey of various musical journals reveals that none included fiction, only poetry—thus my identification of the first work as a poem. Bondurant's statement about the second work is even vaguer and more confusing. Among the many Frank Leslie publications, there was none named simply *Frank Leslie's Journal*. *Frank Leslie's Ladies Journal* was being published from 1871 to 1881; in the 1860s, however, Kate Bonner requested the loan from Cary Freeman of what she designated as "Frank Leslie's Journal" (Note to Cary A. Freeman in Walthall-Freeman Collection). Here she was most probably referring to *Frank Leslie's Illustrated Newspaper* (1855–1891). A search through incomplete files of both the *Ladies Journal* and the *Illustrated Newspaper* failed to turn up "An Exposition on One of the Commandments," which I assume was a short story, though Bondurant in his uncertainty

In the late fall of 1872, with backing from the Millses and his mother, Edward set himself up as a merchant in Dallas and sent back glowing reports. His family, however, began to sense the depth of Kate's discontent and to worry about her separation from Edward, one family member feeling by January that it would be "judicious" for Kate to join him soon. Still hopeful about his prospects, Edward returned in May to bring his wife and daughter back with him to Texas. It was this period in Texas that brought matters to a head. Holly Springs, where the society of family and friends diverted Kate from her own dilemma, was quite different from Dallas, where she knew no one, where the full duties of running a household oppressed her, and where she found even the landscape depressing.[24]

Here, in isolation, was born her resolve. She would go north, strengthen her education—the inadequacy of which made her always feel guilt and discontent—and earn a living as a literary woman. She vowed not to be at the mercy of Edward and his dreams, trapped with a man who would never understand her and whom she did not respect. The design would, of course, necessitate leaving Lilian behind, in the care of some family member. Kate's first plan, as her initial schemes so often were to be, was wild and impractical. She was fascinated by Vassar, the first women's college to offer the same curriculum as a men's college. She determined to leave Lilian in the care of Mrs. McDowell and register there. Evidently failing to consider the financial end of the busi-

---

was willing to call it only a "piece." Given Bondurant's phrasing, one cannot be sure that the "piece" was even published, merely that it was "sent" there. I go into this matter in such detail because it has confused everyone working on Sherwood Bonner since 1898.

It is possible that Sherwood Bonner's bibliography should also include three other early published works—a question that also has proved confusing to several scholars. Kate Bonner's diary entry for January 21, 1869, written at the Shepard plantation near Mobile, reads: "Today Mr. R[ichard] S[hepard] went to Mobile & carried with him my Italian story to be mailed to Mr. Capen—'Maniac' & two little poems so-called to Mobile for Editor of Sunday Times—Ah! suspense! suspense!" It seems clear to me that, while the Italian story was being mailed to Nahum Capen in Boston, "Maniac" and the two poems were being sent to the editor of the Mobile *Sunday Times*. Kate Bonner does not mention in the diary the acceptance of the last three works. She also never mentions the acceptance of "The Heir of Delmont," however, so her silence does not rule out the possibility that these other three works did appear in the Mobile newspaper. Unfortunately the most nearly complete file for that paper ends in 1868.

24. Mary M. Mills to James R. McDowell, Jr., January 8, 1873, in Stephenson Collection.

ness, just how she would support herself in the village of Pough-keepsie, she wrote Nahum Capen, her old literary advisor with whom she had maintained contact, telling him of her plan. Capen replied, commenting not on the financial impracticality of the scheme, but on the matter that would outrage all—that any such plan would involve leaving her child. Terribly upset by his disapproval, she scribbled a reply on the back of an old page of manuscript. Her hauteur was at the fore as she wrote: "I see you do not approve of my plan—so I will not intrude further upon you." She then adopted a lofty moral and social tone in defense and justification of herself:

> As for my child. I did not propose to be separated from her—except temporarily—as I proposed procuring a boarding place for us both in Poughkeepsie as soon as I could.
> Her grandmother is most anxious for me to send the baby to her. She loves her as fondly as any mother could, and is much better fitted to train her than I, both morally and physically, and in parting from her the only "serious matter" I can imagine would be the trial to my *affection*. I do not belong to that class whose exponents consider that the accidental circumstance of birth renders the parent the only possible guide or instructor of the child. I am conscious enough of my own deficiencies to know that, as I am, I am unfitted for such a responsibility, and unselfish enough to sacrifice my affections for what would certainly eventuate in the child's good.

She was floundering and, on one point, lying; for Mrs. McDowell knew nothing of the matter. But the draft ends with an honest and touching statement of her hopes and fears: "I longed for the discipline and development that I hoped the college course might give me. I am so placed that I constantly retrograde." The draft was too haughty, and she probably sent a much toned-down version, but she now realized that even literary people would not totally approve of what she wanted to do.[25]

She then refined her plan and took it to Edward. She would go to Boston, the literary capital of the country, the place where she had gained her first success; and there she would help to support them by writing. She reported later that Edward had agreed to the plan, though he was to deny it. He actually may well have—given

25. The draft of the letter to Nahum Capen is written on the back of page 16 of the "Seven Nights at Edgewood" manuscript (Stephenson Collection).

Bonner House, Holly Springs, Mississippi, as it looks today
Courtesy Holly Springs Garden Club

The residence of J. W. C. Watson, Holly Springs, Mississippi, in the late
nineteenth century. This house, where Kate Bonner finished her days as a
schoolgirl, was also the cultural and social center of her Holly Springs circle.
Courtesy the late Mrs. Lanier Robison

The McDowell cottage on Salem Street, Holly Springs, as it looked in the
late nineteenth century
Courtesy David McDowell III

Edward McDowell in his early forties
Courtesy David McDowell III

Kate McDowell soon after her flight
to Boston
Courtesy David McDowell III

the financial reverses he was now experiencing in Dallas; given his earlier attraction to the noble and romantic idea of a literary woman supporting her family "by her pen"; and given his own laziness, dreaminess, and lack of will. At any rate, whether he at first supported her and later denied it through fear of family and public disapproval, or whether he was merely counting on the Bonners and McDowells stopping her, he agreed to let Kate and Lilian return to Holly Springs.[26]

On August 20, 1873, after almost four months in Texas, the young woman and her baby returned to Mrs. McDowell's house on Salem Street. Both the Bonners and McDowells were warm and loving, but, as they hovered over her and Lilian, Kate knew that she had a secret which would shock them all. As she talked with them, as she received her friends, she gradually faced the truth: none of them would support her. First and foremost, she could not tell her father, the man who had forbidden his little girl to join the drilling company. She waited for two weeks until things again seemed more settled and she and Lilian seemed again most familiar to the two families. Then, after packing her trunks for the Memphis train, she went in and announced the plan to Edward's mother. Mrs. McDowell was astounded, and, to express her disapproval, she ordered that Lilian be immediately taken down the street to Dr. Bonner's. She refused to have the child left in her care; she would not play her part in this scheme. But Kate did not allow her own resolve to be shaken. The trunks were in the carriage, she bade good-bye to her child with tears held back, and then she was off for the train. On September 3, 1873, Kate McDowell left the Holly Springs station on her journey to Boston. She knew only one person there, and him merely through correspondence. She carried only a meager sum that she had managed somehow to save and borrow over the last several months. But she possessed now a will of iron.[27]

26. Kate McDowell to Ruth Bonner, November 13, 1863, in Stephenson Collection; Edward McDowell to Cora Watson, January 13, 1869, in Cora Carey Collection.
27. Custody Suit.

Chapter Three

The Birth of Sherwood Bonner

WHEN KATE MCDOWELL stepped off the train in Boston on a beautiful fall day, she was both elated and filled with misgivings. She had done it. She had left behind all of the things that had stifled and thwarted her. She was free. At the same time, the gaining of her freedom had launched her into a sea of uncertainties. While there were now no barriers, there was also almost nothing to hang on to. The severing of old ties left her without excuses, and her flight from home and responsibilities made the stakes so high that she had to be a success. She had now only will and talent to fall back on. As she looked about herself at this active, forbidding city, she found herself thinking, "I wonder whether I ever will have a home on this earth!" [1]

She tried to leave no space for such thoughts. She arranged lodgings at a hotel and began to refine the plan for her siege of Boston. Her first step was a note to Nahum Capen, her old mentor, who had urged her not to abandon home and family. Within a day, she was on the cars to Dorchester to meet that literary man at last.

Kate McDowell was most fortunate in her one Boston acquaintance. At seventy, Mr. Capen could look back on a long, distinguished, and varied career. While quite young, he had become a partner in the Boston publishing firm of March, Capen, and Lyon, whose authors included Washington Irving and Nathaniel Hawthorne. Capen had also written several books and edited more than one periodical. In addition, he had been instrumental in securing the first copyright law, establishing a permanent census bureau, and forming the first mutual insurance company in Boston.

1. Kate McDowell to Ruth Bonner, November 13, 1873, in the collection of the Reverend Dr. George Royster Stephenson of Jackson, Mississippi (hereinafter cited as Stephenson Collection).

He was deeply interested in politics. Though a staunch Unionist, he was also an impassioned Democrat who counted among his friends Jefferson Davis and who was particularly sympathetic to the plight of the postwar South. The young woman found such a man fascinating; and he, from the beginning, was prejudiced in her favor because she was a southerner and thus a victim of Republican abuse—a most unusual attitude for Boston, the old center of Abolitionist fervor and still a place where anti-southern sentiment ran high.[2]

When Kate McDowell approached the Capen address, "Mt. Ida, at the foot of Bowdoin Street," she discovered a mansion, staffed by three domestics, on a large estate of farmland. Here was old Boston—an early Capen forebear had been a proprietor and original grantee of Dorchester—in a house which had opened its doors to some of the most distinguished literary and political figures of the century. Her reception was warm, and in a short time she had captivated them all: the master, the mistress, the Capen son and daughter (her seniors by a decade), and the various family connections either visiting or living permanently in the large house. They were charmed by her—by her intellect, her gaiety, her grace. More significantly, she won their respect and sympathy. In writing to Dr. Bonner, in fact, Nahum Capen showed that he understood the young woman as no one ever had before. "Your daughter has a very active mind—more ideas and fancies than her judgment has been able to control," he perceptively assessed. "She is doubtless a mystery to herself. She has high aspirations—and she had been unhappy because she could not find or see the means for their development and realization." Capen's sympathy was full as he tried to explain to Dr. Bonner the reason for his daughter's flight: "Her aspirations were stronger than her sense of duty, that is, she felt that she must first do justice to herself, to her own powers, before she could do justice to others." As the letter reveals, Kate McDowell had found real friends at Mt. Ida, and they were to be steadfast friends for the rest of her life.[3]

2. "Nahum Capen," *National Cyclopedia of American Biography*, XXIV (New York: James T. White & Co., 1935), 377–78.
3. Census of 1880, Dorchester, Suffolk County, Massachusetts, p. 53; Nahum Capen to Dr. Charles Bonner, October 12, 1873, in Stephenson Collection.

Almost immediately Mr. Capen set about helping Kate to implement her plans. He secured her admission, tuition free, to the Girls' High School, on West Newton Street; and he found her a room a couple of blocks away in the house of Luther Hunt, a sexton, and his wife. Kate went to work with great zeal and cheerfulness. "She has imposed upon herself," Capen wrote, "a course of severe labor—and a condition of deprivation to accomplish her end." Despite her enthusiasm for this course of self-improvement, the winter was a hard one. Boston had a rich cultural life, and she relished her opportunity for attending lectures and concerts, but she was still terribly lonely. She was twenty-four, considerably older than most of her fellow students at the Girls' High School, and she found few friends there. She was also isolated by her poverty. The southern lady indeed now faced all sorts of unpleasant realities. Her landlords, the Hunts, were nice enough, though to her dismay they did not keep a servant and their boarder had to carry her own coal. She had arranged to take her meals next door, where the food was excellent, but she stopped after three days because of her disgust at the table manners of the daughters of the house. Cut off by penury from her peers, she refused to lower her standards, so she retreated to her room to meals of crackers and cheese supplemented by ginger snaps. The money saved took her to more lectures, to the edge of the great world that she wanted to be a part of. And there were other problems besides her immediate Boston situation. While she had not yet formed a real connection with the great world, she had also not made her peace with the little world of family and friends that she had left. Ten weeks after her departure from Holly Springs, no one in the Bonner family except her sister Ruth had written; and Ruth's letters were full of exhortations about duty. Kate replied to one: "Your letter just this moment received has almost put me beside myself with my longing for my baby. I don't know how I can live without her through this dreary winter." Her resolve, however, was still strong, for she followed with—"But I do feel that it will be for the best good of all concerned for me to stay. It is imperative that I learn how to work and to deny myself—and heaven knows I am doing it now." That strength of resolve did not blur for Kate an awareness of just what her old friends thought of her course. She asked that Laura Robinson, the rector's niece, write, "unless she disapproves of me so entirely as to refuse me even a letter." Through this dreary period of poverty and isolation, living with the uncomfortable awareness of almost universal disapproval, Kate McDowell was sustained by an unshakable confidence in her own abilities. "I have faith that I will succeed in my writings," she told Ruth. "The more I see of other minds," she insisted, "the more certain I am of my capability . . . to earn my own bread and butter at least."[4]

Unfortunately her writing was not earning her bread and butter at the moment, and her funds were running low. She had received only one letter from Edward. He had informed her that his uncle Robert Mills of Galveston was bankrupt, that they were now beggars, and that he took no interest in her present course. Though she might not have wanted to take money from Edward, that was no longer even a possibility. Dr. Bonner, the only other source of funds, would not even communicate with his daughter. Kate had been working as an occasional assistant to Nahum Capen on his lengthy tome *The History of Democracy*; but she needed now a real job. Desperately she wrote to Theodore William Dwight—an old McDowell family friend, the dean of Columbia Law School, and a man with deep literary interests—sending him Lilian's picture and some of the stories that she herself had written and seeking his aid as mentor and, perhaps, employer. Dwight, no doubt fearing involvement in family controversy, did not reply for two months, while, as the weeks passed, Kate wrote demanding the return of, first, the stories and, then, Lilian's photograph. When he did respond, it was to express his affection for Edward McDowell, counsel her that Edward was her "proper protector," and advise that the work under his disposition was "of another sort than you can perform." He added wisely: "Boston is a far better location for you than New York as woman's work and place are appreciated there better than in any other city in America." Luckily, by the time that Dwight's letter arrived, Kate McDowell had found a position in the office of Dr. Dio Lewis, 17 Beacon Street.[5]

In the winter of 1873–1874, part of the country considered Dio

4. Capen to Bonner, October 12, 1873 and Kate McDowell to Ruth Bonner, November 13, 1873, both in Stephenson Collection.

5. Dorothy Gilligan, "Life and Works of Sherwood Bonner" (M.A. thesis, George Washington University, 1930), 16; Theodore W. Dwight to Kate McDowell, February 21, 1874, in Stephenson Collection; [Elizabeth Avery Meriwether], "A Southern Authoress," *Meriwether's Weekly*, August 11, 1883, p. 2.

Lewis a charlatan, a part revered him as a saint, but all had seen his name in the headlines of their newspapers. When he was a young man, lack of funds had cut short his study at Harvard Medical School, and he held only an honorary degree from the Homeopathic Hospital College in Cleveland, Ohio. He now classified himself not even as a homeopath but simply an "eclectic physician," and he held membership in no medical association. His career, however, had not been limited to medicine. In various parts of the country, he had served also as a schoolmaster, a magazine editor, and a lecturer on temperance and hygiene, especially women's hygiene. No matter what the endeavor, he was filled with enthusiasm and assurance, so it followed rather naturally that he and his family had finally settled in Boston, the center of reformist zeal. In 1861, he founded the Boston Normal Institute for Physical Education, which during its seven-year history graduated over four hundred men and women and gained the support of such prominent citizens as Bronson Alcott, Edward Everett, Dr. Oliver Wendell Holmes, James T. Fields, and President Felton of Harvard. About this time, Lewis introduced the wooden dumbbell and the gym bloomer for women; and, in 1862, his book *New Gymnastics*, which argued that exercise classes be included in every curriculum, made him widely known in both this country and England. During this period he also operated a sanitarium and gymnasium and a large girls' school in partnership with Theodore Dwight Weld—the reformer, Shakespearean scholar, and husband of one of the famed Grimké sisters. All of these enterprises having run their course, in 1868 Lewis purchased the property on Beacon Street across from the Boston Athenaeum and erected there an eight-story private hotel, the Bellvue, which boasted Boston's second passenger elevator and the finest Turkish baths in the country. From the Bellvue, Dio Lewis took to the lecture circuit, being a speaker for the Redpath Lyceum Bureau from 1869 through 1874. During this time he gained his greatest fame.[6]

6. The most detailed source on Lewis is Mary F. Eastman's *The Biography of Dio Lewis, A. M., M. D.* (New York: Fowler & Wells Co., 1891), which is clearly unbalanced in its unrelieved encomium. Two other works—Robert Lewis Taylor's *Vessel of Wrath: The Life and Times of Cary Nation* (New York: New American Library, 1966) and J. C. Furnas' *The Life and Times of the Late Demon Rum* (New York: G. P. Putnam's Sons, 1965)—are equally unbalanced in the levity of their treatment of the man.

The son of an alcoholic father, cured of his habit by a zealous wife, Dio Lewis had early been won to the temperance cause and to an appreciation of women's potential power in that movement. Leaving for the moment his other interests in health, exercise, and education, Lewis now concentrated his energies on the question of women-in-temperance and delivered a series of emotional lectures on the subject. On December 13, 1873, at Fredonia, New York, those in Lewis' audience were so moved that they formed the Woman's Christian Temperance Union of Fredonia the next day. The flame lit at Fredonia had become a general conflagration by the twenty-fourth, when Lewis spoke at Hillsboro, Ohio, and the women picketed and shut down every saloon. As the movement spread through the state of Ohio, the newspapers labeled it the "Women's Crusade."

Lewis was the center of bitter controversy for two years. Many newspapers branded him a demagogue. They sneered at his evangelical fervor and reported that he was making fifty dollars a day from his pious lectures. Many of his audiences, however, felt that they were hearing God's voice. The truth about Lewis obviously lay between these extreme views. Kate McDowell herself found him a sincere man. A few months after she had entered his employ, a southern editor asked her for an exposé. "Send a letter for my paper," he urged. "The temperance movement headed by Dr. Lewis seems to be grinning all over, and really invites criticism." She could reply only that, though she was not an enthusiast, the movement and its originator had won her respect; and she spoke of Lewis' "single-hearted zeal, his high and noble traits of character that render him eminently fitted for the accomplishment of a work which requires in its leader a rare blending of mental clearness and moral strength."[7]

Whatever Dio Lewis' other attributes, he proved to be Kate McDowell's salvation. He was receiving hundreds of letters on temperance alone, and he still had a number of other projects which required attention; he needed a secretary with some literary ability. Consequently, he could provide Kate with the sort of position that would sustain her in Boston until she could support her-

7. Katharine McDowell, "From the 'Hub': A Southern Girl's Experience of Life in New England," Memphis *Avalanche*, March 15, 1874, p. 2.

self by her own writing. The benefits of the association, however, were more than financial. At the Bellvue she came in contact with interesting elements of Boston society. First, because of Lewis' old connections, she was introduced to people like the Alcotts and the Welds, families long active in reform. Second, and more important, she also came to know a number of intelligent women of her generation, young feminists who had gathered under the banner of the women's temperance movement.

Three young women of this latter group were to become her particularly close friends. The first was Cornelia Boardman, a native of Great Barrington and four years Kate's senior, who had been working as superintendent of the staff at the Bellvue since 1871 and saving money to complete her studies as a doctor. To know Cornelia well was also to know the friend whom she called "my Nellie Willard." Helen Willard, always called Nellie by her intimates, was more typical of a particular mold of advanced maidenhood in Boston. Her deceased father Simon Willard had been a prominent Boston merchant, and Nellie lived in a large apartment in the Pavilion on Tremont Street with her mother, whom Kate described as a "very dainty, fastidious, aristocratic old lady," and her brother Zabdiel. Nellie devoted herself to intellectual interests and worthy causes. The third acquaintance was in the early Boston years Kate's closest female friend. Carrie Jenness came from Grantville, an area attached to Needham, and she was connected with wealthy families originating there, the Wheelers and the Southers, Henry Souther being founder of a Boston brewery and president of the Broadway National Bank. Carrie, however, had moved into Boston to earn her livelihood as a bookkeeper about the time of Kate's arrival. How different these three women were from the female friends of the young southerner's past. For these Bostonians, heroism and romance were attached to things like the underground railroad, and the young women were so earnest and moral: not even the elder Watsons in Holly Springs could match their tone of high seriousness. To them in the beginning, as to the other Bostonians whom she met, Kate McDowell was, as she ironically realized, *rara avis*. In a fundamental way, she would always remain so. She would always be drawn to life's gaiety and color; she would never feel much of the reformist's zeal.

Still, they liked her. The initial curiosity soon turned to affection; they indulged her vagaries; they tolerated frivolities in her that in other people would have drawn their scorn. And on Kate's part, in addition to the appeal of their softer personal qualities she felt a bond in their feminism—their particular sense of independence and purpose.[8]

But these friendships were just forming in the early winter of 1873, when, still experiencing periods of bitter loneliness, Kate McDowell took the bold step that was to provide her with great advantages in the literary world and that, in a variety of ways, was to help establish her reputation in Boston. She wrote seeking an audience with the country's most revered poet, Henry Wadsworth Longfellow. The note, sent on the eighth of December, was simple and direct:

> I am a Southern girl away from my home and friends. I have come here for mental discipline and study—and to try to find out the meaning and use of my life. It would be to me a great happiness and help if I might know you. May I come and see you please? and if so will you appoint a day and hour?

She closed, "with deep respect," and then abjuring the name Mc-Dowell, she signed herself "Katharine Bonner." Longfellow answered within three days, and the interview was arranged for the next week.[9]

When she entered the large yellow house in Cambridge and met Longfellow face to face, she was struck with the truth of Bret Harte's judgment that here was the "ideal poet." Longfellow was

8. Valuable information on Cornelia Boardman, as well as on other of the Boston figures, is contained in the city directories of the period. Letters from both Cornelia Boardman and Helen Willard to Henry Wadsworth Longfellow are in the Longfellow Collection, Houghton Library, Harvard. Kate McDowell to Carrie Jenness, February 22, 1876, in Stephenson Collection. Two articles by Carrie Jenness are particularly revealing of the women's social and moral views—"Dr. Mary J. Safford Blake," *Cottage Hearth*, III (May, 1876), 113–14; and "Building of the House," *Cottage Hearth*, III (December, 1876), 227.

9. This first note to Longfellow, along with fifty other of her letters, is in the Longfellow Collection, Houghton Library, Harvard. Of the more than fifty-seven letters that the poet wrote to Kate McDowell, unfortunately only one copy of a letter and one original postscript survive. I am grateful to Professor Andrew Hilen of the University of Washington, editor of *The Letters of Henry Wadsworth Longfellow* (the final two volumes of which are now being prepared for publication by Harvard University Press), for providing me with the information on letters to Mrs. McDowell, her family, and friends noted in Longfellow's Letter Calendar.

almost sixty-seven. She described him as of "medium height, well made, with no sign of age in figure or walk." "His head and face," she wrote

> are eminently poetic. His forehead is broad, benignant and full. The great charm of his face centers in his eyes of an unclouded blue, deep-set, under over-hanging brows; alternately dreamy or bright, they hold an indescribable expression of tenderness. Though seamed with many wrinkles, his face is rarely without the rosy flush of health, and would appear that of a much younger man but for its frame of snow white hair. Hair and whiskers are long, abundant and wavy, and give to the poet the look of a grand old patriarch.

The heroes of her girlhood—the Glendowers of the tournament fields and the Byronic lovers—had been replaced recently by the figure of the gray eminence. Nahum Capen, for instance, was to her "a saint." Clearly here in Cambridge was *the* gray eminence, the great venerable literary man. William Dean Howells, who met Longfellow after he himself had achieved some fame and had settled in Boston as an editor for the *Atlantic Monthly*, wrote of the poet: "It was fine to meet him coming down a Cambridge street; you felt that the encounter made you a part of literary history, and set you apart with him for the moment from the poor and the mean." How much more exciting her first meeting with Longfellow must have been for this young woman from Mississippi—such an unknown, so poor, so lonely, so very ambitious.[10]

His surroundings, moreover, were perfect to those young Mississippi eyes. The yellow mansion on Brattle Street was filled with objects of art and fitted with rich carpets, ornate gilded mirrors, and pieces in mahogany, walnut, and rosewood. Emerson, with his Puritan blood, might object to all the show and glitter as diverting one from the true sphere of art and truth. "If Socrates were here," he remarked in his journal, "we could go and talk with him; but Longfellow, we cannot go and talk with; there is a palace, and servants, and a row of bottles of different colored wines, and wine glasses, and fine coats." With her far less ascetic southern spirit, Kate McDowell found the luxury and elegance a fit setting for a

10. Sherwood Bonner, "Sherwood Bonner's Letter: Longfellow's Home—Its History," Memphis *Avalanche*, December 26, 1875, p. 2; Kate McDowell to Ruth Bonner, November 13, 1873, in Stephenson Collection; William Dean Howells, *Literary Friends and Acquaintances* (New York: Harper & Brothers, 1902), 196.

great literary man. She reveled in the "beauties of art, curiosities from every land, and sacred relics"; and she luxuriated in the servants and the pomp. Indeed, as she stood in Longfellow's study, surrounded by the portraits of Sumner, Emerson, and Hawthorne, and examining the inkwell which had belonged to Coleridge, while this other great poet stood by her side, she knew that at last she had entered the great world. She intended to remain in it.[11]

Her warmth of feeling for the poet was matched by his response to her, and his emotions were surely a good deal less complicated. His genuine kindness toward all hopeful artists was heightened by the fact that this one was a beautiful and charming young woman. Throughout his life Longfellow was particularly susceptible to female attractions, and since the death of his second wife Fanny Appleton in 1861, he had formed a number of friendships with women markedly younger than himself. This youthful Miss Bonner—or Mrs. McDowell, as she, with embarrassment, was forced to correct him before the interview was concluded—was both delightful and handsome. A friend of those early Boston days described her as "of distinguished personal appearance—tall, willowy, graceful, and of the fairest complexion, with hair of a rich golden auburn color, that almost touched the carpet when unloosed, and eyes of ever-changing brilliance, that sparkled with the sunniest humor and animation whenever they relaxed from their usually almost austere dignity of expression." Kate McDowell found no reason to project that austere dignity in Longfellow's presence, and he relished not only her beauty, but also her spirit. "Your joyous nature," he would later say to her, "drinks in the sunshine and repels the shade." That hour which they spent together was for him too one of unalloyed pleasure. When Kate McDowell left the yellow mansion, she had formed another friendship that would last for life.[12]

    11. The Emerson journal entry is quoted by Newton Arvin in *Longfellow: His Life and Work* (Boston: Little, Brown and Company, 1963), 52. Bonner, "Longfellow's Home."
    12. "Katherine S. (Bonner) McDowell," *Appleton's Annual Cyclopedia of the Year 1884*, XXIV (New York: D. Appleton & Co., 1890), 609. Longfellow's statement is quoted by B. M. Drake in his essay "Sherwood Bonner," *Southern Writers: Biographical and Critical Studies*, ed. William Malone Baskerville (Nashville and Dallas: Publishing House of the M. E. Church, South, 1903), I, 85. Professor Drake had several of Longfellow's letters to Mrs. McDowell in his possession at the time that he wrote this piece. Because the Longfellow letters subsequently vanished, Drake's quotations from them make his essay particularly valuable.

The winter now seemed less bleak. Kate continued to receive the kind attentions of the Capens, she was enjoying the companionship of her female circle, she was beginning to meet more people at the Bellvue, and she now had the regard of an eminent literary man. She was most pleased when Longfellow thought of her and composed a letter on Christmas day, and by spring she was referring to him with easy irony as "a great man and a poet, who enjoys the additional distinction of being my very good friend." The financial security insured by her position in Dio Lewis' office also produced a better atmosphere for work on her own projects. She had finished her schooling, and while she labored on her fiction, she hit upon a scheme that would both begin to establish her name and add to her still slim purse: she would try to interest a newspaper in her impressions of Boston. She wrote the Memphis *Avalanche*, the liveliest newspaper in that Tennessee city to which her native town was closely attached. The response was enthusiastic, and in mid-March she began an association with the *Avalanche* that was to last for the next three years.[13]

The first *Avalanche* sketch, which the editor presented under the headline "From the 'Hub': A Southern Girl's Experiences of Life in New England," has as its dateline "'Moral Lighthouse,' March 4, 1874." The contents of the piece are well reflected in the subhead—"What a Bright, Educated, Witty, Lively, Snappy Young Woman Can Say on a Variety of Topics." Before the writer launches into her free-wheeling series of impressions, however, she establishes a persona shaped to win a southern audience. She presents a young woman who shares their sympathies, one who will look askance at the culture of this alien city, where "the South is not in good odor." She begins by examining the smugness of these Bostonians, the certainty that "there is no subject connected with the heavens above or the earth beneath that they have not sounded with their plummet lines and touched its bottom." She delivers her view of social success in the Lighthouse:

> For the native Bostonian there are three paths to glory. If his name be Quincy or Adams, nothing more is expected of him. His blue blood carries him through life with glory and straight to heaven when he

13. Katharine McDowell, "The Hub's Good Side: Ralph Waldo Emerson Interviewed by a Fair Southron," Memphis *Avalanche*, April 12, 1874, p. 2.

dies. . . . Failing in the happy accident of birth, the candidate for Beacon Hill honors must write a book. This is easy. The man who can breathe Boston air and not write a book is either a fool or a phenomenon. One course remains to him should he miss fame in both these lines. He must be a reformer. Nothing must be too huge to tackle, or too wild for him to advocate.

She then sketches this center of "isms and ologies and reforms":

Labor Reformists talk the wildest communism, and evolve ideal societies from their muddled brains where brotherly love is to rule the roost and property distinctions are to be abolished. Spiritualists receive mysterious communications telling how things are carried on in Jupiter. Dress reform women stalk about the streets, followed by awe-struck gamins, and snickered at by profane counter jumpers. Moral reform clubs meet, and men and women discuss the proper relations that should exist between husband and wife in an ungloved way that I don't dare illustrate for a Southern paper. Young virgins mount the rostrum and decry "legalized prostitution," and ventilate advanced theories about love.

Having won the audience by her ironic picture of this alien culture, Kate McDowell goes on to take her own stance—one not necessarily theirs. She accomplishes the maneuver most skillfully as she responds to a remark made to her by Louisa May Alcott. "I like your Southern women; they are very pretty and refined and well bred," Miss Alcott had said. "But do you know they always seemed to me like dressed up dolls." "Sweet women of the South!" the *Avalanche* correspondent exclaims.

I thought of you as I had known you. In your homespun dresses or your plain black robes—your eyes shining with faith and hope—your steady white hands binding ragged wounds, or pointing the way to heaven to dying eyes—your toil, your suffering, your courage in those stern, sombre days when our beautiful country stood all bleeding and desolate and despairing. Dressed up dolls! Quarrel then with angels because their snowy wings are fair.

But after this spirited defense comes a turn. "But oh! Southern women," the correspondent asks in the next sentence, "when will one among you arise with head enough to do justice to your hearts?" Almost before the reader can gauge the full effect of the passage, the writer is off again, constantly turning her kaleidoscope of impressions, and shifting her tone a dozen times. Only the careful reader may note that throughout the essay, while even the persona herself does not escape being satirized, the women's rights movement alone receives consistently serious treatment. The delight, however, obscures the instruction in the sprightly, humorous pastiche.[14]

For the next article, one on Ralph Waldo Emerson, Kate McDowell, with journalistic amorality, secured an audience under false pretenses. In a note sent on March 23, strikingly reminiscent of the one to Longfellow, she wrote:

> I am a Southern girl. I have left my home and friends and have come here to strive to solve for myself the problems of a life that has grown very wearisome to me—because, perhaps, I did not understand its possibilities.
>
> You sir, have helped so many struggling souls—will you help me? May I come and see you? and if so will you appoint the day and hour?

The note is probably half a sincere reflection of her seeking and hero worship and half a mirror of her opportunism. At any rate, this Concord meeting was as complete a failure as the Cambridge one had been a success. To give her credit, however, the resulting sketch treated Emerson with respect and made fun of the correspondent's own vanity, dealt a blow when the great man failed to notice a knot of violets in her hair. The remaining *Avalanche* piece, describing the various memorial observances for Charles Sumner, shows her increasing familiarity with the Boston scene, its great figures, its conventions. She had attended a private service, probably escorted by Longfellow; and the correspondent was clearly happy moving in the great world.[15]

Shortly after she finished this last sketch, Kate McDowell prepared for her first visit home. Although she longed to see Lilian and her family, she nevertheless realized that she would now have to face squarely all the disapproval that she had avoided by the secrecy of her flight eight months before. As the train brought her nearer and nearer, she was brooding over the confrontation when

14. This piece, under the name Katharine McDowell, appeared in the *Avalanche*, March 15, 1874, p. 2.
15. McDowell, "The Hub's Good Side." Mrs. McDowell's note to Emerson is in the Emerson Collection, Houghton Library. Kate McDowell, "From the 'Hub': A Personal Chapter on Sumner, Schurz, Wendell Phillips, Garrison, Oliver Wendell Holmes and Others," Memphis *Avalanche*, May 17, 1874, p. 2.

suddenly the "glory of summer in the blossoming woods" filled her with joy just to be back in the "dear, dear South." At home, Lilian knew her mother at sight, and all were happy at her return. Even their disapproval, though still strong in principle, was softened by the fact that this young woman, pampered from birth, had managed to support herself and that she was making a name for herself, locally at least, through the *Avalanche* articles. They were, furthermore, genuinely impressed by the two letters that she received from Longfellow during the visit. In early June, she left family and friends to return to Boston under a more favoring wind than she had expected.[16]

This trip north was far different from the earlier one. Now she was traveling to a city where she had a number of friends, where she was beginning to establish herself. As she wrote Longfellow, it was almost like "going back home." Among the warmest welcomes was that of the poet himself. He was increasingly interested in advancing her career, and pleased to introduce her to members of the literary establishment. In September, he arranged the meeting that she probably desired most—an interview with William Dean Howells, editor of the *Atlantic Monthly*. Elated, she wrote to Ruth:

> He is a man I've long wanted to meet, and I'm all a flutter of delighted anticipation. Have had my black silk fixed short and will get some fawn-colored gloves & new bonnet strings and curl my hair—Hope to strike his majesty favorably tho I hear he's a stern business man. And I hope I may be very much impressed—as it takes one nail to drive out another you know!

Despite the bravado of her conclusion, she staked great hopes on winning Howells' favor. Publication in the *Atlantic* was always to be her goal, a goal that she was never to achieve. Howells, unfortunately, joined that small group of people whom, in those early Boston days, she could neither bewitch nor even win to her side.[17]

While Longfellow was introducing her in the highest circles, she was also becoming acquainted on her own with some Bostonians

16. Kate McDowell to Henry Wadsworth Longfellow, June 1, 1874, in Longfellow Collection; Longfellow's Letter Calendar.
17. Kate McDowell to Longfellow, June 1, 1874, in Longfellow Collection. Katharine McDowell to Ruth Bonner, September 22, 1874, in Stephenson Collection.

who neither were Brahmins nor held Brahmin aspirations. Among these, the most colorful and the most apparently unlikely to gain her warm friendship was James Redpath, one of the leading radicals of the time. The Redpath Lyceum Bureau, an important Boston enterprise that he had founded in 1868, sent lecturers and readers over much of the country to bring entertainment, culture, and instruction to the American public. On the Redpath list for 1874, as for the last several years, was Dr. Dio Lewis. When Kate McDowell met Redpath at the Bellvue, however, she encountered not just the entrepreneur who had solidly launched the lyceum movement, but a man with a crowded history of intense endeavors.

Born in 1833 in Scotland, James Redpath had been a bright youngster whose father early set about educating him for the ministry. By the age of fourteen, he had passed his school tests and completed his formal training; he had also questioned his father's theology and rejected the ministry as a calling. He chose to learn the printer's trade instead, and in his sixteenth year he collaborated with his father on a small volume, *Tales and Traditions of the Border*. Shortly afterward, the family emigrated to America and settled in Michigan, where James Redpath worked on newspapers in Kalamazoo and Detroit. From Michigan his writings attracted the attention of Horace Greeley of the New York *Tribune*, who brought him to New York as an editor when the young man was just nineteen. Redpath had become by this time an ardent abolitionist, and he spent the years from 1854 to 1859 touring the southern states and visiting the battleground of Kansas. His impassioned reports from both sides were published widely in newspapers and then collected in 1859 in two books—*The Roving Editor, or Talks with Slaves in the Southern States* and *A Handbook to Kansas Territory*. To the essays which made up the first book, Redpath attached a bold preface. "I do not hesitate," he wrote there, "to urge the friends of the slave to incite insurrections, and encourage, in the North, a spirit which shall ultimate in servile and civil wars." He dedicated this volume to a man whom he had encountered in Kansas, with the emotional words: "You, Old Hero! believe that the slave should be aided and urged to insurrection, and hence do I lay this tribute at your feet." John Brown was then relatively unknown, but, with Redpath's help, he would not be for long.[18]

In 1857 Redpath had married and settled in Malden, Massachusetts, outside Boston. From his house there, a stop on the underground railroad, he served as Brown's publicist; and he made connections for Brown with influential New England reformers. In 1859, Redpath traveled to Haiti, later boasting in print that he had gone to examine the benefits of slave insurrection. On his return, he founded the Haitian Emigrant Bureau and arranged the transportation of two thousand ex-slaves to the Negro republic. Virtually all of Redpath's actions during these years directly supported the conspiracy that ended at Harper's Ferry. Even during Brown's trial, as other conspirators denied their complicity or fled to Canada, Redpath would not be silent. "Living he acted bravely; dying, he will teach us courage," he wrote of Brown in a Boston newspaper. "A Samson in life; he will be a Samson in his death. Let cowards ridicule and denounce him; let snake-like journalists hiss at his holy failure—for one, I do not hesitate to say that I love him, admire him, defend him. GOD BLESS HIM!" The next spring when the senate committee investigating the incident at Harper's Ferry subpoenaed Redpath, he refused to appear. Expecting to be seized by federal authorities, he vowed to fire at the first intruder. The committee failed to enforce its subpoenas, and within a few months after Brown's execution Redpath published the first, the legend-making biography—*The Public Life of Captain John Brown*. For Redpath, the war itself was surely less exciting than its fiery prelude, though he did serve as a correspondent for the *Tribune* at the battles of Atlanta and Nashville and at the surrender of Charleston. At the close of the war, he was for several months superintendent of schools in Charleston, where he reorganized the

18. The two best sources of general information on James Redpath are Charles F. Horner, *The Life of James Redpath* (New York: Barse & Hopkins, 1926), and Marjorie Harrell Eubank, "The Redpath Lyceum Bureau from 1868 to 1901" (Ph.D. dissertation, University of Michigan, 1968). Material on his role in the John Brown conspiracy is given in Stephen B. Oates, *To Purge This Land with Blood: A Biography of John Brown* (New York: Harper & Row, 1970); Tilden G. Edelstein, *Strange Enthusiasm: A Life of Thomas Wentworth Higginson* (New Haven: Yale University Press, 1968); and Jules Ables, *Man on Fire: John Brown and the Cause of Liberty* (New York: Macmillan, 1971).

system, established a public reading room and library for freed-men, recruited the first Negro militia companies, and founded a Negro orphanage. Before he left the city, he had also begun the first observance of a memorial day for the Union dead. From Charleston he returned to Boston, where he resumed his career as a journalist and where he soon established his lyceum agency.

Redpath maintained his ardor for reform, becoming after the war an advocate of women's rights, labor reform, and strict Reconstruction measures in the South. He had established the Lyceum Bureau, in great part, as a forum for reformist lecturers; and his early lists included Frederick Douglass, Wendell Phillips, Charles Sumner, Thomas Wentworth Higginson, Julia Ward Howe, Caroline H. Dall, and Mary Livermore. But he was also interested in entertainment, and added to the lists were performers like Josh Billings, Petroleum V. Nasby, and Mark Twain. His relationship with Twain, in fact, reflects well another side of the ardent reformer's nature. Twain considered Redpath "competent good company of an evening & companionable in his working methods," and Redpath proved a skillful and tactful manager of the temperamental artist. The business arrangement in time grew into a warm friendship. "The chief ingredients of Redpath's make-up," Twain later commented, "were honesty, sincerity, kindliness and pluck." Despite the intensity of his various enthusiasms, despite the excesses to which he was often given, Redpath was a convivial man and a kind one. It was Kate McDowell's nature to be attracted more strongly to personalities than to principles. She was drawn, not to the reformer, but to the man of the world, a man who had read widely and possessed broad interests. This man of experience, now forty—described by a friend as "below the medium height, wiry in frame, sympathetic in features uniting strength and gentleness in no ordinary degree, electrical in both facial and bodily movement"—fell immediately under the spell of the southern beauty and placed himself at her service.[19]

19. Eubank, "Redpath Lyceum Bureau," 147; Mark Twain, *The Autobiography of Mark Twain, Including Chapters Now Published for the First Time*, ed. Charles Neider (New York: Harper & Brothers, 1959), 162; Earl Marble, "James Redpath," *Cottage Hearth*, IV (February, 1877), 29.

With the addition of her new sponsor, Kate McDowell's chances for completing her conquest of Boston seemed even surer. As important to her success as her looks and intelligence was another factor: though she had come to Boston in part as a seeker and though it would take her years to work out various problems, socially she was completely self-assured. Greatly amused by the Bostonian's notion that he alone felt the pride of lineage and place, she never cowered before Brahmin snobbery because she never forgot that she was Kate Bonner of Holly Springs. That, she felt, should be enough to satisfy anyone. This basic confidence and pride also enabled her to remain very much her own person. She retained just what she wanted from her southern background; she adopted only what she found congenial in the North. Being a southerner often worked in her favor. She was aware that it gave her a certain social distinction, and that distinction of any sort was hard to come by in Boston. She found it necessary, however, to make one definite accommodation with the Bostonians: in these early days she had to dissociate herself completely from slavery. How could she do otherwise if she were to sit in Longfellow's library under the bust of his friend Charles Sumner, seek introductions from a Harper's Ferry conspirator, or even simply get along with Cornelia, Nellie, and Carrie for that matter? She was served well by her Holly Springs background even in this sensitive area. After his famous eulogy of Charles Sumner, delivered on the floor of the senate in April, 1874, Senator L. Q. C. Lamar of Mississippi was a man of the hour, honored for the noble speech calling for an end to sectional bitterness and misunderstanding. Kate McDowell took pains to establish her long acquaintance with Lamar and to mention his judgment, made to her when she was only a girl, that the finest American poems were Whittier's on slavery. She did her work well enough that a friend would later describe her "hatred of slavery." Nothing in either her professional writing or her letters, however, reflects so strong an attitude. As both she and most Boston friends realized, she was neither an enthusiast nor a philanthropist. She cared most for the moment, for what came under her particular scrutiny. She retained, for the most part, the racial attitudes with which she had been reared.

If her apparent view of racial matters was deceptive, however, it was virtually the only stance that she modified to please her new friends.[20]

In the winter of 1874, with these new friends increasing and her horizons continuing to expand, Kate McDowell faced news that a few months before would have been deeply disturbing. Dr. Dio Lewis, in ill health, was selling the Bellvue and moving to California. She took in stride the termination of her job, the end of a steady income. It was time to move on to new experiences, and she boldly rented two small rooms up three flights on Tremont Place and entered what, for a southern lady, was a distinctly bohemian phase. Her quarters became a kind of salon—"clever men," in her words, "dropping in with fresh gossip and witticism and a breezy air of work." One of the clever men was Daniel L. Milliken, who had begun that year an ambitious and intelligent woman's magazine named *The Cottage Hearth*. When the journal was launched on its second year, filling the first page of the January issue was a piece by a writer who styled herself "Sherwood Bonner."[21]

It was no accident that Kate McDowell's adult debut as a writer in Boston announced a new identity. Certainly she was no longer the pseudonymous Clayton Vaughn who had written the melodramatic Italian story six years before. Clearly she must have felt that she was no longer even the young woman who had arrived in Boston fifteen months earlier so desperately in need of instruction and exposure. She had signed the *Avalanche* sketches Katharine or Kate McDowell, but she quite basically resisted the identity that Edward's name gave her. As she had realized with such embarrassment that first afternoon at Longfellow House, however, she could never be again, even for a moment, Miss Bonner. If she had to be Mrs. McDowell to the world, she could still establish her own

20. McDowell, "From the 'Hub': A Southern Girl's Experience of Life in New England"; McDowell to Bonner, September 22, 1874, in Stephenson Collection; *Appleton's Annual Cyclopedia for the Year 1884*, 609; Drake, "Sherwood Bonner," 84–85. C. Vann Woodward offers interesting evidence of the necessity of a southerner's espousing abolitionist sentiments in order to gain acceptance by northern literary and intellectual circles in the decades immediately following the Civil War. See his chapter "A Southern Critique for the Gilded Age" in *The Burden of Southern History* (Baton Rouge: Louisiana State University Press, 1960).

21. Eastman, *Dio Lewis*, 340; Sherwood Bonner to Daniel L. Milliken, May 7, 1877, in the Milliken Collection, Perkins Library, Duke University.

identity as a writer. She could shuck McDowell; she could forget Kate Bonner, the deluded girl who had made so many mistakes. She would be Sherwood Bonner. The name might be sexually ambiguous or even deceptive, but that was not the primary intent. It was after all a part of her actual name, and it enabled her to present a new self which still encompassed that part of the old that she wanted to retain. She would be Sherwood Bonner, a woman of the world, a literary lady.

In the early months of 1875, the name Sherwood Bonner appeared over three sketches in the pages of *The Cottage Hearth*. Taken together, the essays reveal a person different from either the youthful Kate Bonner or the confused Mrs. McDowell who had fled north. The first, a biographical piece on Dr. J. G. Holland, the editor of *Scribner's Monthly*, is the least interesting. Workmanlike, though florid, it lies very much in the genteel tradition, outlining the subject's worthy life and uplifting works. In her second appearance, however, Sherwood Bonner established her own tone; and her editorial comments provided a strong draught on the first page of a journal whose motto above read: "Home is the Kingdom, and Love Is the King." She observes that her subject, the author Mary Clemmer, had early made a mistake "sadly common among American girls—that of marrying too soon"; and she launches next into a defense of the recent Clemmer-Ames divorce:

> It is with hesitation that we touch on this subject, condemning as we do most bitterly, the intrusive curiosity which seeks to pry into family history, and gossip maliciously over its secrets or sorrows. Yet the world being what it is, ever ready to cast aspersions upon those whose talent has lifted them above the mediocre level of their fellow mortals, and especially apt to charge a woman with fault if there be a lack of harmony in family relations, it may not be out of place here to say that in this divorce case, no shadow of blame has fallen on Mrs. Ames.

Obviously a great deal of feeling went into this passage. Kate McDowell strongly identified with this woman who had begun her literary career through a series of letters to a provincial newspaper, "sparkling as only the letters of a clever woman can be"— this woman who had recently resumed her maiden name. Sherwood Bonner continues to speak very much in her own voice in the third essay, devoted to "the representative woman of America," Julia Ward Howe. Still exploring the problem of marriage, she notes the extraordinarily happy and stimulating Ward-Howe union and comments that "by the average chances of married life, neither a man nor a woman of such exceptional gifts is likely to select a mate wisely." Among Mrs. Howe's many endeavors, she cites particularly the New England figure's work in the cause of women, especially women's suffrage. Finally, Sherwood Bonner draws the whole to a most personal conclusion in her remarks on Mrs. Howe, feminism, and the southern attitude toward women:

> Our Southern friends imagine that a woman who wants to vote, or stands on the platform to make a speech, of necessity unsexes herself, and must be bold, unwomanly, and false to her higher duties. If they could see the "representative woman" . . . with her low, even voice, her quietly elegant manner, her serene face whose every expression tells of purity; or if they could join in the favored circle that collects around her in her beautiful home, where she reigns as beloved wife and mother, their prejudices would melt like wax before the sun. They would take the first step in that march of progress which is before them, that of acknowledging that a woman may read Greek and lead a suffrage party without being one whit the less what they apostrophize as the end and aim of feminine endeavor—a womanly woman.

In both the Clemmer and Howe essays, as she explored boldly her own problems of self-definition, she opened issues of *The Cottage Hearth* on a strong and controversial note. By spring, Sherwood Bonner was becoming known as a vigorous writer who did not hold back her own very definite views.[22]

In May, however, she published the piece of work that established her reputation among many Bostonians. On May 8, 1875, the Boston *Times* printed her satire "The Radical Club: A Poem, Respectfully Dedicated to 'The Infinite' by An Atom." Overnight, she became parochially famous. The Radical Club, founded in 1867 at the Chestnut Street home of the Reverend and Mrs. John T. Sargent, was a relic of the Transcendental Club surviving in Boston's intellectual Indian Summer. Both strains of the old Transcendentalist group, the philosophers and the reformers, gathered here—without refreshments—for lectures and discussions, the

22. "Dr. J. G. Holland," *Cottage Hearth*, II (January, 1875), 1–2; "Mary Clemmer," *Cottage Hearth*, II (February, 1875), 29–30; "Julia Ward Howe," *Cottage Hearth*, II (April, 1875), 85–86.

rooms dominated by venerable New England figures. Into this temple of Boston high-mindedness Sherwood Bonner gained entrance. Then she desecrated it.[23]

Longfellow had arranged her first invitation to a meeting in November of 1874. Subsequently her hostess Mrs. Sargent had taken an imperious interest in the young woman, and by March the dame was calling at Tremont Place to announce a guided tour of Harvard and a visit to Longfellow House the next day. Mrs. Sargent was taking the young southerner in hand, and Kate acceded, "not knowing," as she told Longfellow, "exactly how to do otherwise." That problem was solved within two months. Sherwood Bonner's poem, a parody of Poe's "The Raven," presents the distinguished assemblage as a "free religious wrangling club" and concludes that

In their wild Eutopian dreaming and impracticable scheming
For a sinful world's redeeming, common sense flies out the door,
And the long-drawn dissertations come to—words and nothing more,
    Only words and nothing more.

The poem was a great popular success, and the newspaper was deluged with requests for more copies. A certain stratum, however, was not amused. As Mark Twain was to learn from his speech at Whittier's birthday dinner, proper Boston did not laugh at itself and its prominent figures. And Sherwood Bonner had clearly taken liberties in her treatment of those figures. The Reverend Sargent himself is presented as "Mr. Pompous"; Bronson Alcott as "an ancient Concord bookworm"; and a Boston bishop as a "tall and red-faced member, large and loose and somewhat limber" with a "shakey" creed. What proved most scandalous, however, was Sherwood Bonner's presentation of three revered Boston women. The first was Elizabeth Peabody, on whose behalf Henry James was also censured when he drew her satirical portrait in Miss Birdseye of *The Bostonians*. Sherwood Bonner dared to present "the grandmother of Boston," as Miss Peabody was fondly called, in these lines:

23. Widely differing views of the club are presented in Mrs. John T. Sargent's *Reminiscences of the Radical Club* (Boston: J. R. Osgood Co., 1880) and Van Wyck Brooks's chapter "The Radical Club" in *New England: Indian Summer, 1865–1915* (New York: E. P. Dutton & Co., 1940).

The Kindergarten mother clucked in answer to this brother,
And her curls kept bobbing quaintly from the queer head-dress she
> wore.

The much admired Ednah Dow Cheney was described as "another *magnum corpus*, with a figure like a porpus." Remarkably enough, it seems that equal offense was given by the author's milder treatment of Julia Ward Howe, whom she had recently presented in such complimentary terms in the *Cottage Hearth* essay:

Then a lady, fair and faded, with a careworn look and jaded,
As though she saw the glory of the coming Lord no more,
Crushed the British lion's roaring by a reverent outpouring
Of a faith forever soaring unto heaven's golden door;
She was listened to intently by each member on the floor;
> For her genius they adore.

Though "The Radical Club" first appeared anonymously, the clever men of the Tremont Place salon and other friends knew the author's identity, and soon the whole city did. Moreover, additional salt was applied to the wound when the poem was published in pamphlet form in 1876, this time under the name Sherwood Bonner. Because of its continued popularity, the Boston *Times* reprinted the work again in 1877.[24]

After the ridicule sustained when the poem first appeared, the club changed its name to the Chestnut Street Club. After the pamphlet version appeared, one member felt compelled to bring out his own pamphlet in defense. His piece—entitled "The Radical Club: A Reply to 'An Atom' by a Chip"—compares "those strange rhymes, so '*very* free.' / By 'S.B.'" to "the heartless wit / Thrown at Pope by vulgar Dennis." The author then proceeds to defend and eulogize every member satirized in Sherwood Bonner's parody, pausing most sentimentally on Elizabeth Peabody:

24. McDowell to Longfellow, November 8, 1874, and [March 5, 1875]; Longfellow's Journal, March 6, 1875, in Longfellow Collection. When Kate Sanborn included "The Radical Club" in *The Wit of Women* (New York: Funk & Wagnalls, 1885), she took pains in "leaving out the most personal verses." Those were the sections on Miss Peabody, Mrs. Cheney, and Mrs. Howe (see Sanborn, 96–100). The pamphlet was printed in Boston by the Times Publishing Company in 1876. In the copy owned by the Massachusetts Historical Society, the victims of Sherwood Bonner's pen have been identified by Ellen Sturgis Gurney. I have found no copy of the 1877 version but Gilligan ("Life and Works of Sherwood Bonner," 22) cites a note in Kate McDowell's scrapbook stating that the Boston *Times* reprinted the poem again in that year.

Touch her not: each hair is sacred
On that gray and honored head;
Let the "head-dress" shame the critic:
Babes will weep when she is dead.
Blessed "Kindergarten mother."

In conclusion, he delivers one final shot at Sherwood Bonner:

Therefore, "Atom," when you wander
Into homes, respect each guest.
"Words" may fall on ears unheeding:
Deeds will stand the final test.

"The Radical Club" retained its status as a Boston *cause célèbre* for some years. Between the glee of the mass of readers and the disdain of certain Brahmins, there was still a third response, reflected well by Kate Sanborn's handling of the poem in her 1885 volume *The Wit of Women*. "Sherwood Bonner's hit on the Radical Club of Boston was almost inexcusable," Sanborn commented. "She was admitted as a guest, and her subsequent ridicule was a violation of all good breeding. But like so many wicked things it is captivating, and while you are shocked, you laugh." In the spring of 1875, Kate McDowell could ignore both the outright disdain of some and the qualified disapproval of others. The name Sherwood Bonner was now known all over the city. She was reveling in her fame, basking in the compliments of smart and clever people, enjoying to the full her particular version of *la vie de bohème*. She could ignore the fact that certain Brahmin doors once opened to her were now closed. She would not always.[25]

At the moment, however, she was finding full satisfaction in both her life and her work. The early months of 1875 were particularly productive ones. In the late spring and early summer, she wrote three more articles for the *Avalanche*, all now appearing under the name Sherwood Bonner.[26] Two of them, sketches of various centennial celebrations around Boston, reflect a woman growing increasingly confident and sophisticated in "the Moral

    25. *The Radical Club: A Reply to "An Atom" by a Chip* (Boston: William F. Gill and Company, 1876).
    26. "The Big Celebration: An Avalanche Correspondent's Impressions of the Lexington-Concord Centennial," May 4, 1875, p. 2; "Wendell Phillips Interviewed by a Southern Girl," May 30, 1875, p. 2; "Boston's Centennial: A Southern Woman's Description of the Celebration at Bunker Hill," June 30, 1875, p. 2—all in the Memphis *Avalanche*.

Lighthouse." Like her earlier pieces, they are witty and irreverent. The third, an interview with Wendell Phillips, to whom she had been introduced by Redpath, is a masterpiece of its type—thorough, balanced, and informed. In the spring also came the real triumph, that goal toward which Kate McDowell had directed her most intense efforts, both social and literary, since her arrival in Boston. An important magazine accepted one of her stories.

The letter of acceptance came to her only after long months of exposure and development in Boston. Kate McDowell had arrived in the literary capital with stories, and she had written more in the first weeks. They had been rejected everywhere that she had sent them. Among the critics of this early fiction, the most perceptive was Theodore W. Dwight, who found one "considerable fault— that the influence of your reading is noticeable throughout every composition." "You have told me how much time you used to devote to works of imagination & romance," he commented. "The plan of your story is unconsciously based on the conventional plan. The incidents may be new & the dialogue bright, but under all is the trace of mental habit." Dwight saw exactly what Kate McDowell was doing: she was still writing as she had when she composed "Laura Capello" and the other *Ploughman* stories, observing the conventions of the hundreds of melodramatic and sentimental tales that she had found so appealing since her youth. Now, however, she faced a dilemma. She was still using the old formulas, but she wanted to place her stories in the most distinguished of the American journals, the *Atlantic Monthly* or the *Overland Monthly*. She had, in fact, approached Dwight to recommend her to the latter magazine. Such periodicals were not interested in the "Laura Capello" sort of story; instead they were seeking work bearing the marks of an emerging literary realism.[27]

Kate McDowell was actually quick to sense the power of this new movement, particularly in the person of its leading figure. At the time that she came to Boston, Bret Harte was among the most famous writers in the country. Two years earlier when he had first visited Boston after the great success of his local color stories, he had been lionized. During his second visit in the winter of 1873,

27. Theodore W. Dwight to Kate McDowell, February 21, 1874, in Stephenson Collection.

when Kate herself knew no one, he was again the guest of Boston literati. She went to his lectures, and his immediate influence is apparent in her sprinkling of Harte quotations through the *Avalanche* sketches. Her exposure to Harte surely also accounts for her strong interest in publication in the *Overland Monthly*, the distinguished new journal from whose pages he had suddenly achieved fame. Though she quickly felt the power of the new literary movement, she was slower to embrace fully its principles, to give up her old affinity for the exotic. "The more I understand the literature of the day," a confident Kate had written Ruth in her second Boston letter, "the more certain I am of my capacity to take a rank." She was right, but she had first to make a real effort to forget old tastes. Even at the time of her first visit home after eight months in the city, she was still resisting the lessons offered by new models. "I had a safe and particularly stupid journey," she wrote Longfellow from Holly Springs. "I think that it is only in the delightful pages of Mr. Howells and Mr. Warner that one finds 'dear stupid Real Life' very interesting as seen on steamboat or car in these commonplace days—I can always delight in a painting, though reality might not win a glance." Her next paragraph contradicts everything that she had just said and reveals a close observer of real life, a painter with a pen:

> It was interesting to note the gradual glide into the Southern land and the difference in the "manner and ways" of the people. I assure you my heart gave a bound when I first saw the men in their broad Spanish hats and long love-locks, looking so sweet and Southern and picturesque and barbarous, and the old black Aunties come on board with their gaily turbaned heads, and exclamations of wonder at the Northern pennies that I piled up in exchange for their wares.

Despite her resistance and her demurral, here was a budding realist of the local color school.[28]

The evolution seemed complete by July of 1875, when "Gran'mammy's Last Gift" by Sherwood Bonner appeared on the front page of the country's most widely read magazine, *Youth's Companion*. This was not the *Atlantic* or the *Overland Monthly*, but the *Companion* had such a large list of subscribers because it

---

28. McDowell to Bonner, November 13, 1873, in Stephenson Collection; McDowell to Longfellow, June 1, 1874, in Longfellow Collection.

was not just for children, but, in the words of its later slogan, "For all the family." With its family emphasis, certain subjects were not permitted, but those restraints did not prohibit the publication of a great deal of distinguished fiction. And with this Gran'mammy story, Sherwood Bonner became one of the pioneers in the sort of regional writing that would dominate American journals for more than two decades. "Aunty, within doors, was churning," the story begins. "I, on the back steps, was shelling peas,—for the days of the old regime had gone by, and in our Southern home we had proved that white hands, though not so skilled as black ones, were apt enough in household work." The author had left behind the Italian village of "Laura Capello" and the English manor house of "The Heir of Delmont" to give her readers the postwar South— life as she had known it. The sense of reality is conveyed by closely observed details: the picture of Aunt Martha, an old sunbonnet on her head, bent over a worn copy of Dante as she churns; the flavor of Gran'mammy's dialect and wit—"I dunno what to make o' Ned. . . . I can't do no more wid him dan if he was a lightin' rod. He say 'de man is de head o' de woman'—pervertin' Scripture at me, de blasphemous boy!" The story, a simple one, is centered on the death of the beloved Gran'mammy, former nurse to two generations of the white family. Unlike many of Harte's local color tales, it presents an emotional situation unmarred by sentimentality. The close bond between the three white children and the old Negro woman, the moving moment when she hands them her final gifts, the strong faith that sustains her at the end of her life—all are rendered simply and convincingly, without a touch of the maudlin. "Gran'mammy's Last Gift" is, in fact, one of the strongest genre pieces that Sherwood Bonner was ever to write.[29]

Although this first tale shows a developing strain of realism in Sherwood Bonner, her second published story, "Miss Willard's Two Rings," was to reveal that the old sentimental and melodramatic influences had still not been fully shaken. These two stories, in fact, reflect poles between which Sherwood Bonner would range in her career as a writer. All of her fiction can be classified as local color writing, fiction that reveals, in varying degrees, the cul-

29. "Gran'mammy's Last Gift," *Youth's Companion,* XLVIII (July 29, 1875), 237–38.

ture of a region. But while she was sometimes capable of the kind of local color realism that verges on the more sophisticated realism of the Howells school, often she merely used carefully observed cultural detail to garnish work dominated by the old conventions.

This latter tendency displays itself dramatically in "Miss Willard's Two Rings," published in *Lippincott's* in December of 1875, the first of a series of tales that Sherwood Bonner designated as "Romances." Here she learned that she had only to refine her pre-Boston techniques to capture a ready market. In that very year, Henry Mills Alden rejected a work by George Washington Cable with the comment that "the stories in *Harper's* . . . as a rule, must be love-tales." The public was still hungry for them, and many editors were eager to comply. With an eye ever on the market and with her thorough grounding in the conventions of the periodical romance, Sherwood Bonner was to write a number of them, usually reverting in these love-tales to the "Laura Capello" influences. Yet her reversions were never complete. First, the Boston influences had been too strong. Both Howells' tastes, evident on the pages of the *Atlantic*, and Longfellow's particular brand of Americanism had convinced her that she must start with life as she had seen it. Probably more importantly, most editors, too, no longer wanted the exotic; they wanted at least a dash of local color thrown in with the old formulas. In Sherwood Bonner's "Romances," then, there were to be elements of the real, though often blurred and distorted to give readers and editors what she thought they wanted.[30]

"Miss Willard's Two Rings," one of the poorest of these tales, is a revealing piece of work—a particularly transparent lens through which to view the creative process that was to produce much of Sherwood Bonner's fiction. We may watch here as she quite crudely adds the garnish of cultural detail to the old conventions. The germ of her tale she took from a Civil War experience of Dr. Mary Safford Blake. The Boston woman had served as a nurse, and one soldier, in gratitude for her kindness, had presented her with a crude wooden ring of his own making and begged that she

30. Arlin Turner, *George W. Cable: A Biography* (Durham, N.C.: Duke University Press, 1956), 63; Gillighan, "Life and Works of Sherwood Bonner," 58; Sherwood Bonner, "Miss Willard's Two Rings," *Lippincott's*, XVI (December, 1875), 754–61.

wear it always in remembrance. Kate McDowell found the story striking, and around it she built her tale of two rings—one a crude handmade object, the other a diamond engagement ring. She based her central character too on a type encountered in Boston, the reform-minded New England maiden. She even named her heroine for Cornelia Boardman and Nellie Willard, the two models for the character. Next, the author placed Cornelia Willard's wartime experiences in the little north Mississippi town of Hollywell—obviously Holly Springs.[31]

Even at the beginning of "Miss Willard's Two Rings," conflicting influences are apparent in Sherwood Bonner's blending of sources and ideas. One feels the force of the new realism in the choice of character and setting. With her short unconventional skirts and her sensible hats, Miss Willard, the samaritan who plunges into the "vilest streets of the city," holding out "her strong pure hands to forsaken ones whom she called sister, brother," is graphic and lifelike. Similarly, the village of Hollywell—victim of raids by both armies, leaving it with the marks of both neglect and the torch—is rendered in vivid detail. The diamond engagement ring, however, brings in the element of romance; and in Sherwood Bonner's case that often means a return to the attractions of melodrama and sentimentality. Thus, though the author begins by grounding her tale in the real, she soon forgets the honest rendering of experience in an attempt to wring as much sensation and pathos as possible from her material. Toward this end, she devises a scene in which the northern samaritan, a Negro smallpox victim, and a brutish guerrilla escaped from hanging come together at a small hut outside the village. Here the guerrilla first reveals his humanity by taking Miss Willard's place as nurse to the Negro; then he experiences a Jekyll-Hyde change, assaults the girl, and steals her money (although she is in the process of giving it to him). From this bit of melodrama Sherwood Bonner proceeds to spin a labyrinthine plot leading to a love story and a heavy-handed moral. The guerrilla is redeemed by Miss Willard's goodness. Though it failed to prevent him at the time from slashing her fingers with a knife, later he becomes a gallant soldier in the Union army and

31. See Jenness, "Dr. Mary J. Safford Blake," 114.

sacrifices his life for that of his colonel. Honoring the man's dying request that Miss Willard be given his crude ring in gratitude for her noble example, the colonel falls in love with the young woman—hence the diamond engagement ring. But Sherwood Bonner cannot release the reader until she has concluded the tale with lofty words underscoring the significance of that first ornament: "To each of the lovers it is a sacred thing. It suggests the divine possibilities of humanity; it inspires faith and hope."

Thus we see how the author has used an overlay of closely observed detail merely to give a more fashionable cast to old formulas, and we watch the initial realism of the tale overwhelmed in the flood of melodrama and sentimentality that follows. But "Miss Willard's Two Rings" is revealing in still another way, for it provides a gauge of the literary opportunism of which Sherwood Bonner was capable. She wrote the story for a particular northern audience—the Nellies and Cornelias who saw the South as a cruel and totally unenlightened place. Thus she sought to gratify their expectations in her portraits of Hollywell's citizens. When the sick old Negro woman enters town, a doctor responds to her pleas for help: "If you can pay my bill, I will cure you." The village mayor makes the physician seem benevolent. Hearing the diagnosis of smallpox, the official berates the woman: "A pretty thing! that you should come here to poison the place! Why couldn't you get to hell long ago!" And after the woman has been removed unattended to an isolated location, he drawls, "She will weather it. A nigger has as many lives as a cat." This is the picture that emerges of the "hot, wretched country" that Miss Willard is "too just to pity and too loyal to love." But well into the story Sherwood Bonner becomes uneasy with this pandering to her intended audience, and the narrative voice tells the reader that Miss Willard's nature "revolted at the cruelty of the people, though perhaps she exaggerated it." This startling narrative comment, which only calls attention to the opportunism underlying the tale, completes the wreckage of a seriously flawed piece of writing. Sherwood Bonner was never again to pander to the Nellies and Cornelias—both because of her own obvious distaste for what she had done and because of a growing recognition that northern audiences were more interested in her own view of southern life. But she would continue to show herself a literary opportunist, and she would boil the pot with a variety of mixtures.

These first two stories provide a remarkable mirror of the paradoxical patterns to run through Sherwood Bonner's literary career. On the one hand, she would often display genuine talent and marked originality; on the other, she would often be influenced by the immediate market and her susceptibility to old formulas. The paths that this first pair of tales foreshadowed, however, were still in the future in the summer of 1875. "Miss Willard's Two Rings" had just been accepted, and Kate McDowell, glorying in her success, prepared to leave Tremont Place for a visit to Holly Springs. She now felt vindicated. In the almost two years since she had fled her old life, she had indeed accomplished something. With two short stories about to be published, she was no longer just Mrs. McDowell; she was a literary lady who was beginning to make her mark. As if to confirm the fact, the Memphis newspapers for the first time announced her return from the North; and they referred to her, not as Mrs. Kate McDowell, but as "Sherwood Bonner."[32]

32. Memphis *Avalanche*, July 13, 1875, p. 3.

Chapter Four

A Woman of Two Worlds

THE NEXT THREE YEARS were a crowded, complicated, heady, triumphant time for Kate McDowell. While her new friendships were both expanding and becoming more complex, the old relationships made demands and brought burdens. Though she might be Sherwood Bonner to the world, she was still daughter, mother, and wife in the eyes of her father and those with the strongest claims on her affections. Thus she was forced to move back and forth between the great world that she so desired and the world of family that she loved, resisted, and was compelled to please. Through enormous will and skillful manipulation, she managed to triumph over the forces hostile to her ambition and to live the life she wanted, the life of the literary lady. She spent these full years seizing and savoring experience, tantalizing her admirers, juggling her identities, defying and subverting convention—all to maintain an ingenious control over her own destiny.

In early July of 1875, Kate McDowell returned to Holly Springs in triumph. This time she planned a visit of four months, for she wanted to spend more time with Lilian, with her family, and with friends like Howard Falconer and Helen Craft, the only two people besides Ruth who had kept in close touch since she had gone to Boston. Now she was no longer so fearful of confronting disapproval in Holly Springs. Her success had bred a feeling of greater ease, and she could relax and enjoy the familiar scenes and faces. She was also looking forward to a visit from Carrie Jenness. James Redpath was to make a southern tour to benefit his health and to view the effects of Reconstruction, and he had promised Carrie his escort to Holly Springs.[1]

1. Memphis *Avalanche*, July 15, 1875, p. 3.

Kate never hesitated to bring her various friends together, no matter what their differences; and if they did not get along, their disagreements failed to upset her very much. The earnest but sweet-tempered Carrie was embraced by most of the Holly Springs circle, despite some of her Yankee notions. Redpath was another matter. While many acknowledged his charm and his intelligence, these Democrats, still under the yoke of a government of carpet-baggers and scalawags, found his radical Republicanism hard to endure. Even the generally mild Howard Falconer was enraged by Redpath's statement that southerners should unite with the Republican party because "that was the country." On the same theory of unity, replied Falconer with passion, Queen Mary had undertaken to make all British subjects Catholics. Kate ignored Redpath's political ardor and the sparks it generated. She could not, however, ignore his ardor of another sort.[2]

In her Boston life, Kate had returned to the sort of coquetry that she had often displayed before her marriage. Writing Ruth soon after the flight from Edward, she had vowed: "I never intend to degrade myself by another 'affair' with any human being." She still wanted no involvements; the escape from Edward had been too narrow. Her resolve did not preclude flirtation: she simply expected gallantry from men, and she chose men who were safe. Redpath should have fallen into this category. He had been married for eighteen years to a woman a decade his senior who had filled perfectly the role of mother-wife to her impetuous younger husband. But Redpath was just past the cusp of forty, he was unhappy with his business arrangement, and he was feeling increasing restlessness in the life he was living. He fell desperately in love with Kate, and declared himself during the Holly Springs visit. She must have handled her rejection of him skillfully, for their friendship did not suffer afterward. Still she must have felt great relief on September the sixth when her Massachusetts visitors were at last on the train north.[3]

2. Howard Falconer to Sherwood Bonner, December 6, 1875, in the collection of the Reverend Dr. George Royster Stephenson of Jackson, Mississippi (hereinafter referred to as Stephenson Collection).
3. Kate McDowell to Ruth Bonner, November 13, 1873, in the Stephenson Collection; Charles F. Horner, *The Life of James Redpath* (New York: Barse & Hopkins, 1926), 180, 225–27; Censuses of Malden, Massachusetts, for 1860, 1870, and 1880. Roger Ellis'

Another of her Boston relationships had also deepened, but she continued to find this one completely safe and eminently satisfactory. For Kate, both Nahum Capen and Longfellow had been admiring father figures, standing in contrast to the stern real father who regarded her as a prodigal. Her relationship with Longfellow, however, had early taken a different turn. There was, of course, always the element of preceptor and student, but there was another element too. As some of his friends realized, age had, if anything, sharpened his interest in women. Mrs. James T. Fields was to recall vividly a scene at a formal party in the poet's later years. As he stood at the base of the staircase, she overheard him say to himself: "Ah, now we shall see the ladies come downstairs!" Kate was flattered by his particular attraction to her, and she capitalized upon it. Though she felt real affection and respect for Longfellow, she also saw how helpful he could be in furthering her career.[4]

Because of her strong appeal and her deft handling of the poet, Kate McDowell early came to know a Longfellow still unrevealed to other friends of much longer standing. To many of them he seemed still reserved and formal. He quickly dropped much of his reserve with Kate, however. Within a short time, he was sharing with her rather broad anecdotes—like the story about his old landlady Mrs. Craigie. On her death bed, the grim woman called her young poet-lodger into the room and uttered to him only one sentence: "Young man, never marry; for see how an old woman looks in bed!" Kate, moreover, was subsequently to print the story! She relished his lighter moments, and her letters contain many teasing references to his more habitual reserve and conservatism. Home on her first visit, she had written him quoting Lilian's strange parody of a prayer. "But *you*," Kate chided the poet, "will think this profane."[5]

---

courtship of Blythe Herndon in Sherwood Bonner's *Like unto Like* is based in part on Redpath's pursuit of Kate. In Helen Craft's copy of the novel (in the possession of Mrs. Fort Daniel of Holly Springs), she identified Ellis as Redpath, and beside Ellis' love letter to the heroine, Miss Craft wrote: "This letter I have read before in *manuscript!*" Jefferson Davis to James Redpath, September 5, 1875, in Jefferson Davis Collection, New York Historical Society.

4. Edward Wagenknecht, *Longfellow: A Full Length Portrait* (New York: Longmans, Green & Co., 1955), 172.

5. Wagenknecht, *Longfellow*, 127; Bonner, "Longfellow's Home"; McDowell to Longfellow, June 1, 1874, in Longfellow Collection, Houghton Library, Harvard University.

As the months passed, their easy intimacy deepened. Under the spell of her youth and beauty and her charm, Longfellow's feeling ripened into infatuation. This was not the first time that the poet had so responded to a younger woman. In 1867, he had met Alice Frere, an English girl thirty-four years his junior, and fallen immediately in love. When she wrote him soon afterward from England and announced her engagement to an army officer, Longfellow replied graciously, conceding his misreading of the signs. "I now comprehend fully," he observed, "the look which I often saw in your eyes." He added in a postscript: "The secret I told you I know is safe in your keeping. I could not help telling it to you. It was the cry of my soul. And yet I would not have told it, had I known yours."[6]

Then six years later, Kate McDowell appeared, forty-two years his junior. Unlike Alice Frere, of course, Kate was already attached, albeit ambiguously. But her strange marital arrangement perhaps even strengthened his response since—for a man of his character—it safely removed the relationship to the platonic sphere. And it was not long before his feeling for Kate McDowell found a voice in his poetry, where he paid tribute to her as the central figure in "The Masque of Pandora":

> O sweet, pale face! O lovely eyes of azure,
>   Clear as the waters of a brook that run
>   Limpid and laughing in the summer sun!
>   O golden hair, that like a miser's treasure
> In its abundance overflows the measure!
>   O graceful form, that cloudlike floatest on
>   With the soft, undulating gait of one
>   Who moveth as if motion were a pleasure!

This compliment to her beauty and grace, he followed with lines possessing an added resonance for a young woman so troubled by her identity and name:

> By what name shall I call thee? Nymph or Muse,
>   Callirrhoë or Urania? Some sweet name

6. While presenting for the first time Longfellow's romantic interest in Alice Frere, Wagenknecht (*Longfellow*, 286–88) argues that there is no evidence that the poet was "enamored" with Kate McDowell. The evidence that I present in this biography speaks for itself.

> Whose every syllable is a caress
> Would best befit thee; but I cannot choose,
> Nor do I care to choose; for still the same
> Nameless or named, will be thy loveliness.

Later in the poem after Pandora's grievous mistake, she wishes for death and asks, "What else remains for me?" The response Longfellow wrote no doubt struck Kate McDowell as the most personal passage of all:

> Youth, hope, and love:
> To build a new life on a ruined life,
> To make the future fairer than the past,
> And make the past appear a troubled dream.[7]

Longfellow began the poem in January in 1875, and he had placed the volume in the printer's hands by mid July. As he waited to read the proof, his thoughts turned to Kate. He remembered her aid when he was putting the manuscript together, and he devised a plan to bring her near him more often. Once "The Masque of Pandora" was published, he intended compiling an anthology of poetry written about various places around the world. He wrote offering her a position as his secretary. His offer provided the kind of economic security that Kate needed, but she responded coyly, protesting that this scheme of employment was too altruistic, that it was merely a plan for helping her. In his next letter he was forced to urge. "Certainly you can be of the greatest help to me in the 'Poems of Places,'" he insisted. "It would occupy two or three hours in the morning only, and you would have the afternoons and evenings entirely free. The work itself would not, I am sure, be distasteful to you, as it deals with poets and poetry." Finally she agreed, and her Boston life for the next year began to take shape.

7. In 1898, Professor Bondurant, with access to Kate McDowell's scrapbook and various other papers, remarked that "Longfellow in a poem dedicated to her thus describes her: 'A Cloud-like form that floateth on with the soft undulating gait / of one who moveth, as if motion were a pleasure'" (Alexander L. Bondurant, "Sherwood Bonner," *Publications of the Mississippi Historical Society*, II [June, 1898], 55). Though the poet never actually formally dedicated "The Masque of Pandora" to her, Longfellow's entire description of Pandora (not just the passage that Bondurant misquotes) is a clear portrait of Mrs. McDowell. She slyly acknowledged the compliment tendered in the later lines—"Some sweet name / Whose every syllable is a caress"—by using them in her story "A Shorn Lamb" (*Harper's Weekly*, August 26, 1882, p. 804). I quote the poem from *Longfellow's Poetical Works* (Boston: Houghton Mifflin & Co., 1891), III, 149, 176.

Now they could look forward to those mornings and to their continued intimacy—for both certainly, though in different ways, so very satisfactory.[8]

While Kate's Boston life was assuming a comfortable prospect, Holly Springs itself was presenting an interesting spectacle. "Holly Springs has been very gay for the two past months," Kate wrote Longfellow at the beginning of November. "Two regiments have been quartered here, and for the first time since the war we have all yielded to the fascinations of brass buttons." Since 1873, regiments from New Orleans had been spending the late summer and early fall in Holly Springs to escape the dangers of yellow fever. Sufficiently bitter memories of the war remained to prevent much social contact between the troops and the townspeople; but in the summer of 1875, the situation changed. The agent was Colonel Dixon Comfort Topp, a planter who had come to Holly Springs after the war and purchased the Coxe place on Salem Street—one of the grandest estates in the town, in fact the seat occupied by General and Mrs. Grant during one of the general's Holly Springs stays. Unlike many of his friends, Colonel Topp had emerged from the war with much of his wealth intact, but postwar economic conditions and his own failure to adjust to changing times were now bringing him close to ruin. In his poverty, he agreed to another Federal occupation of the old Coxe place; he took as boarders the Yankee commander and his wife from New Orleans. Though Dr. Bonner had done the same thing at the close of the war, the town was now (perhaps for the second time) aghast. Into the situation then came Mrs. Kate Freeman, still charming, tactful, still the town's social arbiter. Concluding that the time had come for further reconciliation, Mrs. Freeman gave Colonel Topp's gesture her stamp of approval. She took the officers and their wives up and opened the way for two months of gaiety.[9]

8. Samuel Longfellow (ed.), *Final Memorials of Henry Wadsworth Longfellow* (Boston: Ticknor and Company, 1887), 229, 240. Passages from these two Longfellow letters are quoted by B. M. Drake, "Sherwood Bonner," *Southern Writers: Biographical and Critical Studies*, ed. William Malone Baskerville (Nashville and Dallas: Publishing House of the M. E. Church, South, 1903), I, 97–98. Although Drake does not give the dates of this correspondence, all of the evidence points to the passages coming from the letters of August 22, September 10, or September 28, 1875—all noted in the poet's Letter Calendar.

9. Kate McDowell to Longfellow, November 2, 1875, in Longfellow Collection; Helen Craft's annotations of *Like unto Like*, in the possession of Mrs. Fort Daniel of Holly Springs.

Bonner House offered a perfect vantage point for viewing this first warm meeting of old enemies in Holly Springs. The New Orleans regiments, the Third and the Thirteenth, were camped on the old St. Thomas Hall grounds across Salem Bridge; and the Topps lived just a few doors down Salem Street. Since the Topps were close family friends, Kate McDowell passed often through the massive iron gates of their estate, up the long grass-grown walk bordered by untrimmed rose bushes, and into the house whose hospitality was enveloping the whole town. She gained still another perspective next door at the McDowell cottage. Despite her strained marriage, Kate continued to maintain a cordial relationship with Edward's family, especially with his sisters, Lilly and Mary. She had named her daughter for Lilly and still felt a close bond. Intelligent, spirited, and vain, Lilly provided Kate with a great deal of entertainment that summer and fall. Having at first protested the Topps's actions, Lilly later accepted an invitation to ride with General DeTrobriand, a leading Reconstruction figure in Louisiana, and came home claiming that she had still not gone back on her principles in the least. By fall, she was being instructed in military signaling, and she could be seen at the McDowell gate waving a stick with a white handkerchief tied at the end and waiting to have the signal returned by a courting officer. It was a time that called for the bending of principles and that offered opportunities for considerable flirtation. DeTrobriand had brought the headquarters battalion band, and soon the military and the citizenry were alternately sponsoring weekly balls at the Masonic Hall, the military band playing for both.[10]

This Federal invasion had begun before Kate's Boston friends left, and it continued well into October. Kate prolonged her visit; Holly Springs had not proven so interesting in years. And after the troops had gone, she accepted an invitation from the editor of the Memphis *Avalanche*, Colonel Andrew J. Kellar, and his wife. When she returned home from Memphis, her plans for the next year in Boston had taken their final shape. For over a year she had wanted Ruth with her in Boston. Ruth had a fine voice, and Kate wished her to study at Tourgic's Conservatory, but there was a still more compelling reason to remove her sister from Holly Springs.

10. Craft Annotations; John Mickle, "Name 'Bonner House' Stirs Old Memories," Holly Springs *South Reporter*, November 20, 1930, p. 1.

David McDowell, Edward's younger brother, had fallen passionately in love with her. At twenty-one, three years Ruth's junior, David was a handsome, intense young man, highly jealous, and importunate in his suit of the gentle, quiet Ruth. During Kate's long Holly Springs visit, the rest of the Bonner family came round to her point of view: one McDowell in the family was enough, and Ruth's removal to Boston might end this affair. They were finally won over completely when the Capens wrote insisting that both young women spend the year with them at Mt. Ida. The second week in November, the sisters left for Boston—their year, it seemed, mapped out before them.[11]

Longfellow called at Mt. Ida immediately to make Ruth welcome in Boston, and the Capens were delighted with their guests. Both the poet and the hosts were clearly happy too that between them they had arranged for Kate a life quite different from her bohemian existence of the last year. Ruth began her study at the conservatory. Kate began her mornings at Longfellow House aiding with the *Poems of Places*. And in early December Kate received an unusually warm letter from Holly Springs that inspired her to work hard at her writing in the coming months. Answering some doubts that she had expressed about her talents, Howard Falconer wrote: "I think that you have 'capabilities' for anything. They have, however, to a recent period, been as deep-buried and unremunerative as the measureless gold of the Big Bonanza before the drill and pickaxe and the hoisting-chains brought its exhaustless riches up to the daylight. Your mind to you a Big Bonanza is—you have only to dig the gold out of it, to be both rich and great." Cheered by his confidence, so particularly gratifying because it came from home, she went to work to prove him right. But hardly had her routine been set when she made a decision that startled everyone. Shortly after Christmas she suddenly decided to go to Europe.[12]

Mrs. Louise Chandler Moulton, a woman high in Boston's so-

11. Memphis *Avalanche*, October 31, 1875, p. 3; Kate McDowell to Ruth Bonner, September 22, 1874, in Stephenson Collection; Holly Springs *South*, May 3, 1882, p. 2; Howard Falconer to Sherwood Bonner, December 6, 1875, in Stephenson Collection; McDowell to Longfellow, November 2, 1875, in Longfellow Collection.

12. McDowell to Longfellow, November 14, 1875, in Longfellow Collection; George R. Stephenson, "Sherwood Bonner" (a 1932 typescript in Stephenson Collection), 13.

cial and literary circles, was planning a European tour; and she needed a traveling companion. She invited Kate to accompany her, and, despite Kate's obligations to Ruth, to the Capens, to Longfellow, to her own writing, the young woman accepted—for in the trip she saw the fulfillment of one of her most persistent dreams. The glamour of Europe itself was further enhanced by the prospect of seeing it with Mrs. Moulton. Kate had been attracted to the older woman early in her Boston life. In one of her first *Avalanche* sketches, she noted the presence of Mrs. Moulton among the distinguished Bostonians at a private memorial service for Sumner, and she described her as the "successful authoress [who] had not forgotten to be the charming woman." This was the type of woman whom Kate always admired most: a woman of intellect, force, and independence, who, at the same time, displayed femininity and style. Kate then went on to pay the northern writer her supreme compliment. She found Mrs. Moulton "Southern in the sweetness of her voice and the winning grace of her manners." The response of the established writer to Kate was equally warm. From the beginning she showed an interest in the young Mississippian, and by the next year Mrs. Moulton was including her southern friend in the distinguished Friday salons held at her elegant house at 28 Rutland Square, a fashionable South End enclave. And though Louise Chandler Moulton was a pillar of the Radical Club, when Kate wrote her satire, her friend received a treatment different from that accorded many other figures, being described in glowing terms as "a matron, made for kisses, in the loveliest of dresses."[13]

In the aftermath of the publication of "The Radical Club" and the author's increasing bohemianism, when many of Mrs. Moulton's set were closing their doors to Kate, she did not follow suit. Of course she had escaped attack herself, but she was also less rigid than many others of her circle. There was still another reason, known only to a few real intimates, that this woman so highly placed could show such tolerance and display such interest in the unconventional and decidedly ambitious southern aspirant to literary laurels. Despite her husband's wealth and her position, Mrs.

13. McDowell, "From the 'Hub': A Personal Chapter"; Bonner, "Boston's Centennial."

Moulton could see some of her own conflicts reflected in Kate. Louise Chandler had published her first volume of poems and sketches in 1854, when she was nineteen; and six weeks out of boarding school she had married William U. Moulton, the Boston publisher who had accepted some of her earliest work. A daughter had been born to them, to whom Mrs. Moulton was devoted; and she herself had enjoyed great literary and social success. But she was miserable in her marriage. Nearing forty at the time Kate had come to Boston, Mrs. Moulton had written to her old friend E. C. Stedman, disagreeing with his ideas about the value of even imperfect marriages. "I don't think," she insisted, "that a woman had better marry out of her own ideal than not marry at all. I *can't* think that, in the face of experience." Still later she had asked Stedman's advice on divorcing her husband, her only fear being that such a measure would hurt the sales of her works and thus make her unable to support herself. She was never to get the divorce, but such a woman could appreciate Kate's strange circumstances and intense ambition. She could understand the reasons behind some foolhardy actions, and she could also perhaps wish that she shared some of the younger woman's disrespect for convention.[14]

By 1875, Mrs. Moulton had been active on the Boston literary scene for almost twenty years. A prolific writer of poetry, short stories, reviews, and children's stories, she was a regular contributor to the *Atlantic Monthly*, *Scribner's*, *Galaxy*, and *Youth's Companion*. She had helped Kate place her first story in the last of these journals. Now, added to these marks of friendship came the invitation to accompany Mrs. Moulton to Europe. The glamour of it all was too much for Kate to resist. Certainly she would go.

Kate had now to break the news. Luckily, Ruth was very much at home in the Capen family, but that young lady, who had come to Boston after almost two years of her sister's urging, must have

14. Virtually all biographical treatment of Mrs. Moulton has been genteel panegyric that hides a great deal of the real woman. See particularly Lilian Whiting, *Louise Chandler Moulton: Poet and Friend* (Boston: Little, Brown, and Company, 1910). Only Louise M. Young's excellent brief sketch—*Notable American Women, 1607–1950* (Cambridge: Harvard University Press, 1971), I, 595–96—suggests the complexities and tensions revealed in Mrs. Moulton's letters to Edmund Clarence and Laura Stedman in the Stedman Collection, Butler Library, Columbia University. Moulton to E. C. Stedman, n.d., 1873, and October 27 [1873].

been startled indeed. Then too there was Kate's patron at Longfellow House. The poet was quite pleased with their arrangement,
and he was making good progress on what had become a many-
volumed project. Shortly after Christmas he had given a luncheon
for Kate, Ruth, Cornelia Boardman, and Nellie Willard. Charmed
by the youthful spirits of Kate and her friends, he had described
them with satisfaction in his journal as a "very pleasant Quar-
tette." This sort of idyll was ended by Kate's news. Not only disappointed but inconvenienced by this change in plans, Longfellow
still responded generously. Realizing how much the trip meant to
the young woman, he encouraged her, provided her with letters of
introduction to his friends, and evidently gave her money. Next
came the hardest chore of all—announcing the plan to her father,
after he had finally consented to put Ruth in her charge. Kate also
knew that her living in Boston away from husband and child was
difficult enough for her father to accept, but that her separation
from them by an ocean might meet his strong resistance. The full
text of his answer to her announcement does not survive, and he
may have imposed conditions upon her going, but he also reacted
with grace. "I know that this trip has been one of your day dreams
for many years," he wrote, "and that your future can hardly be
compleat without it." Evidently sending her money, he cautioned
her against foolish expenditures; and he added in a postscript:
"Remember that you go for other treasures on which there will be
no custom house charges on your return."[15]

Now that all had acceded, Kate set about completing her arrangements. These included an agreement with both the Memphis
Avalanche and the Boston *Times*, both of which would pay her
ten dollars for each European article that she wrote. She was also
adding to her coffers at the moment. The *Avalanche* had published
her sketch of Longfellow and his home on December twenty-sixth,
Youth's Companion had accepted another Gran'mammy story for
January publication, and she was now hurriedly finishing a three-
part romance of the Revolutionary War, "Which Was the Heroine?" to lead off the first three issues of *The Cottage Hearth* for the

15. Longfellow's Journal, December 28, 1875, in Longfellow Collection; McDowell to
Longfellow, January 14 [1876] and January 30, 1876, in Longfellow Collection; George
Royster Stephenson, "Sherwood Bonner" (a 1932 typescript in the Stephenson Collection),
13.

new year. She was still trying to complete work for Longfellow, and on January fourteenth, she mailed him a copy of "All Quiet Along the Potomac," hoping that he would include it in the new volume of *Poems of Places* that he was compiling at her suggestion—one devoted to the states of the old Confederacy. Early the following Tuesday morning she went to Longfellow House to receive the letters of introduction and to bid him good-bye. Back at Mt. Ida, she was presented bon voyage gifts by all members of the Capen household and by Carrie and Nellie. Then on Thursday, the twentieth, she left with Mrs. Moulton for New York to await the sailing of the *Baltic* two days later.[16]

Kate's adventure actually began in New York, where the two women stayed a night with Mrs. Moulton's friend Mrs. Laura Curtis Bullard, who had a reception for the voyagers. Included in the list of guests where Whitelaw Reid, editor of the *Tribune*; Mrs. Mary Mapes Dodge, author of the children's classic *Hans Brinker and The Silver Skates* and editor of the handsomely printed new children's magazine *St. Nicholas*; Noah Brooks, the successful journalist; John Q. Ward, the very popular sculptor from the Midwest; and Mrs. Moulton's childhood friend Edmund Clarence Stedman, the poet and critic. Here was New York as Kate had wanted to see it, and her pleasures continued when the *Baltic* set sail. Though the crossing was rough, the two handsome literary ladies were seated at the captain's table among a group whom Mrs. Moulton described as "some English swells of the first water." The English were attentive, though patronizing, constantly extolling the superiority of English qualities over American ones. Among them, however, was the dashing Captain Talbot, an officer in the Life Guards and brother of the Earl of Shrewsbury. Other passengers were interesting too. There was George Vandenhoff, the English actor, and a Mrs. Nayfew, going to Ireland on the advice of a New York clairvoyant and expecting to inherit a fortune left by some Irish ancestor. With her usual comic sense, Kate wrote Longfellow that the latter could be "quite a heroine of romance except that she wears spectacles and has her ears stuffed with cotton!"[17]

16. McDowell to Longfellow, January 14 [1876] and January 30, 1876, in Longfellow Collection; McDowell to Carrie Jenness, February 22, 1876, in Stephenson Collection.
17. Sherwood Bonner, "'Sherwood Bonner': An Avalanche Correspondent's Voyage

After the *Baltic* docked at Liverpool, Captain Talbot accompanied the two Americans to London, guided them to the Charing Cross Hotel, and began making plans for their entertainment. They went to the theater three times and had visits from Mrs. Moulton's friend the actress and lecturer Kate Field, but the highlight of the week was a day especially arranged by Talbot. Queen Victoria was opening Parliament for the first time in five years and Talbot had secured one of the much sought-after gallery tickets in the House of Lords. The ticket fell to Mrs. Moulton when the women drew lots, but the alternate invitation that fell to Kate turned out to be the real prize. She was asked to watch the procession from the Horse Guards Barracks. Her hostess there, the brilliant young Lady Lamb, took special notice of the young American, even giving her the best seat at the window. But in the midst of this glamorous setting, Kate was shocked by the arrogance of the distinguished assemblage. When the huge crowd struggling on the street below to get a glimpse of the queen swelled out of control, Lady Lamb was eager for the soldiers to charge them. Looking through her eyeglass as a man was knocked to the ground and a child stunned, another titled lady shuddered and commented languidly: "Dear me, how terrified I should be down there. But I suppose they like it." Kate's reaction was surprisingly vehement. "I felt my Republican blood boil," she wrote, "and all the elegance of the trains and titles that swept and sounded around me could not lessen my first shock in English high life." Her day in society did not end at the Horse Guards Barracks, for there a grand old lady, the Marquise de Vincheaturd, took a fancy to her and insisted that she come to a musical party in the afternoon. Kate found her afternoon impressions also mixed. She described herself as shining "with a reflected glory" and feeling "like a young imposter" but as being charmed with the wife of the Peruvian minister and wishing that they could be friends. She appreciated the Marquise's attentions, but Kate noted that the old lady was "uncommonly fond of port" and that her ears too were plugged, this time with brown sponge. Her report of the occasion

---

Across the Atlantic," Memphis *Avalanche*, February 27, 1876, p. 2; Moulton to Laura Stedman, February 12 [1876], in Stedman Collection; McDowell to Longfellow, January 30, 1876, in Longfellow Collection.

to Longfellow reflects not only the ambivalence toward the titled lady, but also Kate's wavering between self-consciousness and self-assurance: "Still she was good to me—and I should like to accept her invitation to call when we go back to London—But I don't know that I shall—Great folks wear smart gowns, and, I fancy, would drop young women who lived in cheap lodgings, very soon. But *if* I could—*how* I should enjoy the London season! I do believe in spite of my ignorance and lack of accomplishments, I could hold my own even against the great ladies." [18]

The two Americans had prolonged their stay in London in order to accept Captain Talbot's invitations. But the day after the opening of Parliament, they packed hurriedly, for many of Mrs. Moulton's plans depended upon reaching Rome in time for carnival. They spent only two days in Paris, where they enjoyed strolling the boulevards, sampling the cuisine, and shopping. Mrs. Moulton could afford to indulge some of her whims, including buying a hat from Virot's; and Kate finally purchased a pair of French boots, reasoning that "I have slain temptation in so many instances, that I can forgive myself in this." The two wonderful days over, the pair left for Rome, but Kate had determined that she must return to Paris for a long stay. In Marseilles they boarded a French steamer for Naples, and from there they traveled to Rome. Reaching the city just as the carnival began, they established themselves in a comfortable pension. Kate was enchanted. "The fascination of this old city is beyond anything I have ever known," she wrote. "It sinks into the soul, with the sunshine and the perfume of the purple Roman violets." And soon after their arrival in Rome came another experience as memorable as that heady, confusing day in London. On February 21, 1876, the fifty-fifth anniversary of Keats's death, English and American residents of the city were invited to the Protestant Cemetery for the unveiling of the Keats medallion. Kate found the spot itself beautiful. As she stood near the poet's grave looking at the mound surrounded by a small hedge of box and covered by Roman violets and English daisies, she read the epitaph that he had chosen—"Here lies one whose

18. Sherwood Bonner, "'Sherwood Bonner': A Southern Woman's Impressions of England and the English," Memphis *Avalanche*, March 15, 1876, p. 2; McDowell to Longfellow, February 10, 1876, in Longfellow Collection.

name was writ in water"—and she was deeply moved. "Poor Keats!" she mused the next day. "I wonder if appreciation so long delayed comforts him! I wonder if he knows of the violets and daisies blooming above—he who felt the flowers growing over him in those woeful last days, when death was coldly touching his passionate heart?" She thought of the cruelty of fate and of the "love, sympathy and appreciation that almost seem a mockery, because they come too late." Then she closed her reverie by quoting a line to which she would often return—for reasons that she could not have imagined at this moment: "Nor shame nor fancy can scale a churchyard wall."[19]

The next week the women attended a masked ball and enjoyed all of the pageantry and high-spirited confusion of the Shrove Tuesday celebrations. On the twenty-sixth came Kate's birthday. She was twenty-seven, and Mrs. Moulton planned a day in accordance with Kate's wishes. In the morning they explored "quaint old places"; in the afternoon they made a tour of cameo shops, climaxed by a "fete" of ices and macaroons in a little cafe. That evening they were given their introduction to the American colony of the city at a party hosted by Ann Hampton Brewster, an expatriate writer. There, in Kate's witty judgment, they met "many well-dressed and a few clever people." Despite her own cleverness when she came to write about the occasion, however, she knew that she was seeing a part of Rome that she would never have encountered without Mrs. Moulton's sponsorship; and she was enjoying the experience.[20]

Miss Brewster's evening party brought other invitations. A number of the Americans in Rome received once a week, and increasingly the two handsome women were included in the entertainments, filled in Kate's view with "angels in Paris gowns and waving plumes, with faces of rose and pearl." The Americans that the women saw most were artists—sculptors and painters, a group that Kate found eventually to be "a nest of scorpions" in

19. McDowell to Longfellow, February 10, 1876, in Longfellow Collection; Sherwood Bonner, "'Sherwood Bonner': A Southern Woman's Trip from London to Rome," Memphis *Avalanche*, March 26, 1876, p. 1.
20. Sherwood Bonner, "Rome's Carnival," Memphis *Avalanche*, April 9, 1876, p. 2; McDowell to Jenness, February 22, 1876, in Stephenson Collection; McDowell to Longfellow, March 5, 1876, in Longfellow Collection.

their intense rivalries and the gossip that they passed about each other. Henry James had earlier described the situation more gently in his allusion to "the rival houses of Terry and Story." The first of these Yankee expatriates, the sculptor Luther Terry, Kate evidently never met; but she did come to know William Wetmore Story, the sculptor and poet whose name had been made when Hawthorne had used Story's statue of Cleopatra in *The Marble Faun*. Kate and Mrs. Moulton visited his studio and were entertained by the Storys in their sumptuous apartment of forty rooms in the Palazzo Barberini. The women received the most devoted and constant attention, however, from another resident of the Barberini, the New Hampshire born painter J. Rollin Tilton. Henry James, who had met Tilton three years earlier, disliked the man, calling him "the atrocious Tilton." Kate's satiric eye also took Tilton's measure. "He is delightful—delightful I mean in the sense that Dickens would have found him so," she wrote Longfellow. "He hob-nobs with the Princes and is hand-in-glove with so many noble lords and ladies that it really becomes difficult to breathe in the rarefied atmosphere around him. He spends weeks with Tennyson, patronizes Ruskin, and is bon comarade with Browning. His conversation is as full of great names as a plum cake is of raisins; but he is always at the fore with the great folks grouped around him." The literary lady was developing an increasingly sophisticated view of the great world.[21]

She was determined not to miss anything, a single landmark, a single acquaintance, a single impression. Accordingly, she found that she had to work late at night. By the beginning of March, she had written three Roman sketches for the newspapers. These, like the two earlier travel pieces that she had sent, were sometimes sparkling, always lively; but the Roman pieces were obviously more hurriedly composed. She also found time, however, to write an able local color sketch of Holly Springs. Called "From '60 to '65," the work presents her native place again under the name Hollywell and vividly describes both the antebellum town, the

21. Sherwood Bonner, "'Sherwood Bonner': A Picture of Social Life in the Eternal City," Memphis *Avalanche*, May 14, 1876, p. 2; Leon Edel, *The Life of Henry James: The Conquest of London, 1870–1881* (Philadelphia: J. B. Lippincott Company, 1962), 89, 95; McDowell to Longfellow, April 21, 1876, in Longfellow Collection.

"City of Flowers," a tiny capital in the Cotton Empire, and the dramatic events and changes experienced during the war. It is a much fuller treatment of her region, its classes and culture, than she had previously attempted. With the clarity that great distance can give, here in Rome she was going back to the material that she knew best.[22]

Though Rome was proving a "heavenly interlude," Kate soon realized that she was spending too freely; and she feared that her funds would not cover the eight months of travel she had planned. Mrs. Moulton was now planning to linger amid Rome's social set and not go to Paris until September. Kate was determined to visit Paris again, and there she could live more cheaply with a Boston friend now studying abroad, the artist Alice Wheeler. Kate also wanted to see more of Italy while she could, but she did not want to tour alone. By April, she had found a guide. A group of young Americans, met through the active social life of the expatriate colony, had attached themselves to the two older women and vied among themselves in paying court to both. An immediate friendship sprang up between Kate and one of them—a twenty-year-old medical student from Philadelphia named William Kirk. Kate was delighted with this coincidence. His father, John Foster Kirk, the editor of *Lippincott's*, had published "Miss Willard's Two Rings"; and Kate had just sent him the sketch of Holly Springs in the sixties. Through William Kirk, she would eventually develop strong ties with the whole Kirk family. William, she described to Longfellow as "an Infant who is six feet in height, speaks four languages, has a lovely sensitive face, and thinks me an angel." Soon the Infant had insisted that he accompany her on a tour of Florence and Venice. Now that she had found a way to see more of Italy, Kate tried to crowd everything into the days remaining to her in Rome. She and Mrs. Moulton had an audience with the

22. McDowell to Longfellow, March 5 and August 8, 1876, in Longfellow Collection. "From '60 to '65," though highly autobiographical, is anything but straight and unadorned fact, as it has been read by some. Sherwood Bonner gives fictional names to local citizens and often presents composite characters. She makes other changes for dramatic effect—including having the local iron foundry manufacturing cannon, rather than small arms, and appropriating to her persona in the sketch some of the wartime experiences of others. It is interesting that she is also careful to include a compliment to her patron: she shows herself reading Longfellow's *Hyperion* when she and her aunt Ellen Hopeton (Anne Vaughn Martin) encounter a party of Federal soldiers.

Pope, paid a visit to Garibaldi, spent a perfect day at Tivoli, and toured the Villa Borghese, where Kate thought constantly of Miriam and Donatello. Then finally the happy days in Rome came to an end, and she bade the city good-bye with tears in her eyes.[23]

Kate spent three more weeks touring Italy. She was awed by Florentine art, but amused to find herself and other tourists plagiarizing their responses from Ruskin, and she turned the experience into a clever sketch. The next city on her itinerary had long ago cast its spell over her. Years before in the library at Bonner House, she had listened to Ruth, singing from the parlor of "Venice, the bride of the sea." At that moment the place had become the city of her dreams. As she rode down the Grand Canal, she felt dream merge with reality, and she realized anew her great good fortune in getting to Europe. Throughout the tour William Kirk was a delightful guide and boon companion; and at the end he accompanied her to Verona, put her on the noon train for Paris, and vowed to see her there within a few weeks.[24]

By the time he arrived, Kate was finding Paris as exciting as Rome, and her circle there, more varied. For the first few days, Kate grew lonely in Alice Wheeler's apartment on the Rue d'Arcet with Alice away at her studio most of the time. The two, however, dined nearly every day on the Avenue Clichy with a French family, and there she began to have happy evenings with a congenial group that included several French students. Alice's American friends also soon began introducing Kate to Paris. Through them she met the young Count Auguste Vandimir and his sister Marie, who became admirers, taking her riding in the Bois and skating at the romantic Bois rink. Kate loved its "splendid band, flowers, ices, pretty women, and dark-eyed youths." And she found herself gliding to the music there often on the arm of "a young Baron with a romantic name"—Ernest de Lorelli. When William Kirk

23. McDowell to Longfellow, April 21, 1876, in Longfellow Collection; McDowell to Ruth Bonner, [March–April 1876], in Stephenson Collection; Sherwood Bonner's travel articles in the Memphis *Avalanche*—"An AVALANCHE Correspondent's Visit to the Pope," April 20, 1876, p. 2; "A Picture of Social Life in the Eternal City," May 28, 1876, p. 2; "Our Letter from Rome," June 18, 1876, p. 2.
24. "Beautiful Florence," Memphis *Avalanche*, July 9, 1876, p. 2; "At Venice," Memphis *Avalanche*, August 6, 1876, p. 2.

reached the city, Kate had been so occupied with society that she had done almost no touring.[25]

All the while that she had been enjoying the pleasures of Europe, however, there were still complicated ties across the ocean that required skillful management. Upon his return from the South to Boston, James Redpath had set about changing the basic pattern of his life. On October 5, he had sold his interest in the Lyceum Bureau. He separated from his wife, resumed his work as a journalist, and moved to New York. He was a deeply disturbed man, but Kate, as was her nature, remained intensely loyal to one who had been a good friend. In her very first letter to Ruth from London, Kate enclosed a letter to Redpath and asked her sister to find his address and send it on. Later, after Redpath had written a series of inflammatory reports on the South, Kate replied to Ruth's criticism of him: "Poor R—I am wretched about him. Yet I know him to be sincere—He has run into this extreme from the ardor of his nature—& remember it is Southern politicians, not Southerners he hates. At all events now when he is under such clouds *I* shall not turn on him. He has been a true friend and I must stand by him."[26]

Kate's relationship with Redpath made simple demands compared with her intricate maneuvering of Longfellow. She had written the poet first from the *Baltic* a chatty, amusing letter, which also expressed her gratitude, the "tenderness and love" she felt for "those who have made possible such rich enjoyments." She closed by reminding Longfellow of "your promise to write me letters of a friendly love." She sent other letters from London and Paris with the same scattering of sprightly impressions and in the same breezy tone. To the third letter, he dispatched a reply that obviously brought her up short. Writing on his sixty-ninth birthday, he addressed her as "Dear Aurora" and insisted that among his birthday bouquets none was "as sweet as your dear, delicious, rambling letter from Paris"; he closed "With dear affection and recollec-

25. McDowell to Ruth Bonner, May 25, 1876, in Stephenson Collection; McDowell to Longfellow, May 30, 1876, in Longfellow Collection.
26. Charles F. Horner, *The Life of James Redpath* (New York: Barse & Hopkins, 1926), 227, 252; McDowell to Ruth Bonner, February 4 and [May] 1876, in Stephenson Collection.

tion." But in between he included a strange comment. Her letter, he observed, reminded him of "Gray's description of Lady Cobham's house at Stokes-Poges, having 'rich windows that exclude the light and passages that lead to nothing'—nothing, I mean, but what is charming to read, and pleasant to remember." If he were chiding her here for sins of omission, she clearly tried to compensate in later correspondence. "It is no satisfaction for me to write to you my dear—Mr. Longfellow—I have so much that I want to say," she wrote from Florence. "When we meet perhaps I shall be tongue-tied—but it seems to me now if I could only sit by you, and look into your kind eyes with a lurking humor in their depths, I could entertain you a long while." Again toward the end of the letter she speaks of "an impatient feeling at my heart at this poor cold paper." And she ends: "Goodnight—It is better to dream than to write." While she was assuring him of her continued affection, she could still tease him: "There is no fear of my 'Talbotyped.' His luster has long since paled before that of other stars." But she did not often take this tone, and from Florence she sent the comforting information that she would be staying in Paris with a young lady from Boston and that "I shall be eminently proper, and do nothing that you would not like." By the time that she had settled in Paris, Kate was in fact being so careful in what she told the poet that "a young Count and his sister—Auguste and Marie Vandimir" mentioned in a letter to Ruth became in a letter to Longfellow "an old Count Vandimir and his pretty daughter Marie."[27]

Kate did not hide from the poet, however, the happiness that she felt in Paris. "How gay and bright and enchanting everything is!" she wrote. "One feels like doing the simplest thing with an air of hilarity!" From Rome, Kate had burst forth to Ruth: "This rich

27. McDowell to Longfellow, January 30, 1876, in Longfellow Collection. Longfellow's "Dear Aurora" letter of February 27, 1876, is evidently the only full communication now surviving out of the more than fifty-seven letters that he wrote Mrs. McDowell. She gave the letter to her friend Helen Craft Anderson, who made a copy before she sold it many years afterward to an antique dealer. The copy is in the possession of Mrs. Anderson's great niece, Mrs. James Driver of Holly Springs.

McDowell to Longfellow, April 21, 1876, in Longfellow Collection; McDowell to Ruth Bonner, May 25, 1876, in Stephenson Collection; McDowell to Longfellow, May 30, 1876, in Longfellow Collection.

full life drives me mad with all its possibilities!" Now Paris too was presenting increasing possibilities. William Kirk had arrived in late May, and the two had begun their touring. Kate's circle of friends, both French and American, continued to grow. In June, Alice's aunt Mary Wheeler Souther and her husband Henry Souther, president of Boston's Broadway National Bank, arrived in Paris for the summer and moved the two young women to a luxurious apartment on the Rue Mansart. But in the midst of such opulence and merriment, still another tie across the Atlantic was making itself felt.[28]

For those at home, this European tour underscored her derelection as wife and mother. From London, Kate had expressed her fear to Ruth that the McDowells were "deeply incensed" about her going to Europe, and she admitted that "even Lilly has not written." By spring considerable pressure was being brought to bear upon Kate to reconcile with her husband. To win her father's support for the tour, Kate may well have agreed to consider resuming her duties as a married woman upon her return. Finally, from Rome, Kate wrote Ruth, who was ever the voice of duty, that she would probably return to Boston in July and, after a couple of months, "home—Lilian & Edward if he wishes." Immediately she must have regretted yielding to family pressure, and by the time she was settled in Paris, Kate was writing to upbraid her sister: "How did you happen to say to Edward I would go back to him? I said so at one time—but after the way he has treated me it is a different matter." But in late June, Kate was still trapped by her concession and struggling to put it as far from her as possible. She had postponed her date of departure, arguing that "perhaps in addition to other reasons it will be well to give poor Edward a little longer chance of establishing himself at something." Kate could not sustain the false altruism long. Thinking of her own dilemma, she struck out at him in a subsequent passage: "Fatal weakness! fatal lack of purpose! to think of the years one after another that have followed since I first knew him—each more barren of result

28. McDowell to Longfellow, May 30, 1876, in Longfellow Collection; McDowell to Ruth Bonner [March–April, 1876], in Stephenson Collection; McDowell to Longfellow, August 8, 1876, in Longfellow Collection.

than the last." She was bitter. She was also trapped. So she continued to delay her return to America.[29]

Finally, in early August, Longfellow wrote, adding additional pressure for her return. He was saving the volumes of *Poems of Places* devoted to Italy and France for her, and he needed her aid. "I have read your letter again and again to find whether it was compassion for my loneliness or a real desire to have me come back that impelled its writing," she responded. "Perhaps it was a mixture of both; but it has decided me. Yes, it is better that I should go back; I am glad that you have saved France and Italy for me, glad that there is still a place for me in your——library." She wrote Ruth the same day to announce her homecoming. Within ten days Kate had changed her mind again, but, in this letter to Ruth, the prodigal daughter sealed her own fate. Ruth had been ill during the summer. Kate, attributing her sister's poor health to worry over the relationship with David McDowell, called the whole affair a "tragedy," expressed her great love for her sister, and offered this advice:

> Consult your heart and your conscience and decide what to do. The one thing that I would impress on you *above all* is *don't consider your-self bound in any way by anything that is past. No matter what you have done,* no matter what you have promised, do the thing that is right now without reference to what has been. No one has any right over you, no matter what your relations have been. Miss W[heeler] was telling me the other day of a girl she knew who had a lover who had been so beastly . . . as to take advantage of her love and become her lover in the French sense—which is a most intimate connection. Afterward she heard of something disgraceful that he had done, & she refused to marry him. He was so low & vile as to taunt her with what had passed, but she very rightly considered that she had lost no purity in the past but would do so by marrying him when he had lost her love and esteem. I respect that girl from my heart. . . . I am saying all this because I think you would be apt to carry conscientiousness too far!

Clearly those were Kate's motives, but it was now she who had gone too far. By September, this letter was reverberating in Boston, and Kate was indignantly writing Ruth to protest her sister's part

29. McDowell to Ruth Bonner, February 4, [March–April], [May], [June], 1876, in Stephenson Collection.

in a communication received from one of the Boston Channings: "From something that you wrote to Channing he has taken the most *ludicrous idea*—Wrote me a long dissertation on purity & launched out viciously at debonair Frenchmen & implored me not to come home changed by this voluptous French life." Ruth also must have been sending distress signals to Holly Springs, and they were received at the same time Edward McDowell was paying a visit there on his way from Galveston to the Centennial Exposition in Philadelphia. For the first time in three years he saw Lilian. Witnessing this strange meeting of the alien father and daughter, both the Bonners and McDowells now united firmly against Kate and insisted that she come back to her family. "I hear nothing from E. & am not disposed to write," Kate had told Ruth in August. "He has treated me horribly. He has been weak, selfish, capricious, tyrannical, as unworthy of trust as a reed. I too feel sorry for him but I am a little sorrier for myself—my life blighted by marriage with a man utterly unworthy." By September, however, she was sending Ruth a letter to mail to Edward. But even at this point Kate's mind was definitely elsewhere, for her instructions contain an interesting slip of the pen. "Mail this letter to JR," she wrote. Then she crossed out Redpath's initials and substituted the initial *E*.[30]

Still Kate thought that she could put off returning. In the middle of August, she had told Ruth that Mrs. Moulton was coming to Paris in September to join her and that "perhaps I shall stay a few months to study & write." Even a month later when she enclosed the letter for Edward, she refused to commit herself to any departure date. By that time, however, the Fates were arraigned against her. Holly Springs presented a united front. She had realized one of her dreams; she had waltzed around Europe; now it was time to pay the piper. She must return to her responsibilities. Finally, she was overcome, her ingenuity exhausted. She left all the pleasures of Paris and reached Boston early in October.

Living at Mt. Ida with the Capens and her sister, Kate re-

30. McDowell to Longfellow, August 8, 1876, in Longfellow Collection; McDowell to Ruth Bonner, August 8, August 18, [September], 1876, in Stephenson Collection; *McDowell* v. *Craft and Bonner* (Custody Suit over Lilian K. McDowell), No. 1657 in Chancery Docket, Chancery Clerk's Office, Marshall County Courthouse, Holly Springs.

established her old routine. She spent the mornings in Longfellow's study assisting him with *Poems of Places*, she went to work earnestly on her own projects, and she turned her mind squarely to the future. On the sixteenth, she wrote her father to inform him of her safe return and to tell him that she had written Edward that she would join him in Galveston, though she insisted that she was not sure what her husband's response would be. She then stressed her present obligations to Longfellow, but promised to return to Holly Springs by Christmas for "that fatted calf feast." Toward the end of the letter she revealed her own conflicts, her sense of frustration, and her final grim acceptance. She did think increasingly of Lilian. "I wish I had her and a *home* here in Boston," she lamented. "It seems a great pity to leave now, when my literary prospects are so bright. The Editor of the Times is very anxious for me to form a permanent connection with his paper—he says the circulation has largely increased since I began to write for it—and the other night at a reception another Editor told me that I had already made a *name*—that my future was assured etc. Well! sacrifices must be made—and I shall try to make mine without any unnecessary fuss." [31]

The reunion with Edward delayed until after Christmas, Kate now immersed herself in work. In Paris, she had written very little. Though the two months in Rome had yielded not only six pieces for the *Times* and the *Avalanche* but also the Holly Springs sketch for *Lippincott's*, during the four months in Paris she had produced only four newspaper articles. She had done nothing on *The Prodigal Daughter*, a projected novel that Longfellow was encouraging her to write based on her experiences of the past four years. She had told the poet that instead she was concentrating her efforts on a collection of short stories for children, which Mrs. Moulton was sure would be published by her own publisher Roberts Brothers. But Kate had actually spent little time on that either. "From '60 to '65" had been accepted while she was in Paris, and it appeared in the October issue of *Lippincott's* as she was working day and night to get other things ready for publication. First, she wrote a final column for the *Times* on her European travels: next, she

31. McDowell to Dr. Charles Bonner, October 16, 1876, in Stephenson Collection.

finished two French stories for *The Youth's Companion*; and, finally, she produced a flowery sketch of Mrs. Moulton for *The Cottage Hearth*. In the midst of her own work and her services for Longfellow, she still managed a short trip to Philadelphia to see the Exposition and to visit the Kirks and Cornelia Boardman, who was there studying medicine. Ruth had gone back to Holly Springs shortly before Thanksgiving, but Kate remained at Mt. Ida until the week before Christmas. She left feeling some dread of the coming year, but also great eagerness to see her family; and her return to Bonner House, as she described it to Longfellow, was her happiest homecoming:

> As I got out of the carriage I heard voices calling, Kate! Kate! and saw Mary and Lilly in the distance. But I could not wait. I rushed into the house—Ruth met me—Then the folding doors were thrown open, and there were Aunty, Papa, and standing in the light of a great blazing wood-fire—a vision. And the next second that vision was in my arms. Mr. Longfellow, she was the most beautiful little creature as she stood there. I was almost afraid to touch her. There was something unearthly about her. Her hair hung to her neck in light pale gold curls and was tied with a scarlet ribbon. She had on a grey dress with scarlet trimmings, and her cheeks and eyes and lips so beautiful. I never shall forget the picture she made. In all my dreams of her I had never imagined her half so lovely.[32]

Lilian was five years old, and Kate, who had missed some of the difficult years of child rearing, now felt herself a more competent mother. The mother and daughter became closer than they had ever been. In the first month at home, Kate devoted a great deal of time to her child, but she also revised the *Avalanche* sketch of Longfellow and his home for a new volume, *Poet's Homes*, being brought about by D. Lothrop in Boston. The happy days at Bonner House were marred only by Ruth's at last accepting David McDowell's proposal. Kate herself, however, had arranged once again to delay her reconciliation with David's brother, this time until spring.[33]

32. McDowell to Longfellow, August 8, [November], December 25, 1876, in Longfellow Collection; McDowell to Ruth Bonner, December 2, 1876, in Stephenson Collection.
33. McDowell to Longfellow, December 25, 1876, and March 11 and April 17, 1877, in Longfellow Collection.

She accepted another invitation to visit Memphis as guest of the *Avalanche* editor Andrew Kellar and his wife Margaret Chambers Kellar. By this time, the Kellars were Kate's intimate friends, especially Mrs. Kellar, who commented years later that "no woman was ever so dear to me as Katharine." But during this visit Kate met two other people who were also to play important roles in her life. The first was a Confederate general of mysterious origins, one of the acknowledged business, civic, cultural, and social leaders of the city, and its most eligible bachelor—General Colton Greene. Forty-four years old that winter, Greene had had a remarkable life. One of its most decidedly remarkable aspects for many Memphians was the fact that he would divulge nothing of his first twenty years except that he was a South Carolinian. As a very young man, the mysterious Greene had arrived in St. Louis, where in the decade before the Civil War he had begun to amass a fortune as a merchant. When the war broke out, he was already connected with a military organization; and with what a contemporary called "an inherent fondness for arms and a chivalric devotion to the traditions of the South," he offered his sword to the Confederacy and was commissioned a captain under General Sterling Price. A gallant and daring cavalryman who was wounded three times, Greene had risen to the rank of brigadier general under Kirby-Smith in the Trans-Mississippi division by 1865. At the war's end Greene joined an expedition of the western Confederates going to Mexico, but he became quickly discouraged by both the disorganization of the party and the uselessness of a further struggle. He came instead to Memphis to work at reestablishing his own fortune and rebuilding the South. He purchased a large insurance business, which had soon prospered enough for him to invest in manufacturing interests; and he eventually formed one of the important banks in the city. As his fortune increased, so did his sense of civic responsibility, and after investigating thoroughly all sorts of community improvements, he became their disinterested advocate. By the 1870s he was spending part of nearly every year abroad and indulging his scholarly and aesthetic interests, by collecting art treasures and an impressive library of rare editions. Elegant, polished, and convivial, he enjoyed great social prestige. One of the originators of Memphis' Mardi Gras, in 1872 he organized the Mystic Society of the Memphi, the secret society that not only gave the highest social stamp to the carnival, but also through its elaborate pageants (which Greene planned and designed) removed the whole celebration from the realm of the provincial. By 1876 he had also organized the Tennessee Club, the premier club of the city. This was the man on whom so many Memphis mothers had pinned their daughters' hopes, but he had eluded all. Kate met him just at the time that the Tennessee Club had moved into the new quarters Colton Greene had planned for it on Court Street, and she attended the Memphi Ball, further evidence of his energy and taste. Here was the sort of hero Kate had once longed for. Colton Greene was everything that she had wanted Edward to be—a man of broad culture who was also a man of action and a man of affairs.[34]

While Kate tarried in Memphis moving in society and enjoying the attentions of a fascinating man, her father became disturbed enough to make the trip of fifty miles to find out what was happening. At Kate's instigation, no doubt, the next day's *Avalanche* noted that "Dr. Charles Bonner of Holly Springs is in the city, taking a sly peep at the splendors of the Carnival." Upset by the role that Kate, whom he had thought reconciled to the role of wife and mother, was playing in the celebration, he could probably find little comfort in the second strong friendship that his daughter was forming. Elizabeth Avery Meriwether, who had been born four years earlier than Dr. Bonner's own wife and who belonged to a highly regarded southern family, was still not the doctor's idea of a proper southern matron. A Tennessean of New York and Virginia parentage, Elizabeth Avery had been a strong minded and well read young woman when she married Minor Meriwether, a scion of Virginia aristocrats. At the time of the marriage, her wealthy father-in-law was in the process of freeing his slaves; and after his

34. Memphis *Avalanche*, January 23, 1877, p. 2; Margaret Chambers Kellar to Martha Bonner, March 22, 1893, in possession of Mrs. Fred Belk, Holly Springs; "Death of Gen. Colton Greene," Memphis *Commercial Appeal*, October 1, 1900; "Death of Gen. Colton Greene," Memphis *Evening Scimitar*, October 1, 1900; "Memorial Resolutions," Memphis *Commercial Appeal*, October 5, 1900—all in Colton Greene File, Memphis Room, Memphis/Shelby County Library, Memphis: Shields McIlwaine, *Memphis Down in Dixie* (New York: E. P. Dutton & Co., Inc., 1948), 236; Mark Mayo Boatner III, *The Civil War Dictionary* (New York: David McKay Company, Inc., 1959), 355.

death his son followed his wishes and sent them to Liberia. The young bride absorbed the Meriwethers' abolitionist feeling and began speaking out against slavery in the early 1850s. Despite their abolitionism, the family were devoted Confederates, Minor Meriwether serving as a major in the Confederate army and his wife protesting to the end of her long life prejudice against the South and the harsh treatment the South received during war and reconstruction. By the 1870s, however, Mrs. Meriwether had found still another cause. The arrest of Susan B. Anthony for attempting to vote brought the Memphis woman into action on the behalf of women's suffrage, one of the causes she had long espoused. In 1872, Mrs. Meriwether published her own newspaper devoted to the issue. The greatest sensation, however, was created when she rented the largest theater in Memphis for the night of May 6, 1876, addressed a large audience on the question of women's suffrage, and announced that she would vote in the Hayes-Tilden election in the fall. That night she became a nationally known figure, and at the National Woman Suffrage Convention in that year, Elizabeth Cady Stanton was elected president and Mrs. Meriwether vice-president. Here obviously was another of those strong women to whom Kate was naturally drawn. But what would her Boston friends have made of Elizabeth Avery Meriwether—a southern lady, who was an abolitionist-Confederate-suffragette? Many southerners themselves hardly knew what to make of her. The suffragettes were viewed over much of the country as "women of the streets," but people at home could not regard in that way a woman whose brother had been a member of Congress from Tennessee, whose husband was among the most respected of Memphis lawyers, and whose connections were all aristocratic. Still, the highly traditional Dr. Bonner could hardly have been pleased that his daughter was forming a strong friendship with the most outspoken feminist in the South.[35]

At the end of Mardi Gras, Kate returned to Holly Springs,

35. Memphis *Avalanche*, February 13, 1877, p. 2. The best biographical sources on Mrs. Meriwether are her autobiography and that of her son: Elizabeth Avery Meriwether, *Recollections of Ninety-Two Years, 1824–1916* (Nashville: Tennessee Historical Commission, 1958), and Lee Meriwether, *My Yesterdays* (Webster Grove, Missouri: International Mark Twain Society, 1942). Her feminist activity is also covered in Grace Elizabeth Prescott, "The Woman Suffrage Movement in Memphis, Its Place in the State, Sectional, and National Movements," *West Tennessee Historical Society Papers*, XVIII (1964), 87–106.

but only to deliver the disquieting announcement that she now planned a trip to Huntsville, Alabama, to visit Helen Craft, who was teaching there. That visit was short, however, because in Memphis Kate had set in motion a plan that demanded her attention soon in Holly Springs. She had invited Elizabeth Meriwether to deliver a speech "Woman and the Law" in the little "City of Flowers." The lecture was to be Kate's revenge upon the town for their disapproval of her actions. Through the Averys, Meriwethers, Dabneys, and Minors, the Memphis matron was kin or connected with many Holly Springs families. They would have to come; they would have to give Mrs. Meriwether their respectful attention. On the evening of March 7, they did. Introduced by Colonel Harvey Walter, one of the town's leading citizens, Mrs. Meriwether gave her speech before—in Kate's words—"an audience of our best people." But Kate could not let even this victory stand by itself. She had to discuss the occasion in a letter to the *Avalanche* signed simply "A Citizen of Holly Springs." The citizen is lavish in her praise of Mrs. Meriwether, "a Southern lady, elegant in toilet, graceful, modest, self-possessed" with a "sweet Southern voice that falls on the ear like music," but a woman in "thought and theory, one of the 'strong-minded sisters' who generally find their 'spheres' under Northern skies." In contrast, the citizen delivers a severe judgment of local attitudes:

> Holly Springs does not claim to be an advanced town. Sleeping quietly among its hills, it is undisturbed by the tread of faraway feet, and takes little heed of the cries it scarcely hears. The political problem is the only one it tries to solve, and the thought brought to bear upon it is active, bright and resolute. The woman question is not agitated. The women here lead happy, sheltered lives. They have known only chivalry and respect; if their sisters have been wronged in a less happy world, they have not known it; and, educated in a severe conservatism, they dread even the expression of radical ideas dangerous to the peace of order loving minds.

Now Kate too had lectured the citizenry. Pressured by her traditional family to return to a husband for whom she had no respect, she was striking back at the whole town.[36]

36. Memphis *Avalanche*, February 25, 1877, p. 3; unidentified clippings in the Helen Craft Anderson scrapbook, in possession of Mrs. John Craft and Mrs. James Driver, Holly Springs (hereinafter cited as Craft Collection); Memphis *Avalanche*, February 20, 1877, p.

None of this boded well for the reconciliation about to take place in Galveston, and Kate's last letter to Longfellow from Holly Springs also presents a bleak outlook. "Ah me! would success ever delight any human soul as it would mine—because it will be all life can give me," she wrote. Then she added, "That is unjust to my golden-haired Lilian, who is more and more my pride and joy." There was no mention of Edward, and she signed the letter "K.S.B." As Kate was struggling with the question of her future, others were not feeling charitable toward either the wayward wife or her husband. Jimmy Watson, one of their oldest friends, wrote his former sister-in-law Cora (Mrs. Sam Carey now for the last seven years): "I have some curiosity to know what the end will be. I wonder if [Kate] is capable now of settling down and making a good wife and a happy home. It shouldn't surprise me if she should take to 'lecturing'—I mean publicly. Ed. would make a first rate agent—a sort of 'avant bill poster'—and I don't think he would object to it very much."[37]

Near the first of April, Kate McDowell arrived in Galveston without Lilian; clearly Kate did not want to risk the child's becoming attached to her father after his years of inattention. Edward was living with his Mills relatives, and the Galveston household was made up of Edward and Kate, Uncle Robert and Aunt Mary Mills, and a couple of servants. Robert Mills had been a millionaire, known widely as the "Duke of Brazoria." When he went bankrupt in 1873, he had nobly surrendered everything to his creditors, even his great mansion, which was protected by the Texas bankruptcy law. Kate described him now as "an old man, white headed, fine mannered," but withdrawn and self-absorbed. Ever in hopes of a return of his luck, he read cotton statistics constantly; and though he was generally taciturn, whenever he wished to escape a conversation, he simply left the room and went to wash his hands. His sister Mary Mills had long been a favorite of Kate's. She was a lovely, gentle, unselfish old lady, but, unfortunately for Kate, "easily horrified by anything out of the beaten

3; A Citizen of Holly Springs, "Mrs. Meriwether's Lecture in Holly Springs," Memphis Avalanche, March 18, 1877, p. 3.

37. K. S. B. to Longfellow, March 11, 1877, in Longfellow Collection; James H. Watson to Cora Carey, April 5, 1877, in Cora Carey Collection, Mississippi Department of Archives and History, Jackson.

track." Edward and his uncle were also not inclined to let Kate have free rein. Both had objected to her taking *Rousseau's Confessions* from the Mills's library. "They tell me it is not fit for a woman's reading," Kate complained to Longfellow. "Nevertheless I read and am immensely entertained with the naïveté and curious candor of poor Jean Jacques." She had of course enjoyed shocking them, but soon she did begin to long for "a truly sympathetic friend" and to find her one solace in the thought that "perhaps this lesson in *repression* will be good for me."[38]

One thing that Galveston did provide that Kate had lacked in recent months was abundant leisure. The household breakfasted at eight, and Kate then retired to her room where she remained until dinner at four. She had this time for her own work, but she protested to Longfellow that "the 'conditions' are not right." She was not happy, and, as had been the case in her youth, her response to unhappiness was to retreat, to escape her present circumstances by reading and dreaming. So she spent many days with an iced pitcher of lemonade within reach, lost in the world of her books, a world far away from Galveston. She was no longer reading the "trashy novels" of her girlhood. She had brought her volumes of Molière, and Longfellow kept her supplied with books and magazines. Still, she was not doing her own writing. The result of her ennui, as always, was an overpowering sense of guilt—guilt that she was producing nothing and a more general guilt that she was still "uncultivated." "I am in a constant state of wonder at the years I have wasted," she wrote the poet, "and despair of my ignorance." After a time, however, she roused herself to action. She began the study of French with a Parisian living in Galveston, and she began to write.[39]

She had still three projects in mind—the juvenile book, the novel *The Prodigal Daughter*, and several magazine stories. On the juvenile she did nothing. Since her first year in Boston, when Longfellow had encouraged her to write a novel based on her recent experiences, she had always referred to her projected novel by the title that they had together devised. But she was continually changing her conception of the work. At the end of April, she told

38. McDowell to Longfellow, April 17, 1877, in Longfellow Collection.
39. McDowell to Longfellow, April 17, April 30, June 20, 1877, in Longfellow Collection.

him that she had at last written one chapter, but that the novel was now to be set in Virginia and Louisiana before the war. That chapter was as much as she wrote, but she did make progress on the magazine stories. She wrote a Civil War story, "Breaking the News," and a tale set in the seedy quarter on the bluffs at Memphis, "In Aunt Mely's Cabin." She also probably started several other stories. The most important piece of work accomplished in Galveston, however, was a short story that was never to be published. Through the pages of the *Atlantic*, which Longfellow had been sending her, Kate gained continued exposure to the kind of literary realism that William Dean Howells was promulgating. As usual, she ostensibly resisted the influence; and she protested in particular "the wretched and unsatisfactory close of Mr. James's story 'The American.'" The author himself, of course, was later to judge his conclusion unsatisfactory. But James's novel about lovers parted because of differences in their backgrounds may well have proved an influence upon her. Remembering the summer of 1875 in Holly Springs, when North and South met amicably for the first time since the war and when she had had to deal with the suit of the northern radical, Kate wrote a short story about a southern girl who rejects her northern suitor because of incompatibilities in their backgrounds and natures. She was pleased with the work, and she used terms in describing it from the lexicon of realism: "Now as to Emery-bags! I have just finished one. I hope it may prove good enough for the critics to sharpen their needles upon— It is called Like unto Like. It is a character study. There is no incident." [40]

At such times she could lose herself in the pleasures of her work. At other times, however, she felt only an awful sense of frustration at the confinement of her situation. The years spent away from Edward had heightened their incompatibility. Each had married with illusions about both himself and his mate, and the two and a half years they had lived together had shattered most of these. Then, in the more than three years apart, during which they had rarely even corresponded, Kate had seen all the possibilities offered in Boston, in Europe, in the great world. Now more than ever, she could

40. *Ibid.* The manuscript of the short story "Like unto Like" has not survived.

never be satisfied with an idle dreamer, who could not begin to understand her needs and her drive, nor to recognize her great promise. Both were evidently doing little more than going through the motions of this reunion. Her return probably proved a sop to Edward's pride, which like hers was strong; but surely he too was uneasy with the situation. Her more sophisticated view of the world developed in Boston and in Europe may well have proved threatening, and her sardonic wit, likewise, could be discomforting to a man, almost thirty, who refused to face his own failure and instability. Edward was soon involved in another of his schemes to make a fortune, this time through the mining of bat guano in caves along the Texas and Louisiana coasts. He was often away from Galveston, and this new separation probably proved welcome to both. But in Galveston Kate was still very much bound to him, and she was frustrated by the gap between this life she was living and the one she wanted to live. "I want so many things in life!" she broke out to Longfellow in one letter. "Who will help me to them—or can I ever gain them for myself?"[41]

At length, Kate regained her old determination and began laying plans to extricate herself. She first won the family. One means she chose was domestic virtue, and the family's response, particularly to Kate's substituting for the absent cook, was a thing in which she found considerable irony: "Aunt Mary is delighted with my new role. She would not be particularly surprised or elated should I give the world a 'Jane Eyre' or a 'Romola'—but any display of domestic virtues she thinks worthy of all praise. 'O rare Kate,' she said today, 'I begin to believe you are a gifted creature. You can write a book and get a dinner. I had thought you totally unfitted for domestic life, lacking in the homely virtues, but I realize more and more how utterly I was mistaken!'" Of this effusion, Kate wryly noted to Longfellow: "You see even a persistent course of darning socks has its reward." But her patient effort was winning all of them; and by summer she had Edward's support for the idea that she should return to Boston and write her novel. In early July, May French, a friend of Helen Craft from Huntsville, Alabama, arrived for a visit; and gradually it was decided that when Miss

41. Kate McDowell to Ruth McDowell, July 8, 1877, in Stephenson Collection; McDowell to Longfellow, April 17, 1877, in Longfellow Collection.

French left Kate should accompany her to Holly Springs. Kate now had the blessing of all the Galveston family for her return to Boston.[42]

Kate had won a victory. And while she had been gaining the support of Edward and his family, she had also been maintaining her ties in the North. She had kept in touch with various literary people, like Daniel Milliken of *The Cottage Hearth*. She was corresponding with Redpath, and in the spring, before leaving for Texas, she had had Lilian send him a little note, and she had enclosed the child's picture. After her return to Holly Springs in late August, she even played her two staunch supporters, poet and reformer, off against each other—in order to get increased attention. "Some of my friends have wished me to come to New York," she wrote Longfellow. "But of this I can hardly think—not while there is one heart left to care for me in Boston. Is my old place filled in your study? or shall I come again with the morning sun—running through the snow to the warmth within?" Despite this touch of the old coquetry, Kate was giving more serious thought to the future than was her custom. She wanted to have Lilian with her in Boston, and she had won Edward's support here too by suggesting the educational benefit to the child. Perhaps because she was thinking more of herself as a mother, she now began to consider her reputation, about which she had been so cavalier. "In the past perhaps there had been something unusual in my position—something difficult of explanation to a stranger," she admitted to Longfellow. "But as a *mother* living in Boston according to her husband's wish for the education of their child, no gossip could touch me." Kate was developing a new awareness; she was beginning to have some regrets: "I do not know whether I have changed or whether it is the thought of having Lilian with me that influences me in planning my winter. I have lost that slight taste for Bohemianism, that you have gently regretted from time to time; I could even find it in my heart to wish that I had not written the 'Radical Club.'"[43]

42. Kate McDowell to Longfellow, June 20, August 31, 1877, in Longfellow Collection; Kate McDowell to Ruth McDowell, July 8, 1877, in Stephenson Collection; Holly Springs *Reporter*, August 30, 1877, p. 2.
43. Sherwood Bonner to Daniel L. Milliken, May 7, 1877, in Milliken Collection, Perkins Library, Duke University; James Redpath to Lilian McDowell, April 18, 1877, in Ste-

The Bonners, however, were not receptive to the idea of Lilian's living in Boston. They had just lost one family member. Ruth, who had married David McDowell in May, had now gone with her husband to St. Louis, from whence they would move to Illinois, before finally settling on the old Mills place near Trenton, Kentucky. Dr. Bonner was not ready to give up another of his family. Lilian was secure and well cared for at Bonner House, and perhaps he also feared that Kate still lacked a sufficiently strong sense of responsibility. As a sort of compromise, Kate took Lilian to Memphis for a visit, the two staying at the Meriwethers. But Kate had not exhausted her schemes. On the eleventh of October, she wrote Longfellow: "It is an understood thing that [Lilian] is to go back to Holly Springs after a few days visit. I am not sure, however, whether she will not have a glimpse of Boston." She managed to give Lilian just that. On the twenty-fourth, Kate and Lilian, accompanied by Lilly McDowell, arrived at the Capens' home in Dorchester. Longfellow drove out the next day to pay his respects, and the following day he entertained the three Mississippians and Alice Wheeler, now back from Paris, at a luncheon. The headstrong Kate, the wayward daughter, had had her way again.[44]

Once Lilian and Lilly had left for Holly Springs, Kate established herself in rooms on Somerset Street among friends. She must have felt keenly her triumph over circumstance. Though she had been entrapped in Galveston, she had emerged the victor. The return to Boston meant the return of all her bright possibilities. She felt also more settled now than she had for a long time, and the ten months on Somerset Street were the longest period of uninterrupted contentment and satisfaction that the mature woman was ever to know.

On returning to Boston in October of 1877, Sherwood Bonner had published nothing for eight months. But during the Somerset Street period she was to see four stories in print, two in *Lippincott's* and two in *Youth's Companion*. Among them were two stories written in Galveston, as well as the slight tale "Dear Eye-

phenson Collection; Kate McDowell to Longfellow, August 31, 1877, in Longfellow Collection.

44. Memphis *Avalanche*, October 11, 1877, p. 3; McDowell to Longfellow, October 11, 1877, and Longfellow's Journal, October 25–26, 1877, both in Longfellow Collection.

lashes," and an ironic little romance "C. G.; or Lilly's Earrings," set in Galveston and New Orleans with the McDowell girls as characters, but suggested by the mystery of Colton Greene. Her most intense efforts, however, were spent on a novel. She still used the title *The Prodigal Daughter* in speaking of it to Longfellow, but the whole conception of the work had changed once again. The rebellious heroine was a self-portrait, but the setting was neither contemporary Boston nor Virginia and Louisiana before the Civil War, but Holly Springs in the summer of 1875. That "character study" written in Galveston had merged with *The Prodigal Daughter*, and finally Kate changed the title of the novel she was writing to *Like unto Like*.[45]

Longfellow was enthusiastic about the novel, and in early May of 1878, he wrote Harper and Brothers, to whose journals he was a frequent contributor, recommending it. The firm replied immediately that Kate's work would receive their prompt consideration, and within a week she was bound for New York to deliver the manuscript. "The gates are opened and heaven is won!" she wrote to Longfellow on the seventeenth. "*Like unto Like* is accepted. I am so happy—and surprised. How shall I thank you to whom I owe all." Joseph Harper himself had come to see her to deliver the announcement, and later Henry Mills Alden, editor of *Harper's Monthly*, had sent for her, praised the novel warmly, and asked that she write for the magazine "some Southern stories." That day in New York marked the greatest triumph of her life. "It is worth all the suffering I have gone through in having so many cruel and unjust things said of me," she wrote her father. "I believe now that a great future is possible—and I may be a rich woman too by my own exertions, before I die!"[46]

While Kate had been writing her own fiction and working still at Longfellow House on the seemingly interminable volumes of *Poems of Places*, she was also leading an active social life. And during this period when she felt herself on the verge of real literary

45. McDowell to Longfellow, March 9 [1878], in Longfellow Collection; Kate McDowell to Ruth McDowell, 17 [March, 1878], in Stephenson Collection; Longfellow to Millie M. Calkins, February 17, 1878, in Longfellow Collection.
46. Harper & Brothers to Longfellow, May 8, 1878, and McDowell to Longfellow, May 17, 1878, both in Longfellow Collection; McDowell to Dr. Charles Bonner, May 21, 1878, in Stephenson Collection.

success, she gained her greatest social triumph in Boston. The famous Polish actress Helena Modjeska, who was making a tour of the East Coast, had reached Boston in March with a letter of introduction to Longfellow from Mrs. Richard Watson Gilder. The actress charmed the poet and all of Brahmin Boston, who showered her with invitations that she was forced to refuse because of her schedule of ten performances in six days. She was, however, feted at Longfellow House, where she met Kate, and the two immediately became friends. In consequence, the only other entertainment that Madame Modjeska attended was a reception that Kate gave in her honor on the last day of the Boston tour. The preparations on Somerset Street were hurried, and there were disappointments. The people connected with the *Atlantic*—both Howells himself and Harriet Waters Preston, who had been a contributor and a constant reviewer for many years—declined Kate's invitation; and she wished at the last moment that she had asked Longfellow to bring Oliver Wendell Holmes. But many other Boston notables came, and Kate judged the affair "a great success," describing the guests to Ruth as a "distinguished company of poets, artists, and fashionable folks." The dapper Appleton brothers, Nathan and Thomas Gold (Longfellow's brothers-in-law), were there, as were the John Townsend Trowbridges; and James Redpath had come up from New York bringing with him Colonel Robert Ingersoll, the great Illinois orator for whom he was now tour manager, and Mrs. Ingersoll, "elegant in black velvet." The Modjeska reception gave Kate McDowell briefly a social importance that she had never before had in Boston. Though the Brahmin doors shut to her after "The Radical Club" did not now open and though increasingly she was the subject of gossip, the Modjeska reception brought Kate interesting invitations in return—one in midsummer being to an Amherst houseparty, where the other guests included not only her Cambridge mentor, but also Thomas Gold Appleton, at that time the premier Boston wit and bon vivant.[47]

Reading proof of her novel, which Harper's was bringing out in

47. Helena Modjeska, *Memories and Impressions of Helena Modjeska: An Autobiography* (New York: The Macmillan Company, 1910), 358–63, 385; McDowell to Longfellow, March 9 [1878], in Longfellow Collection; Kate McDowell to Ruth McDowell, [March 17, 1878], in Stephenson Collection.

the fall, and enjoying her social life, Kate was spending the happiest summer of her life. In August, however, came disturbing news from the South. New Orleans had been struck by one of the epidemics of yellow fever to which it had been subject for over a century. This one was particularly severe, and gradually refugees from the city brought the disease upriver. Memphis had imposed a quarantine, and by the thirteenth, Grenada, Mississippi, eighty miles south of Holly Springs, reported sixty cases. Noted for its healthful location in the hills, Holly Springs felt itself immune from Yellow Jack. On the same day of the Grenada report, the Holly Springs town fathers, with customary gallantry—and chauvinism—opened the city to all refugees through this announcement to the newspapers:

> There is not even a rumor of yellow fever here. The surgeons report no sickness in the camp of the U.S. troops. The Board of Mayor and Aldermen have ordered the town disinfected, are opposed to quarantine, and expressed the sentiment that the gates of the City of Flowers be opened to refugees from our suffering sister cities. The doctors here do not believe there is any danger of the fever coming here. The town is clean and healthy.

With each day, Kate grew increasingly disturbed, both by reports in the Boston press and by news in letters from home. On the twenty-sixth, she learned that two of the Grenada refugees had died in Holly Springs. Though she had left her child five years before and run away to Boston, though she had later even separated herself from that child by the width of an ocean, when that child was threatened, Kate acted immediately. She began packing. If she could not convince the whole family to leave Holly Springs, at least she could take Lilian away to safety.[48]

Tuesday, the twenty-seventh, as Kate made her final preparations, her Somerset Street quarters were filled with concerned friends. Longfellow came that morning. He was followed by Carrie Jenness and others, including Tom Appleton. Finally, a handsome young Greek, visiting in Boston and obviously taken with Kate, appeared late and insisted on accompanying her to the sta-

48. "Yellow Fever Reports," Memphis *Avalanche*, August 13, 1878, p. 2; McDowell to Longfellow, August 29, 1878, and Longfellow to George Washington Greene, August 30, 1878, both in Longfellow Collection.

tion and putting her on the ten o'clock train. From Cincinnati, where she waited for a train south two days later, she described this final Boston scene to Longfellow with her customary sense of irony. At the last minute, the gentleman had wanted to go in her place. "Imagine," she wrote, "the consternation of my proper and peaceful family at the advent of a big and black-visaged young Greek, demanding that Lilian should be given up to him. But he was very serious, and evidently felt himself a hero." The irony was to vanish when she reached Holly Springs.[49]

The town was hushed and expectant, fearing the worst, yet refusing to believe it. Two days after her arrival, the first Holly Springs citizen, old Colonel Goodrich, for many years the town's mayor, died of a "bilious fever." Still the doctors were unwilling to pronounce the disease Yellow Jack, and Dr. Bonner, despite Kate's pleas, felt that the family should not leave. Face to face with her father, Kate had no will to resist him. By the next day her father and her brother Sam were both ill. Two days later, on Tuesday the third of September, sixty cases were reported; the sick had begun to die; and panic seized the town. This "flight of a people from a plague-stricken place" Kate would always remember: "Trunks were packed hastily with such articles as came nearest to hand; houses were left unlocked, unguarded. In the streets, carriages, buggies, wagons, anything on wheels, hurried along, loaded down with those who, from lack of money or any other reason, could not get away by rail. Dearest friends passed each other with only a hand-grip, or a broken, God bless you! as they parted, fearing never to meet again." The last train to stop in the town left the Holly Springs station on Wednesday morning. The streets leading to the depot were crowded, "every available vehicle was filled with baggage and human beings in one confused rush of frantic fear lest the outgoing train should leave them, and every moment of detention had in it the tick of death." Kate hurried Lilian and Aunt Martha to the train, and then she made her way to the telegraph office where she wired Longfellow: "Help for God's sake. Send money. Father and brother down yellow fever. Alone to nurse."[50]

49. McDowell to Longfellow, August 29, 1878, in Longfellow Collection.
50. I have drawn my account of the yellow fever epidemic from files of the Memphis *Avalanche*; files of the Holly Springs *Reporter*, in the Marshall County Historical Society,

The next day yellow fever was declared epidemic in Holly Springs. All stores and offices were closed. Entire streets had not a single inhabitant. Several of the resident physicians had fallen ill, and those who remained could not attend to all the stricken. The telegraph operator had fled, and the pestilence-stricken town seemed cut off from the world. After all the panic and confusion, there was now an awful silence. "In the streets there was no sound," she recorded, "save, perhaps, the frantic clatter of a horse's hooves, as someone from the country rode in to implore the attendance of a physician, or the rapid rolling of the hearse wheels, as a corpse, followed by no mourner, was bourne to its grave." Dr. Bonner and Sam were both worse, and Kate cared for them alone. At first there had been friends, like Howard Falconer, who would stop for a moment with words of comfort; but now nearly every household was nursing its own; and Howard's father had also fallen victim to the disease. So in the big darkened house at the edge of the town, Kate kept a lonely and constant vigil, broken only by the occasional presence of a physician who had come to observe the progress of his patients and do what little he could. Daily the faces of her father and brother became more wasted and more yellowed, and their agonies more intense. On the evening of Saturday, September seventh, they died within a few hours of each other, both in her arms.[51]

Their bodies, like those of all victims, were hurried into deep graves. Rigid quarantines were now in force over all the stricken South, but the telegraph office had been reopened, and a stunned Kate sent a cable to James Redpath. Somehow, probably through his friends among the military, Redpath arranged for her to break the quarantine, and by Sunday night she was out of Holly Springs and on her way to Cincinnati. Three days later she arrived in Boston. The Capens met her train, and Longfellow immediately went into Boston to see her. "She is in great grief, and almost de-

Holly Springs; Maude Craig Mathews, "Yellow Fever Memories" (MS in Craft Collection, Holly Springs); Helen Craft Anderson, "A Chapter in the Yellow Fever Epidemic of 1878," *Publications of the Mississippi Historical Society*, X (1909), 223–36; and Sherwood Bonner, "The Yellow Plague of '78: A Record of Horror and Heroism," *Youth's Companion*, LII (April 3, 1879), 117–19. Bonner, "The Yellow Plague," 117, 118; McDowell to Longfellow, September 4, 1878.

51. Bonner, "The Yellow Plague," 117; Stephenson, "Sherwood Bonner," 16.

spair," he wrote that night in his journal. While trying to comfort her, he had been struck by Keats's lines:

> There was a listening fear in her regard,
> As if calamity had but begun;
> As if the vanward clouds of evil days
> Had spent their malice, and the sullen rear
> Was with its storèd thunder laboring up.

For Kate, indeed, calamity had but begun. The fever cut across her life and marked the end of a prolonged youth.[52]

---

52. Stephenson, "Sherwood Bonner," 17; Nahum Capen to Longfellow, September 10, 1878, in Longfellow Collection; Longfellow's Journal, September 11, 1878.

Chapter Five

The Early Stories and *Like unto Like*

FROM THE BEGINNING of their acquaintance, Longfellow had taken pleasure in introducing Kate McDowell to his friends as one destined to make a name in literature. The eleven magazine stories published by Sherwood Bonner before the appearance of her novel had indeed established her in the second or third rank of those writers satisfying the American reading public's appetite for periodical fiction, but she had failed to produce anything of permanent interest. She had spent much of her time enjoying the great world and making the most of her social opportunities. Never a disciplined person, she still had difficulty meeting deadlines. As a result, though nearly all of the stories display some of her special lightness and charm, most of them seem improvised and hurried.[1]

For the most part, in these early stories she left that ground she had seemed to stake out for herself in her first published story, "Gran'mammy's Last Gift," that well executed and delicately controlled piece, a sort of genre painting. Instead, she turned out more little romances, often sentimental and melodramatic, though never as extreme as "Miss Willard's Two Rings." The worst of these pot boilers was "Which Was the Heroine?" a romance of the Revolutionary War that filled the first three issues of *Cottage Hearth* in the centennial year. Two sisters spend much of the story disguised as soldiers, and, after various convolutions of plot, the tale actually becomes pro-British—the "heroine" saving the life of a redcoat, marrying him, and going to live in England. The two stories that Sherwood Bonner drew from her experiences in France are

1. "Sherwood Bonner," *Harper's Weekly*, August 11, 1883, p. 503; B. M. Drake, "Sherwood Bonner," *Southern Writers: Biographical and Critical Studies*, ed. William Malone Baskerville (Nashville and Dallas: Publishing House of the M. E. Church, South, 1903), I, 103.

more tightly constructed than the Revolutionary tale, but still maudlin and melodramatic. "Rosine's Story" is a rather dainty tale, although it is concerned with the shooting of Francois, a communist, by French soldiers as he is sharing food with a little French maid. "Léonie" tells the story of the accidental death of a bright-eyed little girl on her way home from making her first communion. Rounding out this group of tales is "Dear Eyelashes," a story set in an island town in the Gulf (probably Galveston), in which a handsome Creole child, in despair over the circumstances of his penniless widowed mother, responds literally to the casual remark of a wealthy matron that she would give a hundred dollars to have his long eyelashes.[2]

Even when Sherwood Bonner returned to the Bonner House setting of her first Gran'mammy tale in two subsequent stories, "Gran'mammy's Story" and "Breaking the News," she produced cluttered and contrived works. The story that the old nurse tells of the dramatic meteoric shower of 1833 is awkwardly framed by the account of Kate and her friends watching for another meteoric display thirty years later. And Gran'mammy's vivid narrative of the effect of the phenomenon in the quarters of the Wilson plantation comes to a melodramatic conclusion as she tells of saving the baby Mary Wilson from falling into an open cistern. The plot of "Breaking the News," which is set at Bonner House during the Civil War, strains belief—as, in the space of a few hours, Aunt Sarah Edmandson learns, first, that her son has been killed in battle and, then, that he is alive and waiting for her in the downstairs sitting room.[3]

Despite the decline in quality of the Gran'mammy tales after "Gran'mammy's Last Gift," they had a clear effect on the literary market; and subsequently the pages of *Youth's Companion* and other magazines were often filled with other writers' stories of southern mammies. More often than influencing the reading public's taste, however, Sherwood Bonner was being guided by it. Di-

2. "Which Was the Heroine?" *Cottage Hearth*, III (January, 1876), 24–25; (February, 1876), 52–53; (March, 1876), 80–81; "Rosine's Story," *Youth's Companion*, XLIX (December 14, 1876), 421–22; "Léonie," *Youth's Companion*, L (February 8, 1877), 42–43; "Dear Eyelashes," *Youth's Companion*, LI (March 7, 1878), 74–75.

3. "Gran'mammy's Story," *Youth's Companion*, XLIX (January 6, 1876), 1–2; "Breaking the News," *Youth's Companion*, L (December 27, 1877), 441–42.

alect was a basic component of the local color movement, and as the movement steadily gained in popularity, dialect stories were increasingly marketable. Though in her very earliest stories she had limited herself to presenting only one dialect, that of the southern Negro, she soon expanded her range. In "C. G.; or, Lilly's Earrings," probably influenced by the popularity of George Washington Cable's stories, she included a rendering of the speech of the Louisiana Creole—though the attempt is remarkably crude, the accent being conveyed too often merely by changing all *t* and *th* sounds to *z*: "I went wiz one of ze good Sisters of our Church into ze city hospital. And zere I found my brozer, his head shaved, raving wiz fever! He had been fighting, zey told me, wiz one of ze guerrilla-bands around ze city; had been captured and brought zere wounded dangerously." "In Aunt Mely's Cabin" contains still another dialect, that of the poor white of the Deep South. Here Sherwood Bonner is more successful: "I lifted my rifle, thankin' God there wuz a load in it, an' shot. I'd as lief ha' hit 'em both; but on'y Tom Jack dropped, and Little Betty stood screamin' over him an' wringin' her han's. I flung down my rifle an' run to the woods. I wuz thar all that night an' yesterday, walkin', walkin', till another night come; an' I swum the river befo' sun-up this mornin'." Though Sherwood Bonner was never scrupulously accurate phonetically, nor even always consistent, in this instance and others she captures well the spirit of the dialect.[4]

The best of her early stories—after "Gran'mammy's Last Gift"—are "C. G.; or, Lilly's Earrings" and "In Aunt Mely's Cabin." Both reflect expanding vision and developing technical skill. The former tale is the story of Stella Tresvant, the narrator, and her romantic sister Lilly, orphans being reared by an uncle and aunt in Galveston. It chronicles their long-dreamed-of trip to New Orleans' Mardi Gras, where they fall victim to crafty Creoles, who play upon the girls' sense of romance to trick them out of a set of diamond earrings. Sherwood Bonner filled this tale with local color—sketches of Galveston and New Orleans, another of her wise mammies, Creole lore. But through the gentle irony of the narration, she avoids an overly picturesque effect and brings a sense of

4. "C. G.; Or, Lilly's Earrings," *Lippincott's*, XXII (September, 1878), 362–73; "In Aunt Mely's Cabin," *Lippincott's*, XXI (February, 1878), 245–50.

unity to a story containing a wide variety of elements. The opening lines, proclaiming that this is to be no typical southern story suffused in antebellum memory, reveal some of Sherwood Bonner's particular charm:

> Not since the day on which we heard of Lee's surrender had there been such a commotion in the house. We who had grown up since that date had ceased to expect anything in the way of pleasure, for "the war" was a ghost that wouldn't be laid. Did we want fine dresses, we were asked where the money was coming from, now that Uncle David had lost all his property by the war; did we vainly long for a trip to a Northern city, we were consoled by the announcement that, if it had not been for the war, Uncle David would have taken us to Europe; if we complained that we had to keep our own rooms in order and sweep the parlors besides, a dignified reference was made to the former number of servants in the establishment; and when we roundly declared that life wasn't worth living without a dessert for dinner every day, somebody would say that it could hardly be expected we should set such a table as we did before the war. Positively, we didn't know how old we were, for Aunt Nanny declared that her memory wasn't a yard long, on account of the trouble she had had during the war, and the family Bible had been "confiscated" by a pious private of taking propensities.

This same light touch is sustained throughout the story, a gently antiromantic tone restraining and harmonizing disparate, patently romantic elements.[5]

"In Aunt Mely's Cabin" represents a new direction for Sherwood Bonner in both setting and character. Like most local colorists, she had concentrated her attentions on the picturesque, but in this story, set in a southern city on the bluffs of the Mississippi, her opening description of moonlight on the river serves only as contrast to the dirty, seedy daylight scene:

> The sun rose gloomily, and in its light the place that had been almost poetic the night before showed all its squalid ugliness. The street near the river, once a fine and fashionable promenade, now seemed built of the very skeletons of houses, so busily had decay been at work, and so

---

5. Unfortunately the version of the first Gran'mammy tale that is now in print is "Gran'mammy's Last Gifts," the revised and artistically diminished version that Sherwood Bonner included in *Suwanee River Tales*. "Gran'mammy's Last Gift" (without the *s*) can be read only in its original printing— *Youth's Companion*, XLVIII (July 29, 1875), 237–38.

little had been done to stop its advance. The very flowers had lost their purity, and hung heavily with little particles of cotton that had blown upon them from the wagons continually passing, and blackened in the coal-dust. . . . With the sun awoke noisy life. The cotton drays raced along Front Row, their black drivers standing in them, hatless, shoeless, and ragged, urging on their mules with discordant cries. The bleating of goats was heard from the darkey settlement on the side of the cliff as queer old aunties and uncles hobbled out to milk them. Down on the flat the whir of machinery began; grimy men flung oaths or rough jests at each other; flatboats appeared on the river; and the air grew dense with smoke from the mills.

The exact location of the city is unspecified but the model is clearly Memphis with its busy Front Row. Let us place Sherwood Bonner's description of the scene alongside one written fifty years later by another writer from northern Mississippi, William Faulkner, in *Sanctuary*:

They reached Memphis in midafternoon. At the foot of the bluff below Main Street Popeye turned into a narrow street of smoke-grimed frame houses with tiers of wooden galleries, set a little back in grassless plots, with now and then a forlorn and hardy tree of some shabby species—gaunt, lopbranched magnolias, a stunted elm or a locust in grayish, cadaverous bloom—interspersed by rear ends of garages; a scrap-heap in a vacant lot. . . . From the bluff, beyond a line of office buildings terraced sharply against the sunfilled sky, came a sound of traffic—motor horns, trolleys—passing high overhead on the river breeze; at the end of the street a trolley materialized in the narrow gap with an effect as of magic and vanished with a stupendous clatter. On a second storey gallery a young Negro woman . . . smoked a cigarette sullenly, her arms on the balustrade.

Despite the changes that fifty years had brought, both in history (the replacement of mules by motor vehicles) and in literary style (the influence in the Faulkner passage of the Imagist poets), the two artists produced strikingly similar descriptions. Their pictures share the same composition—the decay, the smoke, the noise, the blighted look of nature, and the presence always of the Negro. And the juxtaposition of the two passages reveals Sherwood Bonner as a precursor of "Southern realism."[6]

6. William Faulkner, *Sanctuary* (New York: Random House, Inc., 1931), 137–38.

Though set in the seedy black quarter of Memphis, "In Aunt Mely's Cabin" is concerned primarily with a social stratum that the author had previously ignored in her fiction. Fascinated by Walter Scott's depiction of simple Scottish folk, she had long studied the plainer folk of her region, though her early interest had been markedly condescending. "Went on a poor circuit last week & enjoyed it amazingly," she had noted in her diary at twenty. "The poor wretches do show human nature so deliciously." Her disdain was still apparent seven years later when she wrote "From '60 to '65," where she first treated "that class of the population called by the negroes 'po' white trash'": "They owned no slaves, and lived in log houses through whose chinks sun and rain entered freely; the men supplied the larder by hunting and fishing; the women dipped snuff, moulded tallow candles, and 'raised' tow-headed children who rejoiced in princely and historic names." The poor white protagonist of "In Aunt Mely's Cabin" (published just two years later) is presented, however, without condescension. Phil Vickers is a man, not merely a member of a subspecies; and the skill with which Sherwood Bonner conveys his character keeps the story from descending into pure melodrama. Returning home from hunting one night, Vickers sees through a window his wife and his friend Tom Jack in an embrace. He shoots Tom and then swims the river to seek asylum in a friendly old Negro's hovel on the bluff. His pursuers find him in the cabin, and he learns that he fired not at Tom, but at Tom's sister Nancy, who was dressed in a Mardi Gras costume of Tom's clothing and clowning with Betty Vickers. At this moment, Betty appears to announce that Nancy is out of danger. The pursuers, whose code permits such punishment for adultery, now understand Phil's firing the shot; and husband and wife are tenderly united. In the midst of such turns of plot, Phil Vickers' guilt and confusion strike a strong, true note amid the melodrama and the sentimentality. Here, as in some of the other stories, Sherwood Bonner's strengths shine through, in spite of her old habits, her reliance on conventional effects.[7]

The occasional glimpses of literary skill offered by these early

7. Kate Bonner Diary (MS in collection of David McDowell III, of Batesville, Mississippi), May 30, August 8, 1869.

stories do not adequately foreshadow, however, Sherwood Bonner's work that deserves much more serious attention, her novel *Like unto Like*. Still, there is some adumbration in the stories of both the novel's setting and one of its themes. Sherwood Bonner had begun exploring the literary uses of Holly Springs in her first two stories, "Gran'mammy's Last Gift" and "Miss Willard's Two Rings"; and she had continued to mine local material, in a limited way, in the subsequent Gran'mammy tales. But it was not until the autobiographical sketch "From '60 to '65," published in October of 1876, that she attempted a broad treatment of the town, its history, its various social strata, its pursuits and pleasures and prejudices. Significantly, in virtually every piece where she used the Holly Springs setting, she also tried to assuage the still bitter feelings between North and South. Of course she was a southerner writing for a primarily northern market, and her stance was only politic. But she had also grown up in a household that had tried to heal the wounds of war; it was her father who invited the Yankee colonel to church at the close of the war and who had later become the intimate of his lodger General Ord. And in her Boston life she had been an agent of reconciliation herself. All of these influences no doubt led her, in writing of the war, to cite instances of heroism and nobility on both sides. She had already, then, brought setting and theme together before she saw their full possibilities. In the fall of 1877, however, drawing upon her view two years earlier of the barriers finally crumbling between the Holly Springs citizenry and the army of occupation, she began work on a novel. Presenting her whole native milieu and using her own wider experiences of the meetings of North and South, she produced in *Like unto Like* one of the early examples of what was to become a popular literary type in the eighties and nineties—the novel of sectional reconciliation.[8]

Her subject allowed Sherwood Bonner full range for the display of her skill as a local colorist. The three settings of the novel—a country town in the Deep South, a cotton plantation, and the city

8. A particularly solid discussion of the type and many of its individual examples is given in Paul H. Buck's *The Road to Reunion, 1865–1900* (Boston: Little, Brown and Company, 1937), chapters 8 and 9. Marcia Jacobson also offers valuable insights in "Popular Fiction and Henry James's Unpopular *Bostonians*," *Journal of Modern Philology*, LXX (February, 1976), 264–75.

of New Orleans—are all rendered with a sure touch. But it is the picture of the town, Yariba, that is her most interesting achievement. Yariba is a composite of Holly Springs and Huntsville, Alabama. The latter place, two decades older than Holly Springs and bearing a similarly aristocratic stamp, the author uses primarily for its picturesque setting in the Appalachian foothills. No doubt hesitant to reveal to Boston readers the relative youth of either southern town, however, the author suggests (as she had in "From '60 to '65") a long history for her fictional place. Yariba, which is said to be in Alabama, seems to move westward in the course of the novel; and despite the mountain setting and the mythologizing suggestion of greater age, the vivid picture that Sherwood Bonner renders is, in the main, one of her native town.[9]

Yariba, that sunny place where "all talk to each other as if they were members of one family" and which most citizens consider the finest spot on "God's green earth," Sherwood Bonner presents with warmth and not a little irony:

> As to the people of Yariba, they were worthy of their town: could higher praise be given them? They lived up pretty well to the obligations imposed by the possession of shadowy ancestral portraits that hung on their walls along with wide-branched genealogical trees done in India-ink. . . . They had . . . the simplicity of manner that comes of an assured social position. They were handsome, healthy, full of physical force, as all people must be who ride horseback . . . and do not lie awake at night to wonder why they were born. Their self-consciousness never took the form of self-questioning; it was rather a species of generous pride—for pride blossoms in as many varieties as if it were a seedling bed. That they were Southerners was, of course, their first cause of congratulation. After a Northern tour they were glad to come home and tell how they had been recognized as Southerners everywhere—in the cars, shops, and theatres. They felt their Southern air and accent a grace and a distinction, separating them from a people who walked fast, talked through their noses, and built railroads.[10]

To bring to life this charming, chauvinistic little place, the author draws a gallery of well-executed portraits—the drawling, gra-

9. Helen Craft's annotations of *Like unto Like* (in the possession of Mrs. Fort Daniel, Holly Springs) reveal just how Sherwood Bonner drew on both Holly Springs and Huntsville to create Yariba. The use of the Alabama town was also acknowledged by an enthusiastic reviewer in the Huntsville *Democrat*, December 4, 1878, p. 2.

10. Sherwood Bonner, *Like unto Like* (New York: Harper & Brothers, 1878), 16–17.

cious, shabby-genteel Tollivers, who have as summer tenants the Yankee commander and his wife; the town arbiter Mrs. Oglethorpe, who takes the Yankees up and forces the citizenry to follow suit; the Episcopal rector Mr. Shepherd, possessed of "a very fine manner, and a great deal of it"; that "Oracle of the Square" Squire Barton, perhaps the greatest Yariba chauvinist; the old grandmother Mrs. Herndon, who cannot forgive God for letting the South lose the war; and those from other stations, the Negro servants and the poor white Mrs. Roy.

There is some caricature, but most of the portraits are subtly shaded, and many display Sherwood Bonner's gift for comedy of manners. Take the narrator's introduction of Captain Silsby of the Thirteenth: "Captain Silsby produced a more dazzling effect, with his blue coat and gold lace, his brown eyes, Greek nose, and little curled mustache. One felt instinctively that his had been a victorious career on the gentle fields where croquet-balls clash, and that he had been a hero in the ballroom strife." Or the description of the sectarian reaction to the call of Mrs. Oglethorpe, an Episcopalian, on the town's military guests: "After the first shock the ladies of her own church upheld her nobly; but the Baptist congregation 'wondered at it' for a week, and the Methodist sisters said it all came of being an Episcopalian and having no real feeling about anything; although the undertaker's wife, a notable woman at prayer-meeting, remarked that she should call herself, as it was only right that 'our set' should pay some attention to strangers. And at last all Yariba reduced its dignity to the size of a pocket-compass and decided to follow in the forgiving steps of its leader."

There are comic touches too in Sherwood Bonner's treatment of the sectional reconciliation motif. When it is first suggested to the Yariba coquette Betty Page that she receive some of the officers, she brands such hospitality traitorous to her country—"the beautiful, persecuted South." Later she not only enjoys the attentions of the apolitical Captain Silsby, but she also goes riding with the hated Reconstruction figure General Van de Meire, losing all patriotic fervor in her whirl of pleasure. Sherwood Bonner, however, grants the theme more serious treatment by presenting a spectrum of sectional feeling. Old Mrs. Herndon, with her coldly flashing diamond and her coldly flashing eyes, is at one extreme. In a haunting sleepwalking scene, she desecrates the graves of a group of Union soldiers—a measure of the bitterness she still feels a decade after the death of her Confederate son. The radical journalist Roger Ellis, at the other extreme, still regards the South as permeated by an Egyptian darkness. The attitudes of the other characters represent gradations between the two; and at the Decoration Day service, though southern feeling is still reflected by Father Ryan's "Furl that Banner" and northern by the "Battle Hymn of the Republic," most realize that theirs is a common heritage of grief. Later, the southern *beau ideal*, Van Tolliver, a moderate Democrat, and Colonel Dexter of the Third, a moderate Republican—though each feels a strong sectional allegiance—are able to speak dispassionately of the mistakes of both parties. Overall, the author treats the cultural effects of the Civil War with refreshing frankness and real insight. Contemporary reviewers found the spirit of reconciliation so pervasive in the novel that virtually all praised Sherwood Bonner's remarkably balanced treatment of both sides—the critic in the Providence *Journal* calling *Like unto Like* "an olive branch in the best and truest sense" and the Boston *Courier* suggesting that "it will probably stand in the future as the best representative of this episode in the national life."[11]

Whatever its political and cultural value to a still divided nation, *Like unto Like*, like the hordes of novels and tales that it prefigured, found its primary appeal in the fact that it was a romance. Though the theme expressed in this genre was sectional reconciliation, a binding of the wounds of the Civil War, the major interest always lay in the means by which the theme was rendered— romance and marriage between appealing representatives of North and South. Over a decade later, Thomas Nelson Page was to express baldly the formula for the type. "Get a pretty girl," he advised Grace King. "Make her fall in love with a Federal officer and your story will be printed at once." The opening pages of *Like unto Like* carefully build expectations for such a formula tale of sectional romance. The news that the Tollivers have taken mem-

---

11. Both the review from the Providence *Journal* (October 13, 1878) and the Boston *Courier* (October 20, 1878) are pasted in Sherwood Bonner's own copy of the novel (hereinafter cited as Bonner Copy), in the Sherwood Bonner Collection, Marshall County Library, Holly Springs.

bers of the army of occupation as lodgers is announced first to not one but three pretty Yariba girls, standing on a rustic bridge and ready for fate to enter in the form of the proper husband. Through the novel Sherwood Bonner continues both to play upon and often to fulfill the romantic expectations of nineteenth-century readers. A group of lovers go on a moonlight picnic, and the northern journalist recites one of Sappho's odes and later writes a long love letter so florid that one reviewer commented, "After this, we know that there are few of the gentler sex who will not be anxious to read more." The narrative voice also does its part in heightening the aura of romance. Witness this narrative commentary and speculation on the heroine: "Life, love, passion, have been to her like close-shut buds of roses of whose sweetness she has dreamed. Has the sun dawned in this fair summer's sky that is to warm them into bloom?" [12]

But even as Sherwood Bonner begins her novel, even as she plays upon all the expectations common to a popular period type, she also shows her divergence from the pattern. Of the three pretty girls on the bridge, two fall into conventional molds. One is vain, selfish, shallow, a coquette; the other is gentle, practical, ladylike, a future devoted wife. The third, however, is the sort of girl not usually found in a southern romance. Blythe Herndon is the village intellectual, ironic, outspoken, and rebellious. Blythe's northern lover, too, is quite outside the usual mold. No dashing Federal officer, Roger Ellis is instead a radical journalist, in the words of the southern coquette, "the blackest of black Republicans . . . forty-five years old and *bald*." Naturally this central pair of lovers would run counter to type since the characters were based on the author herself and James Redpath, both of whom were unusual people. But Sherwood Bonner attempted more than a simple *roman à clef* in *Like unto Like*. Instead she reshaped her material to make her own statement. [13]

Blythe Herndon is a close portrait of her creator, but not of the confident literary lady Sherwood Bonner. The character is in-

12. Edmund Wilson, *Patriotic Gore* (New York: Oxford University Press, 1962), 606; unidentified review in the Bonner Copy.

13. The Craft Annotations show that Sherwood Bonner not only based her central pair of lovers on herself and James Redpath, but that she also modeled other characters on Holly Springs people. The most notable instances are the Tollivers (Colonel and Mrs. Dixon Com-

stead a composite of Kate Bonner, the rebellious and confused girl whose romantic dreams led her to marry Edward McDowell, and of the Kate McDowell who had fled to Boston as a seeker. As the first scene ends, Blythe longs to discover "the meaning and use of my life"—echoing the phrasing of Kate McDowell's first letter to Longfellow. And like Kate Bonner at twenty, Blythe dreams of "a prince on a flying horse" to take her away from Yariba to a "great, satisfying, splendid world" beyond. With a clear view of the person she herself had been, the author reveals Blythe Herndon in all her charm, but also her arrogance and delusion. Roger Ellis is a closer rendering of the James Redpath who visited Holly Springs in the summer of 1875. Sherwood Bonner gives to Ellis her friend's history, his political and social opinions, and his ardent nature. Ellis' happiest days have been spent as an impassioned abolitionist, and he still finds meaning only in fanatical devotion to a cause. But in Ellis too the author makes changes. In appearance, the ugly, tall, balding Ellis is quite different from the small, wiry, not unattractive Redpath. Possibly influenced by the Dorothea-Casaubon attachment in *Middlemarch* (a novel alluded to in *Like unto Like*), Sherwood Bonner also expanded the age difference between her lovers: sixteen years separated the author and Redpath; twenty-five lie between the heroine and Ellis. Both changes heighten the effect of Blythe's attraction to this figure of authority from the great world outside Yariba.

As the novel unfolds, the attraction between this unlikely pair increases. Ellis fulfills Blythe's dreams of a grand passion, for he writes and speaks as ardently as any girl dreaming of love could wish. He is intellectual, literary, worldly; and his radicalism seems to satisfy Blythe's need for growth and rebellion. When he tells her of his work for the abolitionist cause before the war, she replies that she too would have been an abolitionist. She applauds his enlightened view of women, she accommodates herself to his lack of religious orthodoxy, and she accepts his hero-worship of John Brown. With romance in the air—as the coquette Betty Page casts aside her Confederate sympathies and accedes to the handsome,

fort Topp), Mrs. Oglethorpe (Mrs. Kate Walthall Freeman), Mr. Shepherd (the Reverend Dr. James Thomas Pickett), Squire Barton (Colonel A. W. Goodrich), and Betty Page (Lilly McDowell). Mrs. Roy too was drawn from a Holly Springs woman whom Craft does not identify.

shallow Federal officer Captain Silsby, and as the gentle, devoted Mary Barton wins the love of the young planter Van Tolliver— Blythe accepts the proposal of Roger Ellis.

She does so in the face of opposition from many of her friends and family, especially her embittered grandmother. When late in the novel Blythe breaks the engagement, all are relieved, and old Mrs. Herndon even offers the girl her diamond. Clearly the political and cultural incompatibilities that Yariba has seen in the match from the beginning do provide one of the reasons for Blythe's final decision. Ellis is a kind, decent man, but he is such a visionary that he cannot understand the social realities of the Reconstruction South. In his impassioned idealism, he also misjudges character, feeling disdain for some of Blythe's friends because they are Democrats and respect for baser sorts who happen to be Republicans. In the end Blythe is left with more confidence in his sincerity than in his judgment. The breaking of the engagement, however, cannot be taken as a statement that sectional differences are irreconcilable. Ellis, after all, represents an extreme of northern opinion; and Sherwood Bonner carefully throws the weight of the novel in support of the moderates of both sections.

The political and cultural implications of the failure of the romance, moreover, are almost overshadowed by the suggestions of another theme. Blythe's decision is based not so much on political and cultural incompatibilities as on her realization that the union would be destructive to her as a person, and it is Sherwood Bonner's handling of this theme that makes the novel most interesting. Drawing upon the central dilemma of her own life—the conflict between marriage and self-definition—she produced an ostensibly romantic novel built on a groundwork of feminist feeling. Commenting on the tendency of Yariba girls to postpone matrimony as long as possible, the narrative voice notes that they "gather roses while they may; for once married, their day is over, and they reverse nature's order by becoming caterpillars after they have been butterflies." Mrs. Oglethorpe, Yariba's social arbiter, is described as "a—very—resigned widow," far better off without her husband, "a pleasant man, with a fine talent for spending money." Balancing the narrator's playful irony is more serious commentary on man's "rapturous certainty of possession," an emotion "that no

woman ever quite comprehends." That sense of possession is doc-
umented by the story of the mad planter Roy Herrick, who years
earlier had married Blythe's older sister and built a wall around his
grounds "as a sign of his jealous love." Later Herrick had killed
both his wife and himself. Here we can see with particular clarity
Sherwood Bonner's shaping of material to meet the demands of
her theme. The story, which is presented with an air of romance
and mystery, she took from the most shocking incident in her
county's antebellum past, the inexplicable murder of her own aunt
Sarah Wilson Coxe by her husband, the handsome, dashing Toby
Coxe. But the author gives her own cast to events by presenting
the planter as jealous and possessive and by having him build the
symbolic wall.[14]

While the narrative voice is undercutting as much romantic sentiment as it creates, Blythe is presented from the beginning with
the qualities that will make her fall both in and out of love with
Ellis. Her boredom with Yariba leads to the romantic dream of
finding herself through an ideal lover, one who will shape her intellect and soul and carry her off to a splendid world. But she also
holds incipient feminist sentiments. Her father, the narrator tells
us, does not care that to his wife "an English classic was as foreign
. . . as a Greek one," and he believes that "a true woman can be no
more independent than the vine that clings to [a] rock"; whereas
her mother has "a way of dating things from certain notable
events in the lives of her children" and cannot understand why a
woman would want to be independent. Responding to their views
and their example, Blythe feelingly quotes Margaret Fuller: "To
give her hand with dignity, woman must be able to stand alone."
Her arrogance and her rebellion against Yariba's provincial southern values, however, blind her to the conflict between her belief in
woman's necessary independence and her dream of the ideal lover.

Blythe's sense of rebellion and romance combine in her attraction to Roger Ellis. Sherwood Bonner underscores Blythe's romanticism by showing her engrossed in *Clarissa*, with its suggestions
of a grand passion, when she first encounters the northern journal-

14. The "Coxe-Wilson tragedy" is still whispered about by the oldest generation living
in Holly Springs today. The Craft Annotations carefully note whenever Bonner's treatment
of it diverges from fact.

ist. But even as she falls in love, Blythe returns fitfully to her feminism. She comments to Roger Ellis at a crucial point in the novel, "Fancy having written against one's name in the book of fate only this:—born—married—died." He replies, "It is enough if you had said, was born—loved—died." But Blythe cannot agree: "Love," she responds, "could never fill my life." Immediately afterward, Ellis recites a love lyric and gives Blythe her first kiss. Her moment of self-awareness is lost in a flood of high romance, and she accepts his proposal of marriage. Later, however, the haze of romance clears, and she has disquieting thoughts. She realizes that in his complete radicalism Ellis is not "ideal," and she worries about the effect of the relationship on her own sense of identity. At the beginning she had seen him as "a very improving friend," but increasingly she finds such a "mania" in him for expressing his opinions on all subjects that she feels she is being "pelted with hailstones." Having comprehended the intensity of his devotion to causes, she begins to fear her potential fate in the marriage. Early in the novel she fails to note a particularly telling clue to the relative value of politics and love, of causes and woman, for Roger Ellis. After romantically requesting the rose from her hair, he tears it to pieces and throws the petals on the floor in his excitement over a discussion of labor reform. Later, she does perceive that, in spite of his talk about female freedom, his actions show that to him she is *only* a woman. For Roger Ellis, reality lies "among men that are doing the world's work."

As a result of such insight, Blythe eventually breaks her engagement, but this step toward selfhood is a frightening one. Earlier, as she had realized more and more her incompatibility with him, she compared Ellis to chloroform, something to ease the pain. Now, however, she has rejected the drug of romance, and she must herself decide upon her identity, the meaning and use of her life. Her state of mind, she writes in her journal, is benumbed and indifferent. Yet she has taken vital steps toward realizing her own identity. First, she has learned that she has been deluded about herself in many ways: "She had been called romantic, but the most romantic expression of love had failed to satisfy her; she had thought herself liberal minded, but her lover seemed to her a fanatic, and she was not liberal enough to be indifferent to it; she

Henry W. Longfellow in the mid-1870s
Courtesy National Park Service, Longfellow National
Historic Site

The study at Longfellow House (circa 1870), where Kate McDowell first
entered the great world
Courtesy National Park Service, Longfellow National Historic Site

Sketch of James Redpath made in 1877, in his forty-fourth year
Cottage Hearth

Kate McDowell by Sarony of New York in 1878, at the end of a prolonged youth
Courtesy National Park Service, Longfellow National Historic Site

Childe Hassam's *Boston Common at Twilight*, 1885–1886, shows the Common as Kate McDowell would have known it during the bitter winter of 1879–1880. The Hotel Boylston, where she, Aunt Martha, and Lilian had their apartment, is the large building in the background seen through the trees.
Courtesy Museum of Fine Arts, Boston

The mysterious Colton Greene, painted in
his Confederate uniform
Courtesy Memphis Room, Memphis/Shelby County Library

Lilian McDowell about the time of her
mother's death in 1883
Courtesy Bessie Craft Driver

Lilian McDowell at the age of sixteen
Courtesy Bessie Craft Driver

had been impatient of the commonplace, yet she was so commonplace as to desire a smooth and comfortable life."

Her rejection of Ellis, however, is not a complete conservative retreat into her native tradition. To see that Blythe has not compromised her stand there, one has only to think of Van Tolliver's description of "the ideal wife of any Southern gentleman":

> A woman not so beautiful that all her soul is sucked into her face, but not ugly, you understand—fair, fresh, and tranquil, with tender eyes, and lips sweet to kiss. She must be even of temper; not so gay as to pine in the quiet of a country home, nor yet so simple as to chronicle the small-beer of her country life when she goes to town. Well read, but not learned—without ambition—well bred—a lady to her finger-tips—unselfish, without knowing that she is so—of a sweet reticence of soul—with no small coquetries—loving her home, her husband, and the little heads that nestle in her bosom.

Unlike her friend Mary Barton and unlike her own mother, Blythe is still not ready to assume that imposed role. Blythe is still the village intellectual; she is still "literary," an "unfortunate adjective in Yariba, [which] set one rather apart from one's fellows, like an affliction in the family." She is still independent; she has simply said no to the idea of either a southern or a northern master. Yet within the negatives, she has learned something positive as well. There are southern values that remain, however dimly, an important part of her being: "She had openly declared her scorn of 'the narrow and prosaic teachings' of her early life, but their influence held her as tenaciously as the earth holds the roots of a flower, while its blossoms may be blown to the winds." Thus Blythe's rejection of "the most romantic expression of love" involves both negative and positive definitions of self.

Though Blythe Herndon has not reached an everlasting yea, she has passed through the requisite stages leading to it; and there Sherwood Bonner leaves her, confused and waiting—an unusual state in which to leave a romantic heroine in the nineteenth-century American novel. Even to the end, however, with her rhetoric Sherwood Bonner plays upon the romantic expectations already undercut in the novel—providing an overblown coda in whose cadences surely the most romantic of readers could find some satisfaction:

Young and beautiful and sadhearted, she sits by her window, and watches ghosts go by, and tells herself that her romance is ended before her life is well begun. Other women than Blythe have made their sad little moans, and have lived to smile at them. But of one thing be sure: never again will she know the fresh, ethereal madness that, like the Holy Ghost to the kneeling Virgin, comes but once to the human heart, and is called first love. Wider, deeper, richer joys may wait for her in the coming years, like undiscovered stars that earthly eyes have not yet seen; but I who write, alike with you who read, can only guess at what the future holds—for the story of her life is not yet told.

One must almost make his way through this purple passage a second time to realize that buried beneath the verbiage is a most anti-romantic statement: that Blythe has simply received a necessary part of a liberal education, that now with fewer illusions perhaps she can find the meaning and use of her life. Because of the romantic aura cast even at its conclusion, however, most readers to this day have not seen the novel for what it most fundamentally is. For *Like unto Like* is not merely a local color novel and a sectional romance; it is the study of a woman's wavering, confused, but uncompromising attempt to find herself.

Like many a first novel, Sherwood Bonner's contains too many threads. Ideas for several works seem to be emerging in *Like unto Like*, and the author does not always have her material under firm control. Still, *Like unto Like* is a remarkable piece of work. The mass of reviewers concurred. The distinguished critic S. G. W. Benjamin, writing in *Literary World*, found the novel extraordinarily original, "its merits and faults entirely its own." *Publisher's Weekly* judged it the best of the Harper's series, and to all the reviewers *Like unto Like* provided evidence of abundant promise. "The book shows so much talent," noted the *American Bookseller*, "that we should like to know who Sherwood Bonner is." At last Longfellow's protégé had produced a work that gave strong support to the poet's long insistence on the bright literary future of Sherwood Bonner.[15]

15. S. G. W. Benjamin, *Literary World*, IX (November, 1878), 91; anonymous reviews from *Publisher's Weekly*, October 3, 1878, and *American Bookseller*, October 1, 1878, in the Bonner Copy.

Chapter Six

A Woman of Mettle

THE YELLOW FEVER epidemic in which her father and brother died marked the beginning of misfortune for Kate McDowell. Her father's death removed the stabilizing force in her life, leaving her unprotected and faced with staggering responsibilities. Although in the past she had controlled her own destiny through ingenuity, in these last years of her life she was at the mercy of outside forces. The years before the fever had called for cleverness and will; the years afterward were to test her fortitude.

When Kate McDowell reached Boston from Holly Springs on September 11, 1878, *Like unto Like* had been published with a dedication to Longfellow. In the light of her personal loss, the literary triumph seemed empty. She knew that Lilian was safe and well at Aunt Martha's old home in Penn Yan, New York, where the two had fled the Holly Springs epidemic; and Boston friends tried to comfort and divert Kate. But even as she mourned her dead, the list of Holly Springs fatalities continued to grow. Of those who had remained in the little town, over a fifth were to die before heavy frost came in early November; and as Kate read the daily death lists in the newspapers, it seemed as though her whole past was being obliterated. The first citizen to die had been old Mayor Goodrich, the model for Squire Barton in *Like unto Like*. Later there was Miss Lucilla Read, whose Beauregard Institute Kate had attended during the war. Four members of the Fort family, Helen Craft's near relatives, were soon listed as casualties; and Colonel Walter and three of his sons, whose house had been the scene of so many balls and entertainments in Kate's youth, had all fallen. Then, as the weeks drew on, came the worst shock since the deaths of her father and brother. She learned that Howard Falconer, close as a brother, one who had always cared, always understood, always defended and encouraged her, one who had sustained her during the fever itself, was now among the dead.[1]

While she struggled with her grief, there was also the future to resolve. Mrs. McDowell and her daughters had fled to the old Mills place near Trenton, Kentucky, where David and Ruth were living. The family now determined to present a united front, and Edward was dispatched to bring Kate, Lilian, and Aunt Martha to Kentucky. The entire family would wait there until the fever had spent itself and they could return to Holly Springs. Edward arrived in Boston on October 10 and probably indulged a variety of dilettantish whims during the two weeks that he spent on Somerset Street. There is no indication that for Kate this reunion was anything more than a hollow ritual, and one doubts that Edward was motivated by any powerful feelings of sympathy and love for his wife in her grief, for he had waited more than a month after the death of her father and brother to join her. The pair were simply observing certain forms just as they had done erratically in the past. During the visit, Edward was introduced to many of Kate's friends, and before they left on the trip south, the McDowells paid what must have been a strange call at Longfellow House.[2]

Reaching Penn Yan on the last day of October, they learned that Will Holland, the chairman of the Holly Springs relief committee and the hero of the epidemic, had died cruelly after the first frost had come and danger had abated. A nephew of Commodore Matthew Fontaine Maury and the model for the "ultra-Democrat" in Kate's novel, he had also been, all now knew, Lilly McDowell's fiancé. Hearing that he had been stricken, Lilly had left the safety of Kentucky and returned to Holly Springs. Met at the station and forbidden to see and thus excite him, she stayed away until the physicians had given up hope for his life. Then she had gone to him and nursed him until the end. Afterward, almost deranged with grief, she had kissed his lips and worn for days the dress cov-

1. Henry Wadsworth Longfellow to George Washington Greene, September 11, 1878, in Longfellow Collection, Houghton Library, Harvard University; William Baskerville Hamilton, "Holly Springs, Mississippi, to the year 1878" (M.A. thesis, University of Mississippi, 1931), 81, 85; Holly Springs *Occasional*, October 31, 1878, p. 1; Kate McDowell to David McDowell, August 15, 1879, in the collection of George R. Stephenson, Jackson, Mississippi (hereinafter cited as Stephenson Collection).
2. Kate McDowell to Longfellow, October 10, 1878, in Longfellow Collection.

ered with his vomit, hoping to join him in the yellow death. With the specter of another family death now hanging over them, Kate and Edward changed their plans and left Aunty and Lilian in the safety of Penn Yan.[3]

On November 14, Kate wrote Longfellow from the McDowell settlement in Kentucky. Lilly, who was still in Holly Springs, had escaped the fever. Although the scourge was over, Lilly had sent a "desolate account" of the town. Kate attempted a light tone in her letter, but after a few sentences she could not sustain it: "I am trying not to write you of the one subject to which my mind continually swings back; the wonder is that I can write of anything else. Mary McDowell and I go to Holly Springs Tuesday." And she closed: "Write to me in Holly Springs—and as often as you can—some very bitter days are coming."[4]

Kate was right. She found the desolation of the place greater than that during and immediately after the war. The long siege of the fever had left the merchants bankrupt, and few business houses were open. As the refugees returned, most in black, mourning for the dead, the visual and spiritual gloom deepened. Of the 1,440 people stricken during the epidemic, 304 had died. The lovely Holly Springs cemetery looked like a plowed field. And now the bodies of those who had fled and died in other places were being brought back. "I am at home again," Kate wrote Longfellow on the twenty-fifth, "if this great desolate house can be called home." Bonner House had to be stripped, the carpets taken up, the rooms fumigated, the walls calcimined—all to prevent a recurrence of the mysterious Yellow Jack. The exhausting work put her grief at a remove temporarily, but the house was filled with reminders of the dead including in the pocket of her father's dressing gown a copy he had made of the Harpers' letter praising *Like unto Like*. Often she cried until her eyes could not bear the light. Embittered that some of the best had had to die when others had recovered, she was at the same time tortured by guilt. She wondered whether she could have done more during the fever, but she brooded most over her failure as a daughter. "When I think of all I

3. McDowell to Longfellow, November 3, 1878, in Longfellow Collection; information from Charles N. Dean of Holly Springs.
4. McDowell to Longfellow, November 14, 1878, in Longfellow Collection.

might have done to make [my father's] life happier," she told Longfellow, "I am appalled—and choked with unavailing grief." [5]

Through the fall the reviews of *Like unto Like*, sent by Harpers and her friends, lightened some of the gloom surrounding her. Critics were praising the work. Only Paul Hamilton Hayne had found real fault, attacking Sherwood Bonner as a southerner "'yearning towards the tents of the Aliens.'" That was not the sort of charge to bother Kate McDowell, and she was defended against Hayne's criticism later in the same Louisville newspaper. But when the December issue of the *Atlantic* appeared, her highest hopes for the novel were crushed. The reviewer judged *Like unto Like* the product of a "brilliant but shallow mind" and suggested that the work owed its greatest charm to "its *girlishness*." "What a blow Mr. Howells has given me!" she wrote Longfellow. "You know how I dreaded the *Atlantic* and how foolish you thought me for doing so. The unfavourable verdict will do me a mischief in the very quarter where I most wished to be thought well of." Though the unsigned review was written by Harriet Waters Preston, Kate was convinced, despite Longfellow's disagreement, that the author was Howells himself. The poet replied in a kind letter calling the review "unjust and ungenerous," reminding her of his early difficulties with *Hyperion* and adding, "But it was a success, and yours will succeed, has succeeded." The young woman in the gloomy house, however, could not be consoled. [6]

Adding now to other causes of unhappiness were financial pressures. Dr. Bonner had died intestate, so Kate and Ruth jointly inherited the moderate-sized plantation in the country and the property in town, of which their father had been slowly selling small plots to Negroes since the war. But the estate was encumbered with debts, including expenses incurred during the epidemic that

5. John Mickle, "Learned That Frost Doesn't Kill Fever," Holly Springs *South Reporter*, December 10, 1931, p. 12; Hamilton, "Holly Springs," 85; McDowell to Longfellow, November 3, November 14, November 25, December 18, 1878, in Longfellow Collection.

6. Reviews of *Like unto Like* by Paul Hamilton Hayne in Louisville *Sunday Argus*, November 17, 1878, and by R. W. Knott, Louisville *Sunday Argus*, n.d.—both reviews in Sherwood Bonner's copy of the novel, Sherwood Bonner Collection, Marshall County Library, Holly Springs; Harriet Waters Preston to Paul Hamilton Hayne, December 22–25, 1878, in Hayne Collection, Perkins Library, Duke University; McDowell to Longfellow, November 25, December 18, 1878, in Longfellow Collection; Sophia Kirk, preface to Sherwood Bonner's *Suwanee River Tales*, vi.

the Relief Committee had paid. Once Edward and David McDowell arrived in Holly Springs, they pressed their wives to divide the property and sell Bonner House. Kate described herself now as "troubled in every way." She knew that her father would not have wanted them to sell the house, and she herself felt a strong attachment to it and could not bear to give it up. Yet she feared that living there she would be "shut in with sorrow," and she expressed to Cambridge her feeling that "the only possible brightness that I can imagine for the future is to have a home of my very own in Boston, and succeed in my work." In her confusion and despair, and probably influenced by the speculating spirit of the McDowell brothers, she made a surprising request of Longfellow. Her friend Ella Topp, struggling in her own family's poverty, proposed to develop a market garden and ship the produce to Chicago; and she needed an investor with six hundred dollars. Kate asked Longfellow for the money as a loan, suggesting that she could tell people she had received it from the sales of *Like unto Like*. The poet, who had always been generous and who had given Kate a hundred dollars to aid her after the fever, refused—probably quite wisely. She understood his refusal, but in her justification of the request she showed a keen awareness of her own situation. She had wanted "an income that is absolutely my own. Please do not think that I attach undue importance to money. My soul is not a mercenary one. I only ask to live without 'carbling care' and to be free to follow my best wishes." She added, "To a woman who is not independent, life is a bitter, black cup to drink."[7]

Beset by such cares, Kate faced a cheerless Christmas at Bonner House. And as the day approached, she was haunted by memories of what a happy time it had always been—the family gathered together and the great rooms filled with Christmas guests. By the first of the year, however, one problem had been resolved. Aunt Martha had taken a mortgage on the house for $2,400. Kate and Ruth could retain the Bonner property and settle all debts of the estate. It must have given Kate a strange feeling, however, when

7. McDowell to Longfellow, November 25, December 4, December 18, 1878, in Longfellow Collection; Longfellow's Canceled Check File, Longfellow National Historical Site, National Park Service, Cambridge.

she discovered that not only she and Ruth, but also their husbands would have to sign the deed of trust. She had learned another way, according to the law, in which she was anything but independent. Shortly after he had cosigned the deed, Edward left for Texas to indulge in more of his speculations. It must have been with great relief that Kate saw him go, for even in the darkest moments of her despair, Kate had never included Edward in her plans. In her mind her family now consisted of Lilian and Aunt Martha, and she wanted the three of them together in Boston. It was soon arranged that Lilian and Aunty would come back to Bonner House in the spring, and their future course would be decided then.[8]

While awaiting them, Kate accepted an invitation to visit her friends the Kellars in Memphis. That city had also been devastated by the fever, one *Avalanche* headline calling it "GOLGOTHA! Where the Living—Are Too Few to Bury the Dead." But her close friends there had all escaped to safety, the Kellars and Meriwethers to summer resorts and General Colton Greene to Europe. In late January, at the haven of the Kellar home on Washington Avenue, Kate began writing again, after an interruption of six months. In two sittings, she wrote an account of the epidemic, which celebrated the heroism of Holly Springs and mourned the loss of "the cream and flower of our town." She and her family were not mentioned, but the essay was an act of both love and exorcism. It was published in February in Mississippi as a memorial pamphlet, and, in a revised form, in an April issue of *Youth's Companion*. The first week of February, Sherwood Bonner took up her pen again, this time to write for the *Avalanche* her impressions of Madame Modjeska, on the eve of five days of performances to be given in Memphis by the Polish actress. Upon her arrival, there was a warm reunion between the two women, and Kate secured Modjeska's use of the Kellar house for an informal afternoon reception honoring some of her most devoted Memphis admirers and supporters. On Valentine's Day, the morning before the final performance, the *Avalanche* carried a Sherwood Bonner poem in trib-

8. McDowell to Longfellow, December 18, 1878, in Longfellow Collection; Deed Book 43, p. 209, Marshall County Courthouse, Holly Springs.

ute to Modjeska, thanking her for the "happy hours" that she was "weaving into our sad days" in "a land still wet with showers / of tears." When the actress left the city, she also carried an inscribed copy of *Like unto Like*.[9]

Kate was beginning to regain her old spirit. She had enjoyed Modjeska and appreciated the actress' recognition of her as a fellow artist; and she had taken great pleasure in her status in Memphis society as the celebrity Sherwood Bonner. In Memphis, there was also Colton Greene, the urbane man of mystery to whom Kate was increasingly drawn in the years after the fever and who was to play a central, though shadowy, role in the drama of her last years.

Back at Bonner House after a taste of the old life in Memphis, Kate continued to write. She produced a children's story about a family of spiders in the Meriwether attic, which she sent to *St. Nicholas*. She revised her yellow fever piece for *Youth's Companion*, and she mailed the Modjeska poem to *Harper's Weekly*. From the *Companion*, she received eighty dollars, a welcomed addition to the royalties she was getting from Harper & Brothers; for *Like unto Like*, despite its preponderantly favorable reviews, was not selling particularly well. In March, Lilian and Aunty returned from Penn Yan. Once back at Bonner House with all its memories, Aunt Martha felt that she could not leave again, but she agreed that Kate and her child should go to Boston. Edward returned for a brief stay, but soon he and David McDowell were off to Colorado, again to seek their fortunes; and Kate paid another short visit to Memphis.[10]

9. Memphis *Avalanche*, September 5, 1878, p. 1, and February 2, 1879, p. 3; Margaret Chambers Kellar, "Sherwood Bonner," Memphis *Public Ledger*, August 11, 1883, p. 2; Sherwood Bonner, "The Modjeska: Sherwood Bonner's Impressions of the Great Artist," Memphis *Avalanche*, February 9, 1879, p. 4, and "Modjeska," Memphis *Avalanche*, February 14, 1879, p. 4; undated and unidentified clipping on the Modjeska reception, in Helen Craft Anderson's scrapbook, in the collection of Mrs. John Craft and Mrs. James Driver, Holly Springs (hereinafter cited as Craft Collection); Helena Modjeska, *Memories and Impressions* (New York: Macmillan Company, 1910), 385; Marion Moore Coleman, *Fair Rosalind: The American Career of Helena Modjeska* (Cheshire, Conn.: Cherry Hill Books, 1969), 237–38.

10. Kellar, "Sherwood Bonner"; *McDowell* v. *Craft and Bonner* (Custody Suit over Lilian K. McDowell), No. 1657, in Chancery Docket, Chancery Clerk's Office, Marshall County Courthouse, Holly Springs (hereinafter cited as Custody Suit); Kate McDowell to David McDowell, August 15, 1879, in Stephenson Collection; Memphis *Avalanche*, April 3, 1879, p. 3.

Then, in the midst of preparations to leave for the trip north, seven-year-old Lilian insisted that she be baptized at Christ Church. The child's decision ran counter to her mother's wishes. Kate had long ago shed much of the orthodox religious belief with which she had been reared. At twenty, she had recorded in her diary her distaste for "bullying denunciations from the pulpit," and organized religion increasingly became for her a symbol of the confining forces in her background that had so thwarted her. By the time that she fled to Boston, she had broken with the church. Soon afterward, in fact, she had written to Ruth on the question of Lilian's baptism: "I think I will not have my little darling baptized. I do not want her little life to begin by what to me is a meaningless form. There must be nothing in it but what is conscious, true, and an offering of her free will." Kate's views did not change. She commended the religious beliefs of Nahum Capen, who "rarely goes to church," and later in her Boston life, she frequently characterized herself as a "happy heathen." In her fiction the clerical figures are either superficial (the Episcopal rector modeled on the Reverend Dr. Pickett in *Like unto Like*), ignorant and mean (the Baptist preacher in her Illinois stories), or villainous (the priests in "Laura Capello" and "A Volcanic Interlude"), while pillars of the church are usually presented as narrow and hypocritical. Despite her own scorn for organized religion, however, Kate acquiesced to the wishes of her daughter. "I have not much desired this baptism," she wrote Longfellow, "and certainly did object seriously to Mr. Pickett's telling Lilian that we were all, at birth, outcasts and under sentence of wrathful judgment. However, there was no standing against Lilian's vehement pleadings; and I know too that it would have greatly pleased Papa and Sam." Lilian also wished that Longfellow be her godfather. A year earlier he had agreed to serve as godfather for Ruth's first child, so Kate wrote him taking his consent for granted. On April 19, at Christ Church, the seven-year-old girl was baptized with godparents of her own choosing—Longfellow, her aunt Lilly McDowell, and her great-aunt Martha Bonner. The poet was represented in the service by Mrs. Freeman's son and Kate's friend, Russell Freeman, now a young naval officer. Lilian evidently also chose the middle name *Kirk*—for the Philadelphia family, whom she must have met on her visit north two years before. That choice would become strangely appropriate in later years.[11]

Three days after the baptism, Kate and Lilian left for the North, a fresh start, a new life. Kate was now thirty and no longer seemed almost a young girl, as she had six years before. Her figure was fuller, and her gaze more imperious, more determined, and somehow older. But her beauty was still striking, and the magnetism of her presence still strong. A woman friend from this period remarked "a tremendous vigor of body and mind about her, which, but for a beauty peculiarly fascinating to the sterner sex, would have made her appear almost masculine." Her friend hastened to add: "But the golden hair, the flower-like complexion, the soft loveliness of her exquisite white hands made one forget that she could be as sparkling in her wit as Mark Twain, and as bold in her speculations as Robert Ingersoll." The woman noted also Kate's "wonderful power first of attracting friends, and then of attaching them to her." One of those so attracted and attached in these years after the fever was Samuel Stillman Conant, editor of *Harper's Weekly*, who saw in her, as so many men had, "the charms of a ripe loveliness of person" and "the attractiveness of a happy disposition, bright conversational gifts, and a truly feminine soul." "She never made the acquaintance of a man of power, intellectual or social," Conant commented, "without succeeding in making him feel that to oblige her would give him pleasure." The editor judged her a "clever woman," who had "to an extraordinary degree, the faculty of enlisting in her behalf the services of those who would help her, not only in concerns of business, but also in the fashioning of her literary work."[12]

It was to renew such ties that Kate and Lilian now spent five

11. McDowell to Longfellow, April 18, 1879, in Longfellow Collection; Kate Bonner Diary (MS in collection of David McDowell III, Batesville, Mississippi, hereinafter cited as McDowell Collection), September 11, 1869; Kate McDowell to Ruth Bonner, November 13, 1873, in Stephenson Collection; Shirley Carter, "Sherwood Bonner," New Orleans *Times-Democrat*, September 2, 1883, p. 3; Baptismal Register, I, 98, Christ Church (Episcopal), Holly Springs.

12. "Sherwood Bonner," *Harper's Weekly*, August 11, 1883, p. 503. This eulogy is unsigned, but a surviving contemporary letter—Elizabeth Capen to Ruth McDowell, July 31, 1883, in Stephenson Collection—reveals that the author was S. S. Conant, who used material from Sophie Shepard, Ruth McDowell, and Sophia Kirk.

days in New York before going on to Boston. Though *Like unto Like* was not proving to be the success of which Kate had dreamed, it had given Sherwood Bonner an entrée into the Harper publishing empire; and she intended to make use of it. She cultivated the great magnate Joseph Harper himself, and she strengthened her connections both at *Harper's New Monthly Magazine* and at the *Weekly*, where she came to know well not only S. S. Conant, but also his wife, the writer Helen Stevens Conant. Living in New York still, of course, was an older friend—James Redpath.[13]

In early May, mother and daughter arrived in Boston and stayed temporarily with friends on Somerset Street while Kate looked for an apartment. Soon she found one in the Hotel Boylston at the corner of Boylston and Tremont—a suite of four rooms with a view of Boston Common. Haunting second-hand shops and bazaars, she gradually furnished the place and added inexpensive, artistic touches—pieces of oriental handiwork and cheap etchings. She papered the sitting room Pompeiian red, and over the mantel she hung the pastel portrait of herself done in Paris. "This little home of mine that we have all talked so much about," she described in a letter to Cora Carey, the friend since her school days at the Watson home after the war: "It is pretty bare as yet, but it is really lovely, with windows overlooking the Common, and such cheerful bright rooms. It begins to feel like *home*, and I feel a great sensation of peace within its four walls." For the first time, she was listed in the city directory as a resident of Boston.[14]

Hardly was she settled before she was visited by old friends. The Irish-born Harry Charnock of New Orleans, a cousin of the McDowells devoted to Kate and Lilian, spent ten days in Boston. Then Helen Craft came for a shorter visit. As always, Kate immediately brought the southerners into her Boston circle and offered them glimpses of the great world. She took her Holly Springs

13. McDowell to Longfellow, May 1 [1879], in Longfellow Collection.
14. The Hotel Boylston apartment is described in detail in the first three pages of Ellen Olney Kirk, *The Story of Margaret Kent* (Boston: Ticknor and Company, 1886). The portrait of Kate McDowell now hangs in the Marshall County Library, Holly Springs. Kate McDowell to Cora Carey, August 23, 1879, in Cora Carey Collection, Mississippi Department of Archives and History, Jackson.

friend to Longfellow House, and she arranged that James Redpath entertain Helen in New York.[15]

As soon as her guests had departed, Kate went to work with a will on the fiction that she had promised the two major Harper publications. She turned out a trivial, sweet southern tale, "Maddy Gascar and the Professor," for the *Weekly*, which paid her fifty dollars. The *Monthly* gave her a hundred for "The Revolution in the Life of Mr. Balingall," a well-executed story that she based on yellow fever experiences—the night when she had caught the Boston train to go south and face the dangers of the epidemic, and the drama of Lilly McDowell and Will Holland. While working on these pieces, she began to plan another novel. Faced with the necessity now of supporting both herself and Lilian, Kate was surveying the literary market with an even keener eye than usual. Mary Noailles Murfree, writing under the name Charles Egbert Craddock, had published a story of the Tennessee mountains, "The Dancin' Party at Harrison's Cove," in the May 1878 issue of the *Atlantic* to immediate acclaim; and then Murfree-Craddock placed four more mountain stories in the next year. The Cumberland Mountains comprised an area previously unexplored by writers. Realizing the public taste for novelty in their local color reading and envying Murfree's marked success at the moment, Kate decided to write a novel about the moonshiners in that locale. She was sure that Harper's would take the novel, and she determined to go to Tennessee to gather impressions. "It is impossible to write with that truth to nature at which I aim unless I familiarize myself with my localities and see with my own eyes the moonshine folk," she wrote Cora Carey, gilding in the phrasing of the new literary realism an opportunistic scheme. Kate arranged to leave Lilian with friends, and by the twenty-third of August she was in New York on her way south.[16]

This trip remains a mystery in many ways. Kate had planned to be gone only two weeks; she remained away from Boston more

15. McDowell to Carey, August 23, 1879, in Cora Carey Collection; McDowell to Longfellow, June 26, 1879, in Longfellow Collection; memorabilia in Helen Craft Anderson's scrapbook, Craft Collection.

16. McDowell to Longfellow, August 12, 1879, in Longfellow Collection; Kate McDowell to David McDowell, August 15, 1879, in Stephenson Collection; Kate McDowell to Cora Carey, August 23, 1879, in Cora Carey Collection.

than a month. It appears that she lingered in New York, and the reason may well have been James Redpath. The intense Redpath was suffering fatigue and depression that summer and showing all the signs of a man on the verge of a breakdown. He had undergone such an experience twenty-five years before only to be saved by a woman; it is interesting that she was a literary lady, who wrote under the sexually ambivalent pseudonym of Marion Harland. In 1854 in Richmond, alone and in deep depression over what he considered his failure, Redpath took a pistol and walked to the city cemetery to kill himself. Waiting for the place to empty of strollers, he found in his pocket Miss Harland's novel, given him earlier by a friend; and he began to read. Redpath's interest in the apprentice work brought him out of himself, and he vowed to make a great success of the novel that had "saved" him. Though he did not meet the author for two decades, he kept his vow, drumming up wide publicity for the book and immensely enjoying its great success. Now, without the old recuperative boyish spirits, but marked by the same instability, he was devoted to another literary lady, and not quite so disinterestedly. Kate was grateful for his devotion and had remained loyal to Redpath throughout his troubles. The friendship had also survived her using their relationship in *Like unto Like*. Though some might have found the novel a betrayal, she had presented Redpath so sympathetically that Paul Hamilton Hayne had attacked *Like unto Like* primarily on the basis of Roger Ellis' characterization. "How a Southern woman, one Southern in principle could have lingered with such apparent pride, satisfaction and delight over many traits of his ultra Radical nature, and many expressions of his ultra Radical belief" had seemed to Hayne "utterly unaccountable." Kate, however, could not save Redpath in 1879 as Miss Harland had twenty-five years before; and the reformer wanted a great deal more from Sherwood Bonner than he had from Marion Harland. Kate was walking a thin line now in her relationship with him.[17]

She did not arrive at the Maxwell House in Nashville, her proposed first stop in Tennessee, until the second of September. She

17. Charles F. Horner, *The Life of James Redpath* (New York: Barse & Hopkins, 1926), 254–55; Marion Harland, *Marion Harland's Autobiography: The Story of a Long Life* (New York: Harper & Brothers, 1910), 264–69; Hayne, Review of *Like unto Like*.

had told three correspondents that she would then go to Rogers-ville, "where," she had written Longfellow, "I have friends [and] should be at no expense." The Meriwethers were spending the summer at Greenville nearby, but it appears that she never went to the extreme eastern part of the state at all, but that she spent her time between Nashville and Knoxville at Bloomington Springs, where she was to set most of her Tennessee stories. There was an epidemic of yellow fever in Memphis again, though Holly Springs was spared this time, and Nashville and parts east were filled with refugeeing Memphians. It is impossible to know whether she did join friends, though several people whom she knew were through the Maxwell House during the late summer and early fall. Colton Greene stayed there for a time, as did Dr. Pickett of Christ Church, and even the Atheys, who lived directly across from Bonner House. Kate did not return from this now mysterious Cumberland excursion until the eighteenth of September, when she again registered at the Maxwell House.[18]

While Kate was on her trip, Aunt Martha had a change of heart. Her attachment to Lilian was evidently stronger than her feeling for Bonner House, and she decided to leave it in the hands of Ruth and David McDowell and join her nieces in Boston. Shortly after Kate's return, Aunty arrived in the city; and the family at the Hotel Boylston was now complete. Lilian was happy at her school, and Aunt Martha was soon comfortable in Kate's loyal circle—the Capens, Nellie Willard, and Carrie Jenness, who had married Josiah Osgood, a widower with children, the year before. Kate was also seeing a good deal of Louise Chandler Moulton, but she was beginning to detect disturbing traits in the older literary lady and to look at their relationship in a new light. Mrs. Moulton had remained in Europe for almost two years. Launched in London by an invitation to one of Lord Houghton's famous breakfasts, she had moved in the highest social and literary circles—among Browning, Swinburne, George Eliot. In Paris, she had met Mallarmé. She was now grander than ever, and her attentions to Kate

18. McDowell to Longfellow, August 12, 1879, in Longfellow Collection; McDowell to David McDowell, August 15, 1879, in Stephenson Collection; McDowell to Carey, August 23, 1879, in Cora Carey Collection; files of the Nashville *Daily American*, July–September, 1879.

were often patronizing. Though she still on occasion aided the younger woman—she was even now suggesting that they collaborate on a book of children's poetry—she generally used Kate for her own purposes and was inattentive when the Mississippian could not serve her. Even more disturbingly, Kate began to perceive that Mrs. Moulton had not one face, but a dozen, and that she might be using their intimacy to spread gossip and even scandal. As Kate was in the process of reevaluating this old sponsor, distressing news came about another longtime supporter. James Redpath had broken down completely and then disappeared. The newspapers were full of stories speculating on the disappearance, and only a month later did Redpath write to his family from Jamaica. A few months afterward, he surfaced again in San Francisco. In the midst of these disheartening changes in bonds that Kate had depended on, came another person to restore a kind of balance in her life. Mrs. Sarah B. Selmes of Quincy, a friend of several years, established herself and her daughters at the Bellvue for the winter. A maternal figure like Elizabeth Meriwether, Sarah Selmes was highly cultivated, deeply religious, and a devoted feminist. Since the fever, Kate had grown close to this strong and sympathetic woman, and the Selmeses provided much of the comfort and pleasure that Kate received during that long Boston winter.[19]

It was a hard winter for Kate. Her spirit was still often overcast by her memories of Holly Springs and those she had lost. In August of 1879, another of the Holly Springs circle had died, Edward's oldest sister Jennie McDowell Dancy. "How sorrows seem to crowd upon us," Kate wrote David McDowell. "Sometimes when I shut my eyes, I seem to have a vision of graves all around me; and I am continually dreaming of those who are gone." Exorcism, for Kate, took the form of hard work. Keeping up the Bos-

19. McDowell to Carey, August 23, 1879, in Cora Carey Collection; McDowell to Ruth McDowell, December 19, 1879, in Stephenson Collection; McDowell to Longfellow, March 14, April 28, 1880, in Longfellow Collection. This period of Mrs. Moulton's life is covered in chapter 4 of Lilian Whiting, *Louise Chandler Moulton: Poet and Friend* (Boston: Little, Brown, and Company, 1910). Mrs. Townsend in Kirk's *The Story of Margaret Kent* is a detailed portrait of Mrs. Moulton. See particularly pages 19–20, 74–75, for a view of the McDowell-Moulton relationship in the winter of 1879–1880. Horner, *James Redpath*, 254–55; McDowell to Longfellow, 24 [November, 1879], in Longfellow Collection; 1900 Census of Massachusetts, XL, 737. Mrs. Selmes's religious and feminist views are articulated in S. B. S., "Whose Fault Is It?" *Cottage Hearth*, VIII (May, 1882), 164.

ton home was much more expensive than she had anticipated, and she was just beginning to realize how heavy her financial burdens would be with her father gone. Before the trip to Tennessee, she had written one mountain story, "Lost and Found," which she probably took from Mrs. Meriwether's fund of tales garnered when she lived in the Cumberlands as a bride. It was published in *Youth's Companion* in November. The same journal took another tale drawn from a Memphis friendship, "Mars' Colton's Lesson." Neither of these pieces represents Sherwood Bonner's talent at its best. She was turning out anything that she could in order to fill the rapidly depleting family coffers. Her money worries evidently also account for the most blatant literary opportunism of her career. Capable of great originality, at the same time she had always been peculiarly susceptible to literary influence. But in the winter of 1879/80, she baldly set out to copy works by two contemporary writers who were receiving considerable attention. In her mountaineer pieces suggested by Miss Murfree's success, Sherwood Bonner simply appropriated Murfree's setting in order to gain Murfree's audience. But in "A Volcanic Interlude," she copied George Washington Cable's characteristic setting, style, structure, and theme. Somehow, after a quantity of this sort of hackwork, Sherwood Bonner's real freshness of spirit could still break through in her next work, "Hieronymus Pop and the Baby," long considered a masterpiece of the Negro dialect tale. While she was producing these works of radically mixed quality, she was also experiencing real blocks and troubles with other material. The Tennessee novel was not working, and a long story, "Two Storms," which she sent to Henry Mills Alden at *Harper's* in December of 1879, was evidently so flawed that she had to undertake major revisions before she could get it in publishable form a year and a half later. Despite these frustrations, she kept at her desk. Her superb health and her strong drive had always enabled her to work long hours, and a friend had characterized her as "utterly regardless of regular hours for eating, sleeping, or anything else." This winter, however, the effects of the hard work were showing. Friends became worried, and Nellie Willard even wrote Longfellow asking that he reason with Kate.[20]

20. Kate McDowell to David McDowell, August 15, 1879, in Stephenson Collection; Elizabeth Avery Meriwether, *Recollections of Ninety-Two Years, 1824–1916* (Nashville:

There were factors in addition to the pressures of her work, however, that were causing Kate's fatigue and nervousness. Aware for years that she was whispered about, she had at first almost enjoyed the talk: it meant that Sherwood Bonner was becoming known. After the European trip and the months in Galveston, however, she had begun looking at her reputation more seriously; wishing to take Lilian back with her to Boston, she had concluded that as a mother with her child "no gossip can touch me." She had, of course, not taken her child back then. The talk had continued, and she had found the acceptance of *Like unto Like* a compensation for "having so many cruel and unjust things said of me." Returning to Boston after the sorrows of the fever, saddened and determined on building a new life, Kate had brought Lilian and her aunt to a real home in the city—only to find that she was not to have the life in Boston she had counted on. The affronts to Mrs. Grundy had been too great; the base of enemies created by "The Radical Club" had grown; Boston was ready not to forgive her mistakes, but to magnify them.[21]

Kate would have realized the strength of this vituperative spirit even a year earlier had she seen an amazing letter from the nunnish Boston literary lady Harriet Waters Preston to the southern poet and critic Paul Hamilton Hayne. Eager to see Hayne's review of *Like unto Like*, Miss Preston told him that she "'could a' long and very curious 'tale unfold' about the author" if she had sufficient leisure, but that she would give him now the "heads" only. Then the Boston lady continued for several pages to recount her tale of Sherwood Bonner. Like most gossip, it is a mixture of fact, error, and innuendo:

> Kate Sherwood Bonner was the author's maiden name . . . Miss Bonner married a Mr. McDowell and tired of the monotony of living with him in Texas or some such forlorn region; and came to Boston as a literary adventuress and after a rather severe experience became known to Mr. Longfellow, who admired her (she is a statuesque blonde with

Tennessee Historical Commission, 1958), 51–53; McDowell to Longfellow, December 8 [1879], in Longfellow Collection; B. M. Drake, "Sherwood Bonner," *Southern Writers: Biographical and Critical Studies*, ed. William Malone Baskerville (Nashville and Dallas: Publishing House of the M. E. Church, South, 1903), I, 102–103; Helen Willard to Longfellow, n.d., in Longfellow Collection.

21. McDowell to Longfellow, August 31, 1877, in Longfellow Collection; McDowell to Dr. Charles Bonner, May 21, 1878, in Stephenson Collection.

cataracts of yellow hair) and employed her as an amanuensis on his perpetual "poems of places." A malign wit once named them *Merlin and Vivien* and the *mot* became general. Mr. Longfellow has always corroborated Mrs. McDowell's own assertion that her pen and no other was to produce the "great American novel."

Miss Preston then moved to what was obviously to her an even more unsavory area of Sherwood Bonner's life:

> There's another man whose faith has been equally strong and that is James Redpath who has what he is pleased to call a *Lyceum Bureau*; that is he supplies professional lecturers to aspirants for knowledge all over the country. I cannot say when or how Mr. Redpath and Mrs. McDowell became great friends, but there was an extremely clever little satire on the Boston Radical Club written two years ago, which is attributed to their joint authorship, and people of whose *monde* Mr. Redpath is, say that he is most accurately depicted in your friend, the hero of *Like unto Like*. . . . She passed through a terrible ordeal last autumn, having gone with great courage to her father's Southern home when she heard of the outbreak of the fever and arriving just in time to see her father and her brother die. It was Mr. Redpath and not her husband to whom she telegraphed to come and fetch her and her little girl away, but her husband seemed not to have minded it for they are now, I am told, living together in New York. I mean Mr. & Mrs. McDowell.

After this bit of innuendo, Miss Preston revealed to Hayne one of her sources, probably for most of the foregoing information— Louise Chandler Moulton: "In the midst of those awful days at Holly Springs [Mrs. McDowell] wrote a long letter to an old friend of mine who knew her well once when they were in Rome together. My friend whose style is concise and forcible sent the letter on to me as a pschycological [*sic*] curiosity with the comment—'Would it be believed? There she is, *posing* in the very jaws of death!'" Unlike her friend Mrs. Moulton, Miss Preston assured Hayne that she had not allowed herself the possible corruption of frequent exposure to Sherwood Bonner: "Mrs. McDowell I have met once or twice, but last winter when she asked me to lunch with her and meet Mr. Longfellow and Modjeska I declined, and she urged me so long, that I fear she discovered that I did it for no better reason than reluctance to a visiting acquaintance. So you see I'm not likely to get erroneous views of Southern society and character from her personally." Closing her account of Sherwood Bonner, Miss Preston clove to her own rectitude: "All this sounds very badly gossippy [*sic*] but if you knew how much more is said, you would only marvel at my restraint. You saw perhaps, in the *Atlantic*, my notice of her book. I have seldom made a more frantic effort to be impartial." Thus had spoken the author of the most devastating review of *Like unto Like* to the only other critic who had attacked the novel. Though clearly some of Sherwood Bonner's success had been due to her personal magnetism, to her power of attracting influential friends, it is also clear that some of her failures had been due to a similarly strong capacity for arousing antagonism. Moreover, some apparent friends—like Louise Chandler Moulton—had now become enemies.[22]

Despite such gossip, it seems clear that Kate's relationships with both Longfellow and Redpath were not overtly sexual. The nature of the Longfellow intimacy is revealed fully in a letter that she wrote him when she was in Galveston. "The longer I live the more sure I feel that a perfectly well-bred person should never defy the conventionalities in any way," she commented. "That is the lesson you have been trying to teach me is it not?—*While we may be as daring as we please in thought*" (italics mine). Thus she expressed the particular platonism of the seventy-year-old poet. As for Kate herself, the continuing influence of her rearing was still apparent in her frequent command of a high moral tone, and it is further possible that she either was, or thought herself to be, a woman whose "physical temperament was cold"—to use her quaint description of Blythe Herndon. Certainly she sometimes displayed a not particularly positive view of sex. "Let me know if *all is well*. You know what I mean," she wrote Ruth in the first letter after her sister's marriage. And letters to both Ruth and Cora Carey reflect deep fears of childbirth. Indeed it seems most probable that Kate had used her status as a married woman to keep other men, including James Redpath, exactly where she wanted them, at just the right distance. It seems that she had, to quote from a novel that

---

22. Preston to Hayne, December 22–25, 1878, in Hayne Collection. I am grateful to Professor Rayburn S. Moore for making me aware of the existence of this letter. See his "Merlin and Vivien? Some Notes on Sherwood Bonner and Longfellow," *Mississippi Quarterly*, XXVIII (Spring, 1975), 181–84.

pictures her during the Boston years, "laughed, pleaded, tempted, and denied."[23]

Nevertheless, in the year since the Preston-Hayne letter the gossip had continued. Kate began to sense the weight of public opinion, first, through Longfellow's greater distance after her return to Boston. In the late fall of 1879, she had complained to him: "I never see you now-a-days and am trying to accustom myself to the thought that you will soon stop caring for me in the least." She still visited Longfellow House and took friends there, and the poet was generous in presenting little gifts to Lilian, Kate, and Aunt Martha and in sending them tickets to concerts and plays. But he rarely came to the Hotel Boylston, and the days of his escorting Kate were over. The poet's feelings toward his beautiful protégé were evidently unchanged, but someone (probably his own daughters) had obviously made him sensitive to the gossip. Merlin would no more be seen in public with Vivien. Soon Kate was also bitterly conscious that without Longfellow's active public sponsorship she was now being excluded from important guest lists. While spending an evening with her in early December, Joseph Harper had remarked her absence at a literary breakfast that day. Harper, by Kate's account to Longfellow, "seemed not able to conceal his surprise (nor recover his regret) that I was not there. And indeed I should have enjoyed seeing and hearing all those lovely people." Then she burst out to the poet: "Do tell me that it would not have been *possible* for you to have procured me an invitation. It is the only thing that can soothe my regret. Horrid Mr. Howells—he *might* have—." She concluded the letter, "Ah me! what a nervous wearing thing life is!"[24]

Indeed it was for Kate McDowell at the Hotel Boylston. Beginning the winter with high expectations, she had taken much pleasure in her view of the Common, especially when the rose and gold of sunset shone through the elms and covered the snow with varied lights. As winter wore on, however, the stark, bleak elms

23. McDowell to Longfellow, April 17, 1877, in Longfellow Collection; Bonner, *Like unto Like*, 162; Kate McDowell to Ruth McDowell, July 8, 1877, and 17 [March, 1878], in Stephenson Collection; Kate McDowell to Cora Carey, August 23, 1879, in Carey Collection; Kirk, *The Story of Margaret Kent*, 8.

24. McDowell to Longfellow, August 12, [November] 24, December 8, December 24, 1879, and March 14 [1880], in Longfellow Collection.

and the now besoiled snow formed a scene that matched her increasing depression. Through the joint agencies of the McDowell brothers, both her already unpleasant situation and her oppression of spirit were only to worsen. She had always disliked David McDowell, and the previous August he had irritated her sufficiently that she had written to him rather sharply. Asking why he had returned from Colorado so soon, she underscored his habitually directionless state with—"Did you find nothing to do there?" Then she turned her attention to Edward: "Edward writes glowingly of the country, and his prospects, but you know he is apt to speak glowingly in the first blush of anything." Finally she came to the point. David had made a financial request of her—albeit a small one—after having completely misrepresented her fiscal state to Edward: "My dear David I would send Dr. Clements a book with great pleasure, but I have none, nor alas! have I the 75 cts that is needed to buy one. I am actually reduced to my last penny and am waiting for a remittance to pay some little debts for which I am being dunned. Edward remarked coolly that he would send me some money but understood from you that I had $400 in Boston. Where *did* you get such an idea? I am *very* sorry not to send Dr. C. the book; but you know I have to buy them, and since I haven't the money what can I do!" By mid December, Kate was beginning to worry about even more serious deficiencies on David's part. Probably out of loyalty to the husband who was supposed to be managing the Bonner estate, Ruth had not written since Aunt Martha had left Holly Springs. Kate finally communicated with Ruth expressing her concern about "home affairs," and she could not forbear drawing an ironic contrast between McDowell rhetoric and Bonner action: "Edward writes glowingly of the mines and I suppose we shall be tremendously rich some day—In the meantime I keep hard at work with my little pencil." At the end of February, Ruth had still not written, and David's account for the past year was six weeks overdue. On February 26, 1880, Kate's thirty-first birthday, when she must have been taking a hard look at her life and especially her present circumstances, she finally acted. She wrote Ruth that she was appointing an agent in Holly Springs to represent her interests and her aunt's. David was to render to him immediately the last year's accounts. Kate had earlier written to Edward about finances, and she had received no answer; and it was probably on this same day that she had Lilian write her father asking that he pay her school expenses. As her own letter to Ruth shows, Kate was also slowly forming a plan. She mentioned that the family in Boston was thinking of going to Penn Yan in the summer and settling there—"as I find the burden too terrific in keeping up an establishment in Boston."[25]

March, however, brought a clear view of her situation that resulted in a quite different plan for the future. Toward the middle of the month, Mrs. Moulton called to chat about the book of children's poetry on which she and Kate were collaborating, to talk of her imminent departure for Europe, and, particularly, to let Kate know of the entertainment being given by Longfellow's friend the Norwegian musician Ole Bull—a party to which she knew Kate had not been asked. This was the last in a long series of social slights, which Kate now saw as a pattern of exclusion. About the same time, she gained sure knowledge about another aspect of her life. Edward had not answered Lilian's letter. When Kate had finally put aside her pride and called upon him (though indirectly), she learned that he had no intention of contributing to the support of his daughter.[26]

Kate felt her full entrapment. Because she was a married woman who received the attentions of other men, she was whispered about and excluded from the world in which she wished to move. From the man to whom she was married, she could expect, as always, only inflated talk about dim prospects; and tied to him, she would face steadily diminishing possibilities for herself. As early as 1875, when she had first begun establishing herself as a writer in Boston, Kate had talked to a few intimates of divorce. Now she felt that if she were ever going to have a life, she must go through with it. The family of three would go to Penn Yan first; then they would go to a Bonner aunt in southern Illinois, where the divorce laws were reasonable and where Kate could avoid public scrutiny. On March 29, Kate wrote Longfellow that she had let the Hotel

25. Kate McDowell to David McDowell, August 15, 1879; Kate McDowell to Ruth McDowell, December 19, 1879, and February 26, 1880—all in Stephenson Collection.
26. McDowell to Longfellow, March 14 [1880]; Longfellow to Moulton, March 21, 1880; Moulton to Longfellow, March 18, 1880, and n.d.—all in the Longfellow Collection; Custody Suit.

Boylston apartment. "You said I must call on you if I needed help," she said. "I am trying to settle everything—and can come out 'even' with thirty dollars more. Then no more trouble *ever* about finances! What a blessed relief it will be!" In early April, Kate, Lilian, and Aunt Martha left Boston. Kate was to get her freedom.[27]

They paused for a few days in Penn Yan, where Aunt Martha decided to remain for the year in which it would take Kate to obtain her divorce in Illinois. Then Kate and Lilian took the train west to meet their almost unknown relatives. Because the train stopped for fifteen hours on Sunday, the trip took four days; and two of the nights they could not get a sleeping compartment. But Lilian was a good traveling companion, never showing boredom or petulance. As she amused herself for hours spinning the silver dollar that Longfellow had sent her as a going away present, Kate lost herself in *The Newcomes*, trying to forget both her present discomfort and the dilemma that was sending her to Illinois. When they reached the end of the exhausting journey, their relatives greeted them warmly. Aunt Margaret Bonner had been twice married, first to a Mr. Wilkinson, and after his death to Edwin Burbank, a farmer who lived near Du Quoin in Perry County. Through the two marriages, the Bonner connection was extensive in this area of southern Illinois; and Kate rented a house in the larger town of Benton in neighboring Franklin County, the home of Aunt Maggie's son-in-law M. G. Kelso, a lawyer who was to handle the divorce.[28]

This was a poor area of the state with little of the fertile farm land of the northern and central sections, though Perry County did have three strips of prairie, known as the nine-mile, the six-mile, and the four-mile. Also an area dominated by fundamentalist religion, it seemed to Kate a world away from her own plantation country. Holly Springs had had its share of poverty in the last twenty years, but there were also the evidences of an old prosperity and even some traces of grandeur. Though Kate often de-

27. Custody Suit; McDowell to Longfellow, March 29, 1880, in Longfellow Collection.
28. McDowell to Longfellow, April 28 and July 7, 1880, in Longfellow Collection; 1880 Census of Illinois, Perry County, 28; McDowell to Dr. Charles Bonner, May 21, 1878, in Stephenson Collection.

scribed Holly Springs as a straight-laced town, the leaders had been primarily Episcopalians and Presbyterians, and their influence obscured any fundamentalist fervor in the lower ranks. "I can't deny the year to come looks dreary and long," Kate wrote to Longfellow. "I shall have no congenial associates, and the village life seems so peculiar compared to that I have known in the South. I suppose the great wide-halled houses and numbers of servants make the difference. There's one comfort. I am in a fair way of gaining material for the American novel. What diverse experiences come into my life. And this studying humanity 'by the natural method' is exactly what a writer needs and what a woman seldom does." In Boston, Sherwood Bonner had learned the fashionable literary catchwords, but in Illinois she was to prove that she gave more than lip service to the new literary creed. Then, in the next lines, Kate expressed to her old friend both her resolve and the bitterness in her heart at her Boston experience and her present circumstances: "I shall work furiously this year—if I were happier I should be less ambitious. At times I am so tired of the isolation of my life that I could weep my heart away. 'It's a glorious misery to be born a man'—says an old epitaph. I think it *is* to be born a woman unless she is shielded with love from her cradle to her grave." She begged that the poet write often. "Help me afar as you help me anear! It will be like comforting one in prison. Send me a paper some time that I may know the world does move." She signed the letter, "Your troubling Kate."[29]

In Illinois, Lilian was her one comfort. Because Kate found the local children rough, she decided not to send her daughter to school, but to teach the child at home; and she enjoyed having Lilian all to herself. Her love for Lilian had always been strong, even when she had left her infant daughter and run away to Boston. In one of the first Boston letters to Ruth, Kate had written, "Don't let her forget me, Ruth—talk to her every day of me." The child had never forgotten, and though for years the time they spent together was short and Kate's absences long, there had always been a profound empathy between them. Since the fever, the bond had intensified, and this time spent in Illinois, with only each

29. McDowell to Longfellow, April 28, 1880, in Longfellow Collection.

other, was to be the longest span they would have together, and the closest. At eight, Lilian was a beautiful little girl with pale golden hair and large intelligent eyes. Like her mother at the same age, she was precocious; but she was a more serious child with the occasional touches of wisdom that sometimes come to children whose family situations have been unusual and who have early seen the sufferings of adults.[30]

Lilian's companionship, however, was not enough to dispel Kate's profound sense of isolation and abandonment. And now communications from Holly Springs were again unsettling. David McDowell was insisting upon a division or sale of the Bonner property, and Kate was forced to agree at least to a division of the contents of Bonner House. As she found herself wrangling over individual items, she faced the change in the relationship with her sister. They had been close, though Kate had always regarded Ruth very much as her little sister and still thought of her almost as a girl. Now that Kate and David were at odds, Ruth was caught between two people who wanted her support. Ruth never wavered. She was always to be a gently and firmly devoted wife to the handsome, blustery David. Kate knew that another tie had changed forever.[31]

In the midst of the controversy over the division, Lilian began having chills—something that Kate had feared in that malarial country. Though Kate had had her Boston furniture shipped to Benton and was awaiting the arrival of the things from Bonner House, as soon as the child was well, they moved to the Burbank farm near Du Quoin, which Kate considered a more healthful location. Within a short time, Lilian was rosy and tanned, and finding the farm a place of endless fascination. The divorce suit had been filed in August, and in the fall, Kate, whose health had always been magnificent, herself suffered a prolonged illness. The doctor finally diagnosed it, she told Longfellow, "a nervous fever apparently from some mental cause that he could not reach." Probably

30. *Ibid.*; Kate McDowell to Ruth Bonner, November 13, 1873, in Stephenson Collection. The best description of Lilian—better than the many in her mother's letters—is in Kirk, *Margaret Kent*, 10.

31. Undated fragments of two letters [April–June, 1880] from Kate McDowell, one to David McDowell, the other to Ruth McDowell, in Stephenson Collection; information from David McDowell III.

no one could have reached it. Her whole world seemed to be crumbling, and she was looking back over her life and finding it a failure—just as she had before she fled to Boston. Though the doctor administered opiates, for the first time in her life she could not sleep. She had too much to consider and to resolve. By December she had passed the crisis. "It is very plain now that I shall get well," she told Longfellow, "and I mean to get well of more than bodily ills—I shall cast behind me all the morbidity and sadness that pressed my spirit to earth; and meet life more patiently and bravely, striving my utmost." [32]

For Kate now came a long period of frenzied labor. Work, which was necessary for her material sustenance, was also the only thing that could sustain her spiritually. Oppressed by the disorder of her personal life, she found in her art alone a sense of order; and through her fiction she began not only exorcising her personal demons, but also gaining greater artistic control and a new self-awareness. The fifteen months spent in Illinois were the most productive period in her literary career, a time when she wrote nine children's poems, eight stories, and a novella. Among the quite varied works is some of her best fiction.

Soon after Kate came to Illinois, she knew that Louise Chandler Moulton was no longer interested in their collaboration on the book of juvenile poetry; and Sherwood Bonner published the nine poems that she had completed in September and October issues of *Harper's Young People*. In the same journal, she also placed "The Angel in the Lilly Family," a tale based on Lilian's large family of dolls. Late in 1880, appeared two more Negro dialect tales—another of the Gran'mammy stories, "Why Gran'mammy Didn't Like Pound Cake," in the *Wide Awake Pleasure Book*, and a tale based on an incident at the old Mills place in Kentucky during the fever, "Dr. Jex's Predicament," in the *Weekly*. Kate had abandoned the idea of writing a novel set in the Cumberlands; instead she used the material to produce three loosely linked stories of mountain life—"Jack and the Mountain Pink," "The Case of Eliza Bleylock," and "Lame Jerry"—which came out in January, March, and May issues of the 1881 *Weekly*. While often lively, even

32. Custody Suit; McDowell to Longfellow, July 7 and December 23, 1880, in Longfellow Collection.

sprightly on the surface, these mountain tales are dominated by an undercurrent of treachery and deceit. Sherwood Bonner then dramatized the grimmer aspects of another out-of-the-way social system in a story set in Perry County, Illinois. "Sister Weeden's Prayer," published in the April 1881 issue of *Lippincott's*, presents a vivid sense of a backwater community through the narration of one Sister Waller; and in a creek baptism and a meeting of the Baptist Ladies Society, it offers an abundance of local color. It also exposes brilliantly all the hypocrisy and meanness of this fundamentalist culture. The last two works of the period are even more interesting. The April 1881 *Harper's* finally offered its readers Sherwood Bonner's "Two Storms," a story she had first submitted almost a year and a half earlier. Another of the hodge-podges that she occasionally produced, the tale is the most outrageous periodical romance to come from her pen. But after she had dispatched it, she turned her attention to a work that would satirize the whole convention of such literature and present a delightfully sophisticated view of its southern milieu. This novella, *The Valcours*, which appeared in the last four issues of *Lippincott's* for the year 1881, shows an artistic control and a breadth of perspective that Sherwood Bonner had never displayed so fully and so consistently before.[33]

Immediately after her arrival in Illinois, *Lippincott's* had published her tale of miscegenation "A Volcanic Interlude," which far exceeded in sensationalism and melodrama the Cable stories on which it had been modeled; and the editor had received a number of cancellations in protest to the story. *Lippincott's* responded by publishing another Sherwood Bonner story and her novella in the next year; obviously the sensation was helping the career of the literary lady who had for so long enjoyed making a stir. And the steady outpouring of fiction through 1880 and 1881 was adding to an increasingly solid literary reputation. Sherwood Bonner's fiction was now appearing with striking frequency in some of the country's best magazines, often with drawings by F. T. Merrill, A. B. Frost, or W. L. Sheppard, who were among the leading il-

33. McDowell to Longfellow, April 28, 1880, in Longfellow Collection; Lilian McDowell to Mrs. Charnock, September 8, 1899, in McDowell Collection; McDowell to Longfellow, November 14, 1878, in Longfellow Collection.

lustrators of the period. After having taken four stories in six months, Samuel Conant of *Harper's Weekly* at length expressed to her his confidence in her literary status. "I accept your articles now without reading them in advance," he said. "Your signature is enough." [34]

Kate clung desperately to such professional praise, for it was practically all she had to sustain herself in the spring of 1881, as personal pressures yet again began to build. David McDowell made a trip to Illinois to tell her that he intended leaving Holly Springs and settling on his family's Louisiana plantation. He demanded a division of Ruth's interests and hers. When Kate conveyed the news to Penn Yan, Aunt Martha wrote that she would come to Illinois and then the three of them would go to Holly Springs as soon as the divorce was final. She was firmly set against the selling of Bonner House, and she felt that the matter had to be settled permanently. On the fifth of May, Kate, Aunt Martha, and M. G. Kelso went to the courthouse at Du Quoin, and the final divorce decree was granted. Within a week Kate wrote to inform Ruth: "Now Ruth I want nothing but love between us—Some day I mean to write you a letter of about a million pages. At present I can write only a little note for I am ill and weak. . . . There were no embarrassing questions—nothing of non-support—and *nothing* unkind said of E—It all breaks my heart, yet I saw no other way. I shall live for Lilian and hard work." Kate enclosed a letter for Mrs. McDowell, "whom I shall always love," and she begged: "Write to me my only sister—and believe me, Lovingly yours, Kate." [35]

Within a few days Kate was confined to her bed. Her hold on her health had been tenuous, and when the strain she had imposed upon herself by unceasing labor was intensified again by outside pressures, she had experienced a relapse. Facing the reality of the divorce was more than she could bear. She was free now, but she wondered what her freedom meant. Though she never questioned the wisdom of severing her connection with Edward, still her re-

34. Dorothy L. Gilligan, "Life and Works of Sherwood Bonner" (M.A. thesis, George Washington University, 1930), 45; Alexander L. Bondurant, "Sherwood Bonner," *Publications of the Mississippi Historical Society*, II (June, 1898), 53.

35. McDowell to Longfellow, August 7, 1881, in Longfellow Collection; Custody Suit; Kate McDowell to Ruth McDowell, May 10, 1881, in Stephenson Collection.

sponse to the divorce was not elation but confusion. Oppressed by the cruelty of her circumstances in Boston, she had acted to change the only thing that she could, her tie to a man whom she loathed. But the divorce would do nothing to change attitudes toward her there; she could, in fact, expect considerable censure now because she was a divorced woman. Despite her many blows to convention, she still felt keenly the influence of her conventional rearing, and wishing to retain her Holly Springs ties, she was also acutely aware of the reactions of her close but quite conservative old friends there. For years after she had fled to Boston, she had shown great energy and cleverness in extricating herself from uncomfortable positions and in advancing her own future. Now she felt almost helpless before her bitter personal circumstances.[36]

As soon as Kate had recovered enough to be out of bed, Aunt Martha concurred that her niece needed an immediate change of scene; and Kate spent a month with Cornelia Boardman, who had taken her medical degree in Germany and was practicing in St. Louis. Upon her return in early July, she, Aunty, and Lilian left for Holly Springs. Kate and her aunt must have noted with some irony that one of the local newspapers listed them as "guests of Mr. David McDowell" at Bonner House. One of Kate's first undertakings was a walk to the cemetery, where among other graves she visited the recently marked burial place of Howard Falconer. She returned to Bonner House and wrote a poem in eulogy, recalling the last time that she saw him in the midst of the fever, and memorializing his nobility and loyalty. She signed it "Bohemian," as if to proclaim a difference from her fellow townsmen that she was convinced they all felt.[37]

A month after arriving in Holly Springs, she finally composed a long letter to Longfellow, her first to him in eight months. Aware that the time when she had seemed to him a part of the sunshine itself must have appeared far in the past, she began the letter with a long apology: "All this long time I have not written to you, as I continually hoped to have something cheerful to tell you of my

36. Custody Suit; McDowell to Longfellow, August 7, 1881, and Cornelia Boardman to Longfellow, January 20, 1881, both in Longfellow Collection.
37. Kate McDowell to Ruth McDowell, May 10, 1881, in Stephenson Collection; Custody Suit; Holly Springs *Reporter*, July 14, 1881, p. 3; Bohemian, "In Memoriam: Howard Falconer," Holly Springs *Reporter*, July 7, 1881, p. 3.

plans. For so long a time I have approached you only to sadden; and it has often seemed to me that you must grow weary of so repeated a call on your sympathy from one whose life seems more and more a record of failure or a jumble of mishaps." She then detailed for him the granting of the divorce, her breakdown, and David McDowell's plan to put Bonner House up at public auction if she did not act soon to divide the plantation with Ruth and to buy for fifteen hundred dollars Ruth's half interest in the house. She laid the matter before him confident, she told him, that he would help. Then she pled: "And you will help, will you not to save my home—to secure for myself a *retreat* for my ruined life where I may die with dignity." And she closed the letter as a supplicant: "Have I not long held my troubles from you? Love me a little for that—and believe believe my heart is broken—Tell me if it is well with you and those you love—and let me hear from you soon." At seventy-four, Longfellow was feeling the weight of his years. "You are at the beginning of your literary career, and I at the end of mine," he had written in answer to a discouraged letter from Illinois. A weary Merlin could no longer respond in the old way to the witchery of Vivien. His letters were much less frequent, but he still sent books and papers to Kate, and he was generous in his attentions to his godchild. Though at the beginning of the year, he had complained in his journal—"Seventeen letters received today, and all but three asking some favor!"—he was a generous man; and he felt still a warm regard for Kate. He would still offer encouragement and help. On the twenty-fifth of August, he sent a check for five hundred dollars.[38]

By October, David and Ruth and their children had moved out of Bonner House, and Kate's Du Quoin furniture, a part of which had been shipped there from Holly Springs just a year earlier, arrived at Bonner House. The plantation had been divided, and she was making arrangements to borrow a thousand dollars from Judge Orlando Davis. Kate had written Cornelia Boardman early in the year that she had decided of her future course only that "I

38. McDowell to Longfellow, August 7, 1881, in Longfellow Collection; Sophia Kirk, preface to *Suwanee River Tales*, viii; Longfellow Letter Calendar and Longfellow's Journal, January 3, 1881—both in Longfellow Collection; Canceled Check File, Longfellow Historic Site.

do not mean to return to Boston & I shall never live alone." Now Kate, who had wandered for a decade, longed so often for a retreat, and feared that she would never again have a home, had found one—Bonner House, the only home that she had really ever known.[39]

She was also beginning to long for another sort of shelter. Kate, who had spent a decade in flight from the man to whom she was legally bound, was contemplating now the shelter that could be found in marriage. Within the past three years, contemporaries who had not married at the usual age, as Kate had, had begun forming happy unions. At the time of the fever, Carrie Jenness had married an established widower with children; early in 1880 the plain Helen Craft had finally wed Professor Anderson of Holly Springs; and now Kate learned that Cornelia Boardman had married a rich man of mature years soon after Kate had left St. Louis. "Was not C's marriage a thunder-clap?" Kate exclaimed to Longfellow. "Mr. Pulsifer is a very rich man with a beautiful home. I begin to believe 'a genteel sufficiency and love' . . . the all that makes life livable." Certainly wealth and it appears love too could be found in a man who had long ago captured Kate's interest and to whom she had increasingly been directing her attention: General Colton Greene of Memphis.[40]

At Colton Greene's death in 1900, eulogists noted that for all his importance as a civic leader he had been an intensely private man. When we look at his portrait today (hanging in the Memphis Public Library, which he endowed), we see dressed in a uniform of Confederate gray with three gold stars upon the high collar, a figure of distinctly military bearing, with dark closely cropped hair, heavy brows and mustache, a powerful Roman nose, a Middle-Eastern cast to the strong features. He remains inscrutable. A man of mystery in life, he carried his secrets to his grave. That is certainly the case in his relationship with Kate McDowell. No letters survive either between them or about them, and the nature of their relationship must be inferred from Sherwood Bonner's fiction,

39. Estate Papers of Katharine McDowell, File 1656, Chancery Clerk's Office, Marshall County Courthouse, Holly Springs (hereinafter cited as Estate Papers); Boardman to Longfellow, January 20, 1881, in Longfellow Collection.
40. McDowell to Longfellow, August 7, 1881, in Longfellow Collection.

from Greene's strange movements, and from the events of later years.[41]

An intimate relationship is clearly reflected in the fiction, where three stories written over a period of five years contain allusions to Greene. The work that plays most closely upon his name is "Mars' Colton's Lesson," published in March, 1880, the story of a "wild, impassioned, self-willed" South Carolina youth, Colton Grandeis, scion of a hot-blooded race of cavaliers. This violent tale, which remarkably enough appeared in *Youth's Companion*, concerns the boy's lesson about governing his ancestral passions, learned only after a brutal incident in which he plunges his knife into his faithful little body servant's chest. The piece is so strange that one wonders whether the author actually based it directly on an incident told her by Colton Greene—certainly a sign of deep intimacy on the part of the man of mystery. The only clue that contemporaries left as to Greene's strength of passion, however, is a passing reference that "he was as strong in his friendships as in his enmities."[42]

Two other Sherwood Bonner stories show Greene in a more revealing role. "C. G.; or, Lilly's Earrings," evidently completed in the spring or summer of 1878 and published in *Lippincott's* the following September, is her first fictional use of the General. The story centers on a trunk left during the war by a mysterious dark young man—the one clue to his identity being the initials C. G. embroidered upon the garments inside. Two young girls, who find high romance in the mystery of the trunk, are subsequently duped out of a pair of diamond earrings because of their romanticizing of the C. G. legend. To this point, Sherwood Bonner uses her friend merely to play upon his mystery, but the end of the tale introduces a different note. The reader is told that Lilly, the true duped romantic, has vowed never to marry a man with those initials, but that the other girl, the more practical Stella, has indeed married a man named Clément Gardiné, a great Louisiana planter. Sherwood Bonner was still casting a C. G. figure in the role of romantic lover five years later. In "Christmas Eve at Tuckeyhoe," one of the last stories that she wrote, the heroine finally wins the love

41. "Death of Gen. Colton Greene," Memphis *Commercial Appeal*, October 1, 1900, p. 1.
42. "General Colton Greene," Memphis *Evening Scimitar*, October 1, 1900, p. 3.

of still another man with those initials—Cuthbert Gordon. As well as paying compliments to the General, Sherwood Bonner may well have been playing out her own fantasies in these stories. Subsequent events show that Colton Greene must have cared a great deal for Kate, but it is also clear that in the relationship, Kate, the coquette, so often pursued, must have become the pursuer.

The eligible Colton Greene had eluded the belles of Memphis for nearly twenty years now, and obviously he intended to retain his bachelorhood even at the cost of a woman as exceptional as Kate McDowell. After she had gained her freedom and returned South, offering the possibilities of a different sort of relationship, Greene's response was immediate. Within ten days he had booked passage for Europe, where he remained for four months. After his return in the fall of 1881, it seems certain that they were brought together many times in Memphis, and one wonders whether Kate's response to his evident wariness is not reflected in her poem, published in *Our Continent* in April, 1882, "With Her Picture":

> Shade of my wayward face,
>   Painted in daring gold,
> Win thou my lover's praise
>   Passionately bold!
>
> . . . .
>
> Till I, who wait a sign,
>   Hear through the dusk my name,
> And know his heart, like mine,
>   Eternally aflame!

In her fiction appears another pattern that also seems relevant here. Beginning at the time of the divorce suit, Sherwood Bonner produced a series of stories about women deceived or abandoned by their lovers. To this group belong "The Case of Eliza Bleylock," published in March, 1881; "Two Storms," published the following month; and "On the Nine-Mile," published in May, 1882. The last, striking in its bitterness, chronicles the history of a simple farm girl of the Illinois prairie who, after being maimed in an accident, discovers that her fiancé now finds her an unsuitable mate. He must have a proper farmer's wife—strong, vigorous, unimpaired. The depth of feeling in this work may well be traceable to the author's own fear that the divorce made her "unsuitable" for marriage. "I find myself continually whispering that verse which says 'Lover and friend has thou put far from me—' and I find no courage to beat back the wild sad thoughts that crowd on me," Kate had told Longfellow after she returned to Holly Springs with the divorce. By the time that she wrote "On the Nine-Mile," however, she was also acutely conscious of a graver matter.[43]

"There is *something*—I know not what—a hard lump or swelling—growing on my breast!" she had confided to Longfellow in August of 1881, and she had continued:

> *I* who have been so well—so strong—What it is I know not—I have seen but one medical man, an old friend of my father's, and he will give me *no* assurance that it is harmless—but strongly advises that I go East at once and see Dr. Hamilton or some eminent surgeon. He says he does not think it cancer—that my blood is too pure—but it is something on the bone. It hurts—or burns—all the time—and as I pace up and down my room—holding my hand on an iced cloth over the place—you may imagine how I seem to myself one of the lost in the Halls of Eblis—I do not mind dying—but suffering—ah! no, no! my flesh shrinks, my spirit fails—I try not to imagine what may be before me.

Perhaps it was fear, or the apparent glow of health that she saw reflected each day in her mirror, or her concern with other matters—but for some reason she put off seeking an expert medical opinion until the next spring. By this time, her closest friends had become insistent.[44]

On the fourth of March, the division of Dr. Bonner's estate was legally recorded, and Kate had purchased Ruth's share in Bonner House. She wrote Longfellow directly afterward, telling him of the persistence of the pain in her breast, expressing her fears about medical expenses, and asking him again for financial help. In his response, he promised her aid "after the middle of the month." When that time came, however, the feeble old poet was confined to his bed. On the twenty-fifth, Kate received the news that he had died.[45]

43. Memphis *Avalanche*, July 21, 1881, p. 3, and November 30, 1881, p. 3; McDowell to Longfellow, August 7, 1881, in Longfellow Collection.

44. McDowell to Longfellow, August 7, 1881, in Longfellow Collection; Bondurant, "Sherwood Bonner," 53.

45. Deed Book 47, p. 44, Marshall County Courthouse, Holly Springs. This correspondence between Kate McDowell and Longfellow has not survived, but it is discussed and

With Longfellow's passing, Kate McDowell lost her greatest bulwark. He had introduced her into the great world, encouraged and sponsored her work, and provided her with sympathy, understanding, and important financial support. She had often manipulated him, but she had also loved him. "To me through many years he was such a friend as I can never hope to have again," Kate wrote the poet's daughter Alice, "strengthening faith, reanimating courage, sustaining my faltering steps, keeping hope alive in my heart. In the wild misery that followed the cruel death of my father and my brother, when it seemed as if reason itself would desert me, dear dear Mr. Longfellow sorrowed with me and helped me to live through the dark days. Now he too has gone, and my world is desolated."[46]

Longfellow's death had also placed Kate in desperate financial straits, and she inquired tactfully about the letter she had written him immediately before he died—a letter thanking him for his assurance of aid. Alice Longfellow dispatched a prompt reply, sending the money her father had pledged. Kate sent back a long letter of thanks, which contains a touching account of her situation. "Since the fever one care after another has been thrust upon me, until I almost sink under unlooked for burdens," she told Alice Longfellow. "Up to that time I believe I had scarcely done more than play with life." And she concluded her thanks with an honest and brave statement: "I do not win for myself a selfish ease. With my home free from encumbrance, and my beautiful child to educate, I shall have all that I can do. Yet *now* I see light ahead—and before, I dared not look into the future. The chilling fear would cross my mind—that art is cruelly intolerant of the necessity of making a living—and that my work must suffer from the obligation I was under to earn money. But now I am strong and full of hope." Her writing of course had often suffered from the financial pressures upon her, and it would continue to, but these are brave words from a woman who was becoming deeply worried about her health.[47]

Evidently immediately after writing Alice Longfellow and pay-

---

quoted from in two letters from Mrs. McDowell to Alice Longfellow, April 5 and April 28, 1882, at the Longfellow Historic Site.

46. McDowell to Alice Longfellow, April 5, 1882.

47. McDowell to Alice Longfellow, April 28, 1882.

ing Judge Orlando Davis half of the thousand-dollar debt, Kate McDowell left Holly Springs to see physicians in New Orleans. She appeared so healthy that the doctors expressed surprise that she had come, but they sobered as they examined her. At length she demanded the whole truth, and they gave her their opinion: that she had breast cancer in an advanced stage and that she had only a year to live. She took the opinion calmly, and left the building to walk down the streets of a city that she had long loved.[48]

Later in the day she stood beside the desk of Shirley Carter, one of the editors of the New Orleans *Times-Democrat*. Kate was probably staying in the city with her friend Cora Carey, and since Mrs. Carey later wrote for that newspaper, it is probable that Kate had gone to recommend her friend to Carter. Whatever the reason for this first meeting with Kate McDowell on the day that she received her death warrant, Carter has left a remarkable account. Like so many men before him, the editor felt immediately her powerful attraction. "Her superb physique, her imperial step, her fearless eyes will always be remembered as a revelation of material beauty not often seen," he later wrote. "There was a tropical abundance about her that gave an impression of inexhaustible vitality, and an incommunicable charm of manner which, allied with magnetism of her wonderful eyes, made captives of all who came within her orbit." For Carter, she was "an enchantress, smiling at me with vivid brightness and talking gaily of trivial things." Quickly the conversation took a more intimate turn, and the editor began to think her a kind of genius. "There was an infusion of new and radical ideas all through her fluent speech which sparkled with pungent surprises but was not tarnished by a plebeian shock," Carter remembered. "She had clearly cast off the old lines of thought which she considered to have had their uses, borne their fruits, passed into the limbo of worn-out things." She then came to a discussion of "the moral uses of dark" experiences, and finding her new friend such a sympathetic presence, she unexpectedly began sobbing. To the startled Carter, the sophisticated literary lady suddenly seemed "a heart-broken little child." As she told him the news that she had been given that day, it struck him that

48. Custody Suit; Bondurant, "Sherwood Bonner," 53.

"her power to suffer was in proportion to her power to enjoy." It seemed to him "while she spoke of leaving her beautiful little daughter and the dependent household in the dear old homestead that she would die of anguish." After a time, however, Kate made a magnificent recovery of her spirits; and she left him vowing to allow "no room for depressions." She had also left with him an indelible impression of her beauty, her charm, and her courage.[49]

Kate kept the vow made in Shirley Carter's office. She came back to Bonner House with so many plans that there was no time for grief. Hiding the truth of her condition from her family and all but a couple of Holly Springs friends, she announced that she was going to Boston for several months in the interests of her literary career and for further medical opinions. On May 25 she departed Holly Springs to go north for the last time.[50]

So many times now for the last decade Kate had made this trip to Boston from the South. She must have felt in some moods that the last ten years had been simply years of travel, dictated by the complex demands of her circumstances. And she had come to Boston particularly in so many different guises—first, as the confused but determined Mrs. McDowell, fleeing home and family and intent upon realizing her own talents; next, as the confident, magnetic literary lady Sherwood Bonner, who both outraged and charmed; then, as the head of the small close family at the Hotel Boylston, who had discovered that past sins against convention could not be erased; and, now, as the sick woman, hiding her illness from her family and working desperately to amass as much money for them as she could. The four years since the fever had been bitter ones for her, but she voiced no complaints now. "Her health, which had been as rare and noticeable as her beauty, was gone forever," wrote a friend. "But her youthfulness, her buoyant, indomitable spirit were not gone; and her courage was only beginning."[51]

Kate spent the first few weeks in Boston consulting various doctors and listening to a great many contradictory diagnoses before

49. Carter, "Sherwood Bonner."
50. George R. Stephenson, "Sherwood Bonner" (1932 typescript in Stephenson Collection), 20; Bondurant, "Sherwood Bonner," 53; Holly Springs *Reporter*, May 25, 1882, p. 3.
51. Sophia Kirk, preface to *Suwanee River Tales*, viii.

placing herself under the care of one physician. She made a strange choice, Dr. Richard C. Flower, whom she described as "eclectic—magnetic—spiritualistic—heaven knows what? No end of a quack the allopaths would say!" But this ambiguous medical figure had gained her confidence. Once again she had responded to personality, not principle; and the doctor had obviously responded to her. He placed her in a sanatorium for his patients on James Street, came to her instead of requiring she come to his office, and made himself so generally interesting, she wrote, that "I think we both rather forget that I am the victim of a fell disease." This was the tone she sustained in her conversation and especially in her letters home. Writing to Mrs. Addison Craft, whose husband, Helen's brother, had handled Kate's business affairs in Holly Springs for the past two years, the invalid showed her old spirit, but also a new sense of peace: "Tell Helen my steady diet of reading is Marcus Aurelius—delightful old stoic. I have learned a great many philosophical lessons from him—how to die with decency and courage—and to live without vain delusions and impossible hopes. I read choice extracts to my Doctor occasionally—and so the days glide along. . . . And tell Mr. Add . . . I *wish* he could make some money for me. . . . To be ill and hard up too does crowd things too much. Marcus Aurelius *never* had such troubles as mine! and in his most vexatious times he could console himself by burning a few Christians. However, I won't complain. For after all the wind has been a good deal tempered."[52]

Dr. Flower did not allow her to write more than three hours a day, but in the allotted time she was working diligently. Sherwood Bonner had published nothing in the four months following a sketch of mountain life, "The Bran Dance at the Apple Settlement," which had appeared in a November 1881 issue of *Harper's Weekly*. There had been the division of her father's estate to arrange and her family to settle in Bonner House. But during the winter and spring, in spite of growing concern about her health, Kate had written three stories, which appeared in April and May issues of Harper publications. In the first months at Dr. Flower's sanatorium she wrote two light, entertaining tales set at the time

52. Kate McDowell to Mrs. Addison Craft, June 24, 1882, in Craft Collection.

of the Van Dorn raid on Holly Springs, one of which she placed in the new Philadelphia magazine *Our Continent* and the other in the *Weekly*. A primary reason for coming north, however, had been to collect some of her stories and have Harper and Brothers bring them out in book form. In mid July, she journeyed to New York to see Joseph Harper, and on the eighteenth the contract for *Dialect Tales* was signed. The volume would collect eight of her best stories from Harper publications and two from *Lippincott's*, and she agreed to write an additional story to lead it off.[53]

She returned to Boston, tired by her effort; but she was soon surrounded again by the old friends who came often to James Street. The Capens, Nellie Willard, and Carrie Jenness Osgood were all faithful. More than anyone else, however, in the early Boston months, it was Mrs. Sarah Selmes on whom Kate again leaned; and in gratitude Kate dedicated *Dialect Tales* to her: "To my dear friend Mrs. S. B. S. with love and gratitude: Her angel face, / As the great eye of Heaven, shined bright, / and made a sunshine in a shady place." There were other friends too. Sophie Shepard, Kate's intimate from the Hamner Hall days, was now living in Dorchester. Still unmarried, Sophie had long ago shared Kate Bonner's literary ambitions. It was she who had first corresponded with Nahum Capen, and after thirteen years she had moved to Dorchester to be near her mentor. The schoolgirl bonds of the past were immediately renewed. But there was another friendship that was to become even more important. Kate had maintained her ties with the Kirk family of Philadelphia, particularly with William Kirk, who had become a prominent doctor. Now she found William's older sister Sophia in Boston; and the sister was drawn as strongly to her as the brother had been years before.[54]

For the most part, Kate kept her thoughts of death hidden even from her Boston intimates. But in late July, she went to Ipswich with the Selmeses; walking along the seashore with Mrs. Selmes

53. Contract for *Dialect Tales*, in Harper Brothers Collection, Butler Library, Columbia University.
54. McDowell to Craft, June 24, 1882, in Craft Collection; Elizabeth Capen to Ruth McDowell, July 31, 1883, in Stephenson Collection; Kate Bonner Diary (MS in McDowell Collection); Boston City Directories, 1880–1883; Deed Book 47, p. 273, Marshall County Courthouse.

and staring out at the limitless ocean, Kate felt the power of death. "Failure or success will mean nothing to me then," she said. "The line is mine—'nor fame nor shame, can scale a churchyard wall.'" Like others of those who have met early deaths, Kate had always had an almost morbid consciousness of her mortality, engendered perhaps by the sights of her sister and mother dying when she was just a girl. She had felt deeply the line that she appropriated as her own, first, in Rome as she had stood over the grave of Keats— another always aware of the specter and fated to meet it early. But Kate had subsequently changed the line. In Rome, she had quoted it as "Nor shame, nor fancy"; by 1881, when she used it in *The Valcours*, *fancy* had been replaced by *fame*. The altered verse was more appropriate for Kate McDowell: her last months were to be a struggle between her ambition and drive and the pull of death.[55]

In the fall, as her body grew weaker, her spirit actually seemed to strengthen, and she insisted that she would get well. But by winter the truth of her condition was clear to all the Boston friends. She had started several tales and finished one, "The Gentlemen of Sarsar," a story that attacked the hot-blooded chivalric and military tradition of the South. This was the work to begin *Dialect Tales*. Sophia Kirk helped her in reading proof for the volume, and by February, when the book was in the printer's hands, Kate decided to return to Holly Springs. Although insisting that the return home would restore her health, she surely knew that she was going home to die. Sophia Kirk had now become so closely attached to Kate that she could not let her go alone. After leaving Boston, the two evidently paused in Philadelphia; and on March 7, 1883, they arrived in Holly Springs.[56]

So Kate came back, just a few days after her thirty-fourth birthday, to Lilian and Aunty, to Bonner House, to Holly Springs. A shockingly altered woman stepped off the train that day, but a woman who by her own buoyant spirits tried to keep up those of her family and friends. Her days she filled with as much activity as

55. McDowell to Craft; "In Memoriam: Sherwood Bonner," Holly Springs *South*, n.d., in Craft Collection.
56. "Sherwood Bonner," *Harper's Weekly*, August 11, 1883, p. 503; Custody Suit; Capen to McDowell, July 31, 1883, in Stephenson Collection.

she could. *Dialect Tales* was published within the month. Soon afterward the local bookstore was advertising it for sale, and she sent to the Holly Springs *Reporter* a review that placed her volume in the tradition begun by Bret Harte's *Overland* stories. She had now determined to bring out the Christmas juvenile that she so long talked about, and she began collecting and revising the stories for it. When her right hand became paralyzed, she dictated to Sophia, trying as she revised the Gran'mammy tales to gain a clearer focus by dramatizing more and excising most of the exposition. She was also planning a third collection of her fiction to be named *Romances by Sherwood Bonner*, and she was dictating a novel. In all this work she was driven by two forces—her determination to leave something by which the world would remember Sherwood Bonner and her concern that Lilian and Aunty be provided for. Even as her suffering became intense, she refused opiates. Her mind had to be clear for her work.[57]

Through all the work and the pain, Kate still wanted to be a part of the life of her family and of the town. Lilly and Mary McDowell were traveling in Europe, but Kate was reconciled with Ruth, and she enjoyed her frequent visitors, especially the old school friends. The town had never recovered from the loss of its leaders in the fever, but now five years later there were some signs of activity, and she took pleasure in the excitement caused by the telephone lines just going up. She and Sophia also attended the meetings of the Musical and Literary Society, which had been formed by Mrs. Freeman after the fever. Kate insisted on being hostess for the June first meeting, for which she arranged an essay by Helen Craft's husband, music by Miss Lula Potts, and a reading by Sophia. Then abruptly on Monday, May 28, she canceled the meeting, and with Sophia she made a sudden trip to Memphis.[58]

Kate may well have gone to Memphis for medical attention, as she was often now in terrible pain. The two women remained

57. [Helen Craft Anderson], "In Memoriam," Holly Springs *Reporter*, August 16, 1883, p. 3; Review of *Dialect Tales*, Holly Springs *Reporter*, April 26, 1883, p. 3; Sophia Kirk, preface to *Suwanee River Tales*, vi, iii; Gilligan, "Sherwood Bonner," 58, 64; Stephenson, "Sherwood Bonner," 20.

58. Holly Springs *Reporter*, February 16, March 22, 1882, May 24, May 31, June 7, June 28, 1883.

there a week, however, and they were lodged, not with Kate's friends as had been her custom for a decade, but in a hotel. It is known that the following Friday they were entertained at a luncheon by Elizabeth Meriwether. What is not known is whether Kate had come also for a final meeting with Colton Greene—and, if she had, whether he gave her his promise to make Lilian's future secure. That possibility seems likely, for it was evidently afterward that Kate completed her last story with a hero bearing the initials C. G. Within the month, just as he had done after her divorce, the General left the city, this time for a six-week stay in New York.[59]

Back in Holly Springs, Kate continued her dictation amid increasing pain and oppressive weather broken every few days by violent thunderstorms. Late in June, Margaret Kellar came from Memphis for what she knew would be a last visit with Kate. "She loved life, and all bright things this beautiful world can give," Mrs. Kellar later wrote. "She was not one of earth's meek and lowly angels, that are supposed to have a royalty of unselfish goodness. Yet no saint ever showed more thoughtful forbearance or tender solicitude for the happiness and comfort of those about her. Her nature was full of grandeur, and loyalty, and ambition. In the midst of the worst human suffering her gay, bright witticisms rang out, and her clear smile shone." With a gay courage, the invalid had asked her friends to suggest epitaphs, and she selected "She was much loved." On July thirteenth, Kate had her will witnessed by Sophia and two friends from girlhood, Clara Clayton Fant and Sallie Lea Calhoun. The document left everything to Lilian, appointed Aunt Martha and Addison Craft as executors, and expressed "the ardent wish and sincere desire of my heart that my Aunt Martha Bonner shall have the care, custody, and control of the person of my daughter." Someone was now with Kate every moment of the day—either Lilian, Aunty, Sophia, or the old friend and now gentle nurse Ella Topp. In this hopeless state, Kate continued to dictate. Five days after she had signed her will, in the middle of a sentence she was dictating came a long pause. Sophia Kirk looked up into Kate's face. The sufferer had clearly seen the specter. Her literary labor

59. Memphis *Avalanche*, May 29, June 3, July 5, August 31, 1883.

was now over, and for the next four days, in her moments of consciousness Kate's amazing spirit found voice only rarely. "Why I have just begun to write!" she uttered one day; and with almost her last words she said, "It is not death I dread." On Sunday evening, July 22, 1883, Kate McDowell died at Bonner House with the dignity and composure that she had wished and willed. In her death, the romantic young girl Kate Bonner had become the heroine she had always wanted to be.[60]

60. Kellar, "Sherwood Bonner"; "Sherwood Bonner," *Harper's Weekly*; Estate Papers; Custody Suit; Sophia Kirk, preface to *Suwanee River Tales*, viii.

Chapter Seven

The Later Stories and *The Valcours*

THE FICTION THAT Sherwood Bonner wrote during the last five years of her life, the most productive period of her career, reveals a growth of vision and of technical skill; but the pattern of development is obscured by the presence of considerable hackwork. For much of the time she was writing feverishly to meet the financial demands upon her, and she was often willing to turn out anything that would find a ready market. While her ability to produce marketable fiction for different audiences makes her bibliography a good index to the reading tastes of her time, the entries in that bibliography vary widely in quality.

Sherwood Bonner's work from 1878 to 1883 falls into five general categories: light tales for adults, children's stories, Negro dialect sketches, local color short stories, and romances. The least interesting are the light adult tales—"Maddy Gascar and the Professor," "Peacock Feathers," and "A Shorn Lamb"—all written for *Harper's Weekly* and grouped later under the heading "Four Sweet Girls of Dixie" for her collection *Suwanee River Tales* (Boston: Roberts Brothers, 1884). That heading reflects well the tone and quality of the tales. "A Shorn Lamb," which concerns a girl's sacrifice of her long tresses in order to disguise her Confederate sweetheart as a woman and thus prevent his capture, has more plot than the others. However, the critic Dorothy Gilligan, who found "little to recommend this sketch except the facility with which it is written," may well have spoken the last word on the entire group.[1]

The number of American periodicals catering to juveniles burgeoned after the Civil War, and Sherwood Bonner contributed to the leading journals in the field—*Youth's Companion, St. Nich-*

---

1. Dorothy L. Gilligan, "Life and Works of Sherwood Bonner" (M.A. thesis, George Washington University, 1930), 57.

olas, Wide Awake, and *Harper's Young People.* Some of these contributions were obviously not directed exclusively at children. The Gran'mammy tales, for instance, were among her most popular works for a general audience; and her moving account of the epidemic in Holly Springs, "The Yellow Plague of '78," was not written merely for a group of youthful readers. Other works, however, fit clearly into molds already well established in the juvenile magazines. "The Angel in the Lilly Family," a tale of a large family of dolls, and "The Terrible Adventures of Ourselves and the Marshall," which chronicles the exploits of a group of spiders, both fill their places comfortably among their many counterparts. So do stories like "The End of the Dancing School at Danville," in which a rich, spoiled little girl learns a lesson about selfishness and deceit, after dealing unfairly with her poor, virtuous best friend.

The third category into which Sherwood Bonner's work falls, the Negro dialect sketch, is one in which she was a pioneer. The first of her Gran'mammy tales appeared in 1875, three years before the publication of Irwin Russell's celebrated Negro dialect poem "Christmas Night in the Quarters" and five years before Joel Chandler Harris' Uncle Remus tales reached a national audience. Her 1878 novel *Like unto Like* contains a reference to the Tar Baby story a year before Harris first presented the tale to the readers of the Atlanta *Constitution,* and in "Two Storms" (1881) Sherwood Bonner too gave her version of the fable. This, however, was her only use of folk tale, and most of her Negro dialect pieces are simply humorous anecdotes.

The two most popular of the sketches have been "Aunt Anniky's Teeth" and "Hieronymus Pop and the Baby." In the first, Aunt Anniky, an esteemed Negro nurse, is rewarded for caring for her former mistress by a gift of her choice—a set of false teeth. But the teeth are destroyed by another of her patients, an old colored man Uncle Ned, who in his delirium mistakes the dentures for ice. Though the accident breaks Ned's fever, he thinks Anniky has played a joke on him, and he refuses to give her the pig that he had promised in payment for her nursing. Finally the two disputants submit to the arbitration of their former master who, failing to convince Ned that he must pay, hits upon the idea of the marriage of Ned and Anniky—the pig thus becoming community property.

The two agree to this solution, and the arbitrator offers a second set of teeth as a wedding gift. But irreconcilable differences become apparent, and Ned sends a letter reneging on his promise:

> "Anniky Hobbleston," he began, "dat weddin' aint a-gwine ter come off. You cleans up too much ter suit me. I ain't used ter so much water splashin' aroun'. Dirt is warmin'. Spec' I'd freeze dis winter if you wuz here. An' you got too much tongue. Besides I's got anudder wife over in Tipper. An' I ain't a-gwine ter marry. As fur havin' de law, I'se a-leavin' dese parts, an' I takes de pigs wid me. Yer can't fin *dem*, and yer can't fin *me*. *Fur I ain't a-gwine ter marry.* I wuz born a bachelor, an' a bachelor will I represent myself befo' de judgment-seat."

But when the daughter from the big house conveys Ned's message and her own sympathy, it is Aunt Anniky who has the last word: "'It's all right,' said that sensible old soul . . . with a cheerful laugh. 'Bless you, chile, it wuz de teef I wanted, not de man.'"[2]

"Hieronymus Pop," considered for decades a masterpiece in the genre, concerns the misadventures of a young black boy left in charge of his baby brother. Handsomely illustrated by A. B. Frost, the tale opens with the mother's instructions to Hieronymus: "'Now, 'Onymus Pop,' said the mother of that gentle boy, 'you jes take keer of dis chile while I'm gone ter de hangin'. An' don't you leave dis house on no account, not if de skies fall an' de earth opens ter swaller yer.'" The boy eventually decides to put his crying and wretchedly hot baby brother in a bucket and lower him to the bottom of the deep, cool well. The parents return, a frantic search ensues, and the tale ends with the boy's father leading him firmly off to the woodpile.[3]

These two sketches, like Sherwood Bonner's others in the genre, provide comic pictures of an illiterate and childlike, though often crafty, black peasantry. Though few readers today would find them of literary value, for fifty years after the author's death these pieces were the only work that kept Sherwood Bonner's name before the public. "Aunt Anniky's Teeth" was reprinted by Kate Sanborn in her *Wit of Women* (New York: Funk & Wagnalls, 1885). "Hieronymus Pop and the Baby" was included in two collections—*Humorous Masterpieces from American Literature*, ed.

2. "Aunt Anniky's Teeth," *Harper's Weekly*, June 3, 1882, pp. 347–48.
3. "Hieronymus Pop and the Baby," *Harper's*, LXI (June, 1880), 20–24.

Edward Mason (New York: Putnam's, 1888), and *Library of Southern Literature*, ed. Edwin Anderson Alderman and Joel Chandler Harris (Atlanta: Martin & Hoyt, 1907). Three of the late (and inferior) Gran'mammy tales were collected in *Little Classics of the South: Mississippi* (New York: Purdy Press, 1927). Remarkably enough, it is also the Negro dialect sketches that account for the reprinting in the last decade of Sherwood Bonner's two volumes of short fiction, *Dialect Tales* and *Suwanee River Tales*—both appearing as entries in The Black Heritage Library Collection (Freeport, New York: Books for Libraries Press, 1972). Obviously, the interest underlying this recent re-publication is sociological and historical, rather than literary.

Sherwood Bonner's contributions in another category have held up better over time. The local color short stories show well both her development as a writer and her place in literary history. It is striking that, of this group of eight stories, none is set in the cotton-producing part of the South where Sherwood Bonner was born and where she set a number of the light adult tales, children's stories, and, of course, the Negro dialect sketches. It is also interesting that when cultures other than her native one came under her scrutiny her attitude was more harshly judgmental. The result was a group of stories that combined local color interest with marks of the critical realism that would increasingly stamp serious American literature in the decades following her death.

This direction in her literary development first became apparent in the group of stories set in the Cumberland mountains. Of the four, "The Bran Dance at the Apple Settlement" is closest to a simple local color sketch, basing its appeal on the rustic charm and strangeness of these mountaineers. The principal speaker—one Jack Officer, a better educated mountain man than most, who regularly reads the Bible and a weekly newspaper—begins the piece with a description of the Apple family:

> They pretty much rule things round here. 'F one of 'em takes a fancy to a good-lookin' girl, the other boys keep away—they are shooters, them Apples. Thar's a powerful lot of 'em. Old Grandpa Apple—him that started the settlement—is a-livin' yet. He come over from Carliny some sixty years back, in a canopied waggin, with all he had, includin' his gret-uncle, ready to light out fur Jordan, an' a yaller dog—female, that's mothered the best breed o' pups on the mountain. He had two

blooded cows, an' a starvin' young woman for a wife; an' calves an' children came's fast's he could house 'em—faster too, I recken, for they had to tent it one hot summer. The boys they growed up, an' they married aroun' the country, an' somehow they've had luck—big, smart, han'some families. An' their childern is a-marryin' an' child-bearin'. So, you see, old Grandpa Apple he sees the fourth generation. An' I guess the Lord ain't any pleaseder in surveyin' the earth he has made than that old man is a-countin' Apple noses.

This patriarch, Grandpa Apple, who resembles "Santa Claus or the Old Year," presides over the bran dance from his rambling house of logs "worn to a rich polish." The narrator draws a comparison with Hogarth's prints in evoking the scene—the dancing to the fiddling in a rustic arbor and the partaking of Cumberland punch, pure moonshine whiskey. Obviously influenced by the success of Mary Noailles Murfree's first Cumberland story "The Dancin' Party at Harrison's Cove," Sherwood Bonner is here simply drawing quaint pictures of mountain life.[4]

In contrast to the "Bran Dance" sketch, her other three mountain pieces are short stories, and in them Sherwood Bonner attempts a franker treatment of the genteel Miss Murfree's usual young Cumberland heroine. In "Jack and the Mountain Pink," in fact, Sherwood Bonner was among the first writers to introduce what would become a definite stereotype, the sexually promiscuous mountain girl. "I envy you," says an old Nashville man to the young dandy Selden, who is setting out for a Cumberland excursion. "I was brought up in the mountain country fifty years ago. Gay young buck I was! Go in, my boy, and make love to a mountain pink! Ah, those jolly, barefooted, melting girls! No corsets, no back hair, no bangs, by Heaven!" The undercurrent of sensuality is remarkable for local color, though Sherwood Bonner treats the stereotype ironically. Sincerity Hicks, the mountain pink whom Selden meets, is somber, wooden, rough; and she is his superior in strength and physical skill. He can admire her cunning as she aids the escape of a moonshiner from the revenuer who has captured him, but Selden concludes: "A mountain pink! . . . Oh no, a bean stalk—a Cumberland bean stalk."[5]

4. "The Bran Dance at the Apple Settlement," *Harper's Weekly*, November 19, 1881, pp. 779–80.
5. "Jack and the Mountain Pink," *Harper's Weekly*, January 29, 1881, pp. 75–76. Sherwood Bonner's early use of the stereotype was first noted by Merrill Maguire Skaggs,

The mountain pinks in the remaining two stories are presented neither as possibly desirable mistresses nor as Miss Murfree's chaste heroines, but as victims of a crude and brutal culture. "The Case of Eliza Bleylock" concerns two sisters. According to their mother's accurate reading of character, Janey, who constantly fights with her intended, the moonshiner Dick Oscar, is a "spit-fire," while Eliza is different from the usual mountain girl: "Now, Lizy is different. Can't tell why, less'n 'tis I want to camp-meetin' and' perfessed a while befo' she wuz born. Somehow she's always been delicater an' quieter like 'n any of my childern." Eliza shyly accepts the attentions of a disguised revenuer, but she refuses to reveal to him the location of Dick Oscar's still. It is instead Janey, in a fit of rage with Dick Oscar, who proves the traitor. Later, having experienced a change of heart, the fiery girl walks to Nashville and persuades the governor to commute the sentences of the men she has betrayed. But she cannot admit that she had been the informer, and the whole community, including the girls' father, blame Eliza. Unable to bear her state as a pariah, Eliza finally dies "with very little said about it, in the valley."[6]

"Lame Jerry" presents an even gloomier picture. The title character has been an informer in order to get enough money to take his epileptic daughter Cordy away from the mountains. Beaten and almost killed by vengeful moonshiners, Lame Jerry is nursed back to health only to discover that Cordy has taken up with Discoe, a rough mountain man. Waiting weeks for the proper moment, Jerry ambushes Discoe and kills the man who has ruined his daughter. Then he goes to Discoe's cabin to find his daughter and take her away. But the slow-witted girl, who has been happy with Discoe, is only confused by her father's appearance. "You didn't think you wuz doin' anything wrong to take up with Discoe—and no preacher to make it honest?" he asks. "I didn't know what to do. They said you wuz dead," she responds. "An' Discoe said he'd like to have me. An' he's a nice, well-made man. An' I wuz so dull with fright an' grief that I didn't much care. But I care now. An' he's going to marry me, pappy, when—when the baby comes." Refusing to let her father take her away, Cordy awaits Discoe's return

The Folk of Southern Fiction (Athens, Ga.: University of Georgia Press, 1972), 151. Skaggs's book also contains excellent discussions of eight other Bonner stories.
    6. "The Case of Eliza Bleylock," *Harper's Weekly*, March 5, 1881, pp. 155–56.

through the long weeks of her pregnancy. Both mother and baby die in childbirth, and the grieving Jerry continues to live in the hated mountains, though more like an animal than a man.[7]

The four Tennessee stories form a fascinating group for viewing the effects of late-nineteenth-century literary movements upon Sherwood Bonner. She had appropriated Miss Murfree's mountain setting and characters, but she then offered a variety of treatments of the locale, ranging from the local color quaintness of "The Bran Dance at the Apple Settlement" through the critical realism of "Jack and the Mountain Pink" and "The Case of Eliza Bleylock" to the naturalism of "Lame Jerry," in which she explored the lowest depths of mountain life, the squalid lives of its doomed creatures. No group of stories by a contemporary writer reflects so well the pattern of development in American literature from the Civil War to the end of the nineteenth century.

As interesting as the Tennessee pieces are in mirroring Sherwood Bonner's place in literary history, however, her three stories set in Illinois are more successful as works of art. There is greater specificity here, a more vividly realized sense of place, as she uses all the carefully observed cultural detail typical of local color in her exposure of the meanness of a backwater fundamentalist culture. And Sherwood Bonner's growth as an artist is particularly apparent in her skillful use of first-person narrators. All older women wise in the ways of the folk among whom they live, these narrators not only give the reader a vivid sense of their culture, but they also serve as a humanizing norm in the midst of the surrounding pettiness and hypocrisy.

"Sister Weeden's Prayer," the first of the stories to be published, is the simplest and most effective. Beginning with a glimpse of the baptism of the hitherto unregenerate Roland Selph, the narrative moves quickly to a "wool-pickin'" of the Baptist society. There Florindy Daggett asks the group for an opinion on her duty upon discovering another sister in "the act o' backslidin'." As the wise old narrator notes, the whole society warms to the subject: "Well, now, do you know, not one of us had the Christian charity to say, 'Hold you tongue, Florindy.' Truth is, we wuz dyin' to hear what it

7. "Lame Jerry," *Harper's Weekly*, May 28, 1881, p. 346.

wuz: so we jest edged our cheers a little closer together, an' sort of slacked in the wool-pickin'." Sister Daggett reveals that she has discovered the Widow Biscoe and her daughters sewing on Sunday. Silence falls as all await the judgment of Sister Weeden:

> Sister Weeden wuz the impressivest female in the Baptist society. . . . What she said *wuz said.* . . . "I have listened," says she, "an' if what Sister Daggett charges shell be proven true, we must expel Dorothy Bisco from the society an' leave her to the mercy of God."
> Cold shivers ran down our backs: it wuz jest as if she had said *Selah.*

When the Widow Biscoe arrives and is confronted with the charge, she admits that her family had to work through Saturday night and into Sunday in order to make Roland Selph proper clothes for his baptism. Another silence falls upon the society until Sister Weeden again breaks it, this time with a prayer:

> Down we all knelt promiscuous, the wool a-scatterin from our laps, an' Sister Weeden, without stoppin' a minute to think up her words— for prayin' comes to her by nature—began: "O Father, our hearts is vile an' unclean as the wool we've been pickin' out this day; quick to catch at evil as sheep's back to catch at brambles an' briers in pushin' through a thicket; clogged with meanness an' jealousies an' suspicions, till they're got no will nor power to be harmonious with thy Spirit, which is love. O Lord, we'd give up, despairin', if it wuzn't that immortal patience can cleanse them of trash that defiles; if it wuzn't that Immanuel's blood can wash the blackness of blackness away; if it wuzn't that we knew forgiveness wuz held out free as long as breath held body an' soul together. Every day Satan dangles some new temptation before us, an' we fall inter sin. Most especial to-day hev we failed in charity toward our sister here, condemnin' her without a hearin', an' never a-dreamin' that it wuz the Lord's work to which she give his day, as sinless as the act of Him who plucked the ears of corn an' wuz reproached by the lip-servin' Jews. Put it inter her heart, O Father, to pardon us without much more said about it. All for the dear sake of him who died for us. Amen."

With the prayer, a truer, if still somewhat limited, Christian spirit carries the day—but not before Sherwood Bonner has exposed the narrowness bred by fundamentalist religion.[8]

In the last and the weakest of the Illinois sequence, "The Tender

8. "Sister Weeden's Prayer," *Lippincott's*, n.s., I (April, 1881), 399–404.

Conscience of Mr. Bobberts," which was published after Sherwood Bonner's death, she returns to the vicious effects of primitive religion upon a community. But in the middle story, "On the Nine-Mile," another sort of cruelty is the subject. Though the story is often humorously told by the wise and crafty old widow Aunt Fonie, and though it ends with two happy marriages, at its center "On the Nine-Mile" is the bitterest story that Sherwood Bonner wrote. Janey Burridge, the daughter of the household in which Aunt Fonie is boarding, is the most popular girl on the Nine-Mile prairie when she accepts the suit of a young farmer, Charlie Winn. Amid preparations for the wedding, Janey is maimed when she falls upon the blades of a reaper. After almost dying, she finds that Charlie Winn has changed his mind about the marriage:

> "But you know, Janey," he stammered—"you know a man hes to marry a woman ter do her shear o' the work. And you can't do anything."
> "True," says Janey, speakin' very loud an' harsh, "I'm laid on the shelf. An' of course a man marries a woman ter have his meals cooked reg'lar, an' the harvestin' tended to, an' the lard tried out, an' the apple-butter made, an' the geese plucked, an' the house cleaned, an' the washin' done on Monday, an' the mendin' Saturday, an' the odd jobs on Sunday."

This cruel experience behind her, Janey eventually marries a former alcoholic whom she has regenerated. But with Janey's rejection at the hands of Charlie Winn, Sherwood Bonner concludes an exploration—undertaken in "The Case of Eliza Bleylock" and "Lame Jerry" and the romances "A Volcanic Interlude" and "Two Storms"—of the victimization, betrayal, and abandonment of women. And "On the Nine-Mile" offers bitter commentary on the uses of women in the man-woman relationship.[9]

After examining critically these mountain and prairie cultures, when Sherwood Bonner wrote another southern story for the volume *Dialect Tales*, in which she was collecting her late local color works, she produced a work radically different from her earlier Deep South pieces. In "The Gentlemen of Sarsar," Ned Merewether, a romantic, pompous young city man, goes to the remote community of Sarsar to collect a debt of the local chieftain Cap-

9. "The Tender Conscience of Mr. Bobberts," *Harper's Weekly*, March 22, 1884, pp. 190–92; "On the Nine-Mile," *Harper's*, LXIV (May, 1882), 918–28.

tain Andy Rucker, who forces Ned to take part in a "nigger hunt," during which he is led to believe that he has killed the quarry. As a result, the young dupe is happy just to get out of the place and leave the money behind. Obviously Sherwood Bonner has drawn upon a definite tradition here—the southwest-humor tale in which a foppish narrator becomes the victim of a backwoodsman's elaborate and brutal hoax. But she bends some of the old conventions in order to make a contemporary statement.[10]

Rucker and his companions live in the backcountry, but they are not conventional backwoodsmen. In a true southwest-humor story, in fact, they would be considered gentlemen, for their speech is that of educated men, the Captain himself even quoting Shakespeare and Scott. Bonner also links these "gentlemen" with the southern military tradition. Much of Captain Rucker's authority stems from his having been a Civil War hero, and his band of followers, "rigged out like a lot of banditti," have outfitted themselves with "what was left over from their war equipment"— "horse-pistols and bowie knives, cavalry boots and devil-may-care hats." Clearly here and elsewhere in the story, Bonner is suggesting a connection between the gallantry displayed during the war and a residual postwar brutality. Though she did not return directly to her own southern cotton country in "The Gentlemen of Sarsar," still she was obliquely exposing weaknesses that she saw there.

The best representatives from these first four categories of Sherwood Bonner's work—the light adult tales, children's stories, Negro dialect sketches, and local color short stories—she had assembled before her death for the volumes *Dialect Tales* and *Suwanee River Tales*. With the 1972 re-publication of these collections, these stories are all in print today. But the works in the fifth and final category (which she had also intended collecting as *Romances by Sherwood Bonner*) have been lost, some for a century now, in the files of periodicals of the period; and these romances are among her most interesting works. Even the artistic failures present revealing images of both the writer herself and her era; and the group also contains Sherwood Bonner's best piece of work, her novella *The Valcours*.

Here too, however, Sherwood Bonner's development was any-

10. "The Gentlemen of Sarsar," *Harper's Weekly*, December 16, 1882, pp. 802–804.

thing but consistent. The kind of critic who insists upon finding an
unswerving pattern of development would be hard pressed indeed
to explain the author's last contribution in the category, the post-
humously published "Christmas Eve at Tuckeyhoe," a tale of antebellum North Carolina. Unfortunately, the tone and style of the
story are revealed completely in the opening lines: "I—Angela Violett—do not believe in chance. It was never an aimless, blind god-
dess who pointed the path that led to Tuckeyhoe, but a large-eyed
Fate, serene, amiable, and grand as the Ludovisian Juno, who said,
'Go forward; for your appointed work awaits you.'" Angela next
launches into a description of her uncle Judge Violett, "a fine old
Southern gentleman, with a capacious heart and a sort of passionate fatherliness of nature, if I may so express myself." There is no
irony here, either in the speech of the character, or in the authorial
attitude; and the enchanting Angela and her uncle of the capacious heart make their way through a ridiculously complicated
and contrived plot. After many pages, niece and uncle, who is
grieving for his lost scapegrace son, arrive to spend the Christmas
season at Tuckeyhoe, the plantation of John Erskine, where Angela learns through her suitor Cuthbert Gordon that Erskine's
daughter had broken her father's heart too by eloping with the
family tutor. Through Angela's noble scheming, the runaway couple and their cherubic baby return on Christmas Eve. Erskine is
won over by the sight of his grandchild, the husband turns out to
be Judge Violett's lost son, and Cuthbert Gordon declares himself
to Angela. It remains to mention one final touch. The faithful re-
tainer old Mammy Ann has been freed by Erskine in punishment
for aiding his daughter's elopement. At the end of the tale, the
aged slave returns from her exile and joins in the reunion:

> "I thought I'd make so bold ter offer my ole mars' a Christmas-
> present."
> "What is that?"
> She held out a packet: "Dem ole freedom-papers, mars'."
> He took them from her, laughing.
> "Would you mind lettin' me see 'em burn, Mars' John?"
> Mr. Erskine tossed them on the live hickory coals, and Mammy
> Ann, her face beaming with gratitude, took the [baby] off to bed.

Here Sherwood Bonner, uncharacteristically, has sketched the
stock slavery-loving darkey that Thomas Nelson Page would pre-

sent countless times in the following two decades. Aside from that touch, the story contains little of interest except for a detailed account of Christmas customs on a southern plantation. And from its weaknesses one might well conclude that Sherwood Bonner had shown no development in her romances since "Miss Willard's Two Rings" almost a decade before.[11]

But Sherwood Bonner cannot be judged very accurately on the basis of her last works, written when she was desperately ill. And, to give credit to her literary judgment, she never intended to include "Christmas Eve at Tuckeyhoe" in the projected volume *Romances*. That collection was to contain "A Chance in Life" (an unpublished and unlocated story about which I will have something to say in the final chapter), "The Revolution in the Life of Mr. Balingall," "A Volcanic Interlude," "Two Storms," and *The Valcours*.[12]

Sherwood Bonner applied the term *romance* to any of her works that were love stories or thrillers. It was the mode perhaps most congenial to her, but also the one most dangerous for her as an artist, for in it she could so easily indulge her old taste for sentimentality and melodrama. She had learned as early as "Miss Willard's Two Rings" to give her love tales a coating of local color detail, a technique that she was still using in "Christmas Eve at Tuckeyhoe"; but in the eight years between the two stories she had also proved herself capable of serious and effective work within the mode. Her novel *Like unto Like*, itself a love story, is a case in point, as is "The Revolution in the Life of Mr. Balingall," the first story that she wrote for *Harper's* after the yellow fever epidemic.

The theme of "The Revolution," the appeal of a strong and heroic woman, was one to which Sherwood Bonner was drawn more than once. But the subject here, the epidemic of 1878, was so close and real to the author that it checked her usual tendency in the romances to overdramatize. Earlier in the year in which she wrote "The Revolution," she had produced her moving but restrained nonfiction accounts of the fever. The same restraint is apparent in this her only use of the experience in fiction. The heroine of the story, Idalia Carey, a young woman of "large and noble propor-

11. "Christmas Eve at Tuckeyhoe," *Lippincott's*, n.s., VII (January, 1884), 51–65.
12. Kate McDowell outlined and commented upon the volume *Romances* on the back of an envelope, which was in the possession of Sophia Kirk in 1930. Miss Kirk transcribed the notations for Dorothy Gilligan (See Gilligan, "Sherwood Bonner," 45, 58).

tions" who seems "to float rather than walk," is obviously based on the author herself. But the plot is drawn from experiences of both the author and Lilly McDowell—Kate's own rush to catch the night train leaving Boston for the South, where her family remained amid the dangers of the fever, and Lilly's even more heroic gesture in going to the dying Will Holland and facing what all considered certain death. But Sherwood Bonner adds a strongly imagined element to give the story its shape. Mr. Balingall, a young doctor, encounters Idalia Carey as she is hurrying to reach the midnight train that will take her to her sweetheart stricken with yellow fever. Despite the protests of her male companion, who is trying to prevent her trip South, Balingall leads the young woman to the station and places her on board the train. This brief encounter changes Balingall's life. With the image of the brave Miss Carey in his mind, he now sees the shallowness and frivolity of both his fiancée and the life he has planned for himself. Subsequently he breaks his engagement and goes to the southern town that has been ravaged by the epidemic, where he finds that the young woman's sweetheart has died of the fever and that she remains there lost in sad memories. Balingall stays in the town, establishing a practice, helping to revive the people's spirit, and watching from a distance the care-worn young woman. Sherwood Bonner rejects the conventional conclusions, a marriage and a happy ending, nor does she exploit the opportunities for pathos in the story, and the style itself reflects her control of the material. Take this passage describing the race to the train:

> They started off, the girl almost leading with quick, long steps. She would not take the arm of either young man, but walked between them in a silence so magnetic that the whole air seemed to vibrate with her pain. The rain was falling faster now. Around the lamp-posts were little circles of light, and each interval of gloom, as they passed from one to another, seemed longer and blacker than the last. Mr. Balingall felt himself in a dream where all is unreal and nothing natural. The only words that would have come to his lips, had he spoken, would have been: "I did not think a woman could take such long steps."

There is a great distance between the style of "Christmas Eve at Tuckeyhoe" and this.[13]

13. "The Revolution in the Life of Mr. Balingall," *Harper's*, LIX (October, 1879), 753–63.

Sherwood Bonner had quite clearly eschewed restraint of all sorts, however, when she wrote her next romance, "A Volcanic Interlude." Published in April of 1880, "A Volcanic Interlude" was composed during one of the most difficult periods in the author's life, the time when she was finding herself both shut out of Boston society and faced with staggering financial responsibilities. It was also a time when she was guilty of her worst offenses as a literary opportunist. After having earlier made a trip to the Cumberlands in order to exploit the market recently created by Mary Noailles Murfree, Sherwood Bonner next set out to capitalize even more directly on the success of another southern writer. George Washington Cable's Creole stories, which had been appearing in *Scribner's Monthly* and other leading journals since 1873, were collected in 1879 in the volume *Old Creole Days*, which was enjoying great critical and popular success. At the same time, his novel *The Grandissimes*, appearing in installments in *Scribner's* was also being hailed by enthusiastic readers, among them Henry Wadsworth Longfellow, as a great work in American literature. Cable's influence upon Sherwood Bonner is apparent as early as 1878 in her use of New Orleans material in both *Like unto Like* and "C. G.; or Lilly's Earrings." But in "A Volcanic Interlude," she appropriated not only Cable's setting, but his style, some of his character types, and his most notable theme—all to produce one of the most blatant examples of literary imitation in nineteenth-century American fiction.[14]

Many a Cable story opens with a description of a building in the old quarter of New Orleans, one example being "Café des Exilés," first published in 1876:

> That which in 1835 . . . was a reality in the Rue Burgundy . . . is now but a reminiscence. Yet so vividly . . . at this moment the old Café des Exilés appears before my eyes, floating in the clouds of reverie, and I doubt not I see it just as it was in the old times.
>
> An antiquated story-and-a-half Creole cottage sitting right down on the banquette, as do the Choctaw squaws who sell bay and sassafras and life everlasting, with a high, close board fence shutting out of view the diminutive garden on the southern side. An ancient willow droops over the roof of round tiles, and partly hides the discolored stucco,

14. Edward Wagenknecht, *Longfellow: A Full Length Portrait* (New York: Longmans, Green & Co., 1955), 27.

which keeps dropping off into the garden as though the old café was stripping for a plunge into oblivion—disrobing for its execution. I see, well up in the angle of the broad side gable, shaded by its rude awning of clapboards, as the eyes of an old dame are shaded by her wrinkled hand, the window of Pauline.

Compare the opening of Sherwood Bonner's "A Volcanic Interlude":

> Driving through New Orleans at any time before the war, the stranger could scarcely have failed to notice a quaintly-fashioned house in its luminous heart, where half a century ago the fine old French aristocrats lived in a splendor of light and gay life. The house of which I speak stood in the centre of a blooming square. It was built of stone, but the verandas that ran out from it in all directions, and like spiders' legs gave a disproportionate smallness to the main body from which they sprang, were of light wood twisted and woven and curled in a sort of imitation of bamboo. The house itself looked as hoary as if it had been dug out of the earth and then set upon it; but about these verandas there was a newness, a fresh impertinence, that seemed to laugh in the very face of the old mansion.

After this Cable-like introduction—displaying the same narrative tone, the same architectural interest and sense of atmosphere, and a similar use of metaphor—Sherwood Bonner continues to mine the works of the New Orleans writer. The building that she describes houses the exclusive finishing school of Madame Crozat, which includes among its pupils the three beautiful, pampered daughters of Mr. Dufresne, whose name is the oldest and whose fortune is the largest in all of Louisiana. Sherwood Bonner even hints at her debt here to Cable's De Charleu daughters in "Belles Demoiselles Plantation" by giving a steamboat that appears later in her story the name *Belle Demoiselle.*[15]

For all her imitation, or one should say more accurately her appropriation, Sherwood Bonner's literary skill is apparent as she moves the reader at a quick pace through the story, all the while effectively building suspense for the denouement, which occurs in the garden at the Dufresne plantation. There, after having been informed through the agency of their priest Father Marquette that they are illegitimate, the daughters confront their father and demand to know the identi-

15. George Washington Cable, "Café Des Exilés," in *Old Creole Days* (New York: New American Library of World Literature, Inc., 1961), 74; Sherwood Bonner, "A Volcanic Interlude," *Lippincott's*, XXV (April, 1880), 452–59.

ties of their mothers. Enraged by the haughtiness of the older girls, Dufresne tells the first that she is the child of a "pretty, passionate, ignorant" overseer's daughter and the second that her mother was a promiscuous ballerina. He cannot bring himself, however, to tell his youngest child Zoe of her mother; and finally the priest intervenes:

> "Tell her," said the priest sternly. "Or shall I?"
> "Keep it from her," entreated the father.
> "It is no longer possible," said Father Marquette.—
> "Zoe—be brave, my child—your mother was your grandmother's waiting-maid, a slave. She died, clasping the cross to her bosom, when you were born."
> Another silence, more terrible than the first. Zoe drew herself together like a flower that shrinks when the sun goes down. A small stunned creature, she gazed wide-eyed on the priest, whose words had cast her out from the pleasant land of love and hope to an empty and dreadful isolation.

The tragic consequence of miscegenation that Cable had explored with great sympathy and insight in "Tite Poulette" and *The Grandissimes*, Sherwood Bonner uses in "A Volcanic Interlude" to gain the maximum in melodramatic effect. The tale might most accurately be described, in fact, as a George Washington Cable story by the author of "Laura Capello"; for in the sensationalism of her conclusion and in her creation of Father Marquette, Sherwood Bonner goes back to her oldest literary mode. As her white sisters shrink from her, little Zoe falls prostrate at her father's feet, and the priest springs forward. "This one, at least," he said solemnly, "will belong to God."

"A Volcanic Interlude" produced an immediate stir among readers, and the editor of *Lippincott's* received a number of cancellations to protest his having published the story. Cable had received no such northern response to either "Tite Poulette" or *The Grandissimes*, but of course Sherwood Bonner had gone him one better, appropriating one of his major themes, but giving it a far more sensational treatment. That she was quite aware of what she had done is made clear by two of her own comments. Before the denouement, Dufresne accuses Father Marquette of wanting the daughters told of their illegitimacy only "to take their broken hearts and their unbroken fortunes into the healing shades of a convent." The priest replies, "You make me out quite the conventional priest of a third-class romance." That, of course, as Sherwood Bonner knew, was exactly what she had created. Her second comment is even more enlightening, for it implicitly acknowledges her debt to Cable. On the back of an envelope, where she had written instructions for her collection *Romances*, she noted of "A Volcanic Interlude": "Doubtful as to morality of story but neutralized in the book by abundance of other matter, and worthy, I think, of preservation as a typical Southern story of its kind." She also showed prescience in viewing the work as a contribution to what would almost become a miscegenation genre. During the past twenty years "A Volcanic Interlude" has been included in two anthologies—*The Local Colorists: American Short Stories, 1857–1900*, ed. Claude Simpson (New York: Harper & Brothers, 1960), and *Nineteenth-Century American Short Fiction*, ed. William Holmes and Edward Mitchell (Glenview, Ill.: Scott, Foresman and Company, 1970)—in each case as a "typical Southern story of its kind." [16]

The composition of her next romance was begun during the same trying time in Sherwood Bonner's personal life. On December 8, 1879, she wrote Longfellow that she had finished what she referred to as "my long story" and that she awaited the verdict of Henry Mills Alden, editor of *Harper's*, with "more anxiety than usual." That long story, "Two Storms," did not appear in *Harper's* until April of 1881; obviously Alden had insisted upon revisions. One wonders about the nature of the original submission and of the subsequent changes, for "Two Storms" is the most confused work that Sherwood Bonner ever published, a crazy-quilt of plots and subplots, a pastiche of set-pieces, a confused mixture of literary influences. [17]

The story takes its title from two tropical storms separated by a span of twelve years. In the first, the mother of Dina Mabyn meets her death. In the second, Dina not only learns of the perfidy and lasciviousness of men, but also regains the affection of the father who has ignored her for twelve years in his grief over his wife's death. Most of "Two Storms," however, is devoted to an account of the courtship of Dina by the novelist Marion West, a man twice her age, who rescues her from a scene of violent hoodoo rites to which she has gone with her beloved mammy. Fearing the influence of the

---

16. Gilligan, "Sherwood Bonner," 45.
17. Kate McDowell to Henry Wadsworth Longfellow, December 8 [1879], in Longfellow Collection, Houghton Library, Harvard University.

worldly older man upon the naïve girl, Miss Sims, an old friend of Dina's mother, insists upon taking the virtual orphan in her charge. She removes Dina from her Galveston home to Last Island, a fashionable resort off the Louisiana coast. But West follows and arranges a midnight rendezvous. In the midst of the lover's meeting, a hurricane hits the island. When Dina's father reaches the scene of destruction, his daughter and West are miraculously among the few survivors. West then confesses to Mabyn and Dina that he is a married man, and the girl swoons into the arms of her now loving and caring father. This summary, incredible as it may appear, hardly does justice to the plot of "Two Storms." [18]

Much of the wrenching of plot in the story is due to the fact that "Two Storms" is comprised primarily of a series of set pieces, for which all congruity of story line is sacrificed. The story opens with young Dina weaving flowers into her mother's hair, a scene sketched by Longfellow in a letter to Sherwood Bonner, which she had evidently first used to open one version of her abortive novel *The Prodigal Daughter*. At the time that she was working on this version, she had also hinted that the poet provide her with "a little fairy story for some one to tell my little prodigal." By the time that she incorporated the scene into "Two Storms," however, the fairy story had been discarded for a Negro folk tale, "The Tar Baby," which Maum Dulcie tells the child Dina—an obvious attempt to appeal to a public that was responding so enthusiastically to the work of Joel Chandler Harris. But Harris' influence is not the only one apparent in "Two Storms"; both the conjure woman Sinai and a hoodoo dance scene are a clear debt to George Washington Cable's *The Grandissimes*. These set-pieces are often masterfully rendered by Sherwood Bonner, but they are quite gratuitously included in "Two Storms." [19]

In this pastiche, the author also foregoes any attempt at consistency of characterization. Francis Mabyn, recalling the mad planter Roy Herrick in *Like unto Like*, is first presented as the jealous proprietor of his wife: "He possessed in an extreme degree that sense of appropriation which made it a positive pain that the least

18. "Two Storms," *Harper's*, LXII (April, 1881), 728–48.
19. Sophia Kirk, preface to *Suwanee River Tales*, vii; McDowell to Longfellow, April 30, 1877, in Longfellow Collection.

smile from his wife's eye should shine on another man. All men are more or less Turks at heart, and I really think Francis Mabyn would have liked to shut his wife away in a guarded palace." Later, Mabyn's grief brings obsession and eccentricity. He can think of nothing but speculation in cotton, reading cotton statistics with a deep absorption and then leaving the room always to wash his hands. Thus has mad Roy Herrick metamorphized into Edward McDowell's uncle Robert Mills of Galveston, a most unsettling change. Even stranger is the character Marion West. His being presented as a novelist neither advances the plot nor lends verisimilitude, but it does allow Sherwood Bonner this commentary on the "fashionable author":

> He was certainly quite as clever a man as his admirers supposed him, though in a different way. With a keen intellectual perception and a good memory, he still owed his success in life to a sixth sense with which he was gifted, for so his genius for imitation might be called. He used authors as a chemist his simples, blending and compounding with exquisite nicety. The results were curiously fresh; and if there was one merit over another for which the critics lauded Mr. West, it was for his native American originality.

One wonders whether Sherwood Bonner is engaged in an attack on one of her contemporaries or whether she is feeling guilt at her own sins of imitation and appropriation over the past two years. Whichever is the case, the characterization of West here has little to do with her later treatment of him as a lustful cad.

This side of West's nature alone gives the final two-thirds of "Two Storms" whatever unity of effect that it possesses, and Sherwood Bonner treats the attempted seduction of Dina Mabyn with surprising boldness for the period. In the Mabyn garden during her father's absence, West tells Dina, who does not fathom his meaning, that they are like Paul and Virginie. As the days pass, his desire increases: "Cost what it might, she must be his," the narrator reveals. "Afterward? Of that, I believe, he did not think, any more than a man thinks what he will do after he is dead." The naïve, sheltered Dina still fails to understand his purpose, though her mammy has sung her to sleep often with the pointed lyric—

> Ere de moon has risen
> De bird ob night dost sing,

> Guard dy heart like any prison
> Till dou hast a ring—
> *Till—dou—hast—a—ring.*

And at the rendezvous on Last Island, West is about to gain his desire when the storm breaks upon them. Despite the reader's knowledge of West's concupiscence, the revelation to Francis Mabyn that forms the climax of the story is still pure melodrama. "I loved her," West confesses. "I would have taken her away with me. She seemed of no particular value here. And I wanted her. But I am already married." After this lurid touch, the author manages to give her story a happy ending only through a reconciliation of father and daughter that brings a wince from any post-Freudian reader. "Safe in the purest love man ever gives to woman," Sherwood Bonner tells us, "[Dina] rested on her father's heart."

As I have suggested, the story does contain some good writing, not only in the set-pieces, but also in the descriptions of Galveston and Last Island and of the storms; but too often the author interjects this lurid tone: "Ah, Dina! pretty Dina! poor Dina! danger is near—danger from the beast you have maddened!" And the sensational conclusion is matched by the earlier death scene, when the delicate Mrs. Mabyn succumbs of heart failure at the sight of a corpse hurled by the first storm into her drawing room. Withal, "Two Storms" is perhaps the ultimate periodical romance of late-nineteenth-century America, just the sort of fiction that William Dean Howells kept out of the *Atlantic Monthly*: outrageously plotted, overwritten, and melodramatic.

Interestingly, it was soon after Sherwood Bonner had mailed to Alden her final version of "Two Storms" that she produced a tour de force, *The Valcours*. During her fifteen months' residence in Illinois waiting for her divorce, she wrote not only her most outrageous romance, but also her most sophisticated one. And perhaps it was the descent into the awful hackwork of "Two Storms" that enabled her in *The Valcours* to parody brilliantly the genre in which she had so recently committed so many offenses.

During this period, she had also thoroughly assimilated another influence that helped to shape *The Valcours*: the novels of Thackeray. On the train to Illinois, she had read *The Newcomes*, and it is probable that she read more of his novels during her residence in

Illinois. Though *The Valcours* contains an allusion to *The Virginians*, the primary model for Bonner is *Vanity Fair*. Her four principal characters owe something to Thackeray's George Osborne, Amelia Sedley, Dobbin, and, particularly, his Becky Sharp; but a more pervasive influence is apparent in Bonner's adaptation of the Thackerian narrator. Inspired by his narrative mode, she was able for the first time to demonstrate fully her great gift for irony. Thus Sherwood Bonner did not simply appropriate the English novelist's work as she had done Cable's. Instead, Thackeray's influence was a liberating one, one that served to release her own imaginative powers.[20]

With Thackerian irony, Sherwood Bonner wrote a long periodical romance (appearing in four installments in *Lippincott's*) that would both delight the devotees of such romances and, at the same time, expose the illusions underlying the genre. The complicated plot is masterfully conceived; and the reader is invited not to find all contrivance believable, as he is in other of Bonner's romances, but instead merely to enjoy the author's cleverness. A host of old conventions are presented—a romantic hero and heroine, disguised identity, a deathbed scene—but after the author has involved the reader in these stock devices, she then proceeds to show their theatrical quality. Working in a romantic, conventional mode and playing it off against real life, Sherwood Bonner achieved a delicate balance unparalleled in her fiction.

At the center of *The Valcours* are Garry Valcour, the handsome son of a hot-blooded old general; Eva Charenton Leacock, a beautiful, gentle heiress, whom her admirers call the Peri; David Church, a young newspaper editor; and Church's sister Buena Vista, spirited, talented, and scheming. Around these characters, Sherwood Bonner weaves a complicated plot audaciously outlined in the opening lines:

> When General Valcour rose in his stirrups and made a speech, he knew not "the subtle ways" into which it would lead. In itself the speech was not as bright as a comet's head, but it had a longer tail. Because of it a saucy editor was horsewhipped, a good girl was turned into an artful little schemer, and a peri was evolved from somewhere

20. McDowell to Longfellow, April 28, 1880, in Longfellow Collection.

who set everybody by the ears with her beauty, her wealth, and her extraordinary papa. Furthermore, a wicked deed was bared to light, and General Valcour's son got a wife.[21]

The fiery extemporaneous speech, delivered in answer to the harangue of a radical Republican, eventually results in the General's removal to Hot Springs for his health—but not before David Church's satiric treatment of the General in his newspaper has caused Garry, first, to horsewhip the editor, and, later, to become his staunch friend. The expensive trip to the spa also necessitates the selling of a cottage on the Valcours' Louisiana plantation to a Mrs. Charenton of New Orleans and her granddaughter Eva. In Hot Springs, the Valcours also accidentally met the old reprobate Phillip Hamilton Leacock, who is subsequently revealed to be Eva's father, long ago banished by Mrs. Charenton. Having returned from Hot Springs, Garry falls in love with Eva, while David, also worshipping the Peri, watches faithfully from the wings; and Buena Vista, who is in love with Garry herself, smarts with jealousy. Conveniently, as in so many periodical romances, a death occurs, that of Mrs. Charenton; and Buena Vista can now involve herself in Byzantine schemes to end Garry's courtship of the Peri. Learning accidentally about old Leacock, she convinces Eva to summon the father whom she has not seen since childhood. The dissipated Leacock arrives, General Valcour forbids a match connecting his distinguished name with that of the reprobate, and the stage if now set for an ingenious exposure of intrigues, a weaving together of all strands, and, of course, a happy ending.

Along the way to this denouement, Sherwood Bonner presents a panorama of southern life in the days of social upheaval following the Civil War. She begins the cultural portraiture with the picture of old General Valcour of the race of "fighting Valcours," the man who had once commanded a Confederate brigade, but who is now commanded by his own prejudices. Her portrait of the General leads to a sketch of the species to which he belongs:

> None could take their places, for they were a picked lot, born of the time and social conditions. Brought up to fight chickens, race horses,

21. *The Valcours* appeared in *Lippincott's*, n.s., II (September, 1881), 243–58; (October, 1881), 345–61; (November, 1881), 444–62; and (December, 1881), 555–70.

drink whiskey, punctual at the communion-table, chivalrous toward women, not insensible to beauty but demanding wives like Caesar's and intrusting their names grandly to such gentle keeping, generous but inflexible masters, ready to kill their best friend for a nice point of honor, finely familiar with the classics but indifferent to modern literature, excelling in all bodily exercises, consecrating their intellectual forces to a mastery of the science of government, they were for the most part superb figures. Memory lingers on them with satisfaction, for they are becoming as extinct as dodos.

Not only through such narrative commentary, but also through the General's speech filled with Walter Scott's rhetoric, and the elder Valcour's consistent bluster, Sherwood Bonner offers her most effective ironic treatment of the blue-blooded, hot-tempered, chivalric southern gentleman. Completing the Valcour family are a properly decorative wife, and the son, Garry, who finds himself in a "drill-world of transition." Though still influenced by his father's fierce code of honor, Garry's sense of humor provides him, first, a double vision of the "fighting Valcours" and, eventually, a consistently ironic perspective. That perspective is gained partly through the agency of David Church. While Church is not of the planter aristocracy, coming instead from a Kentucky family who owned no slaves, he too has a fiery ancestry, his grandfather being a Mexican War hero. But after the violent death of his father, David has rejected the chivalric code and become a man of peace who only scoffs at challenges.

Adding to this picture of a ruling class whose values are being tested in changing times and a more humble strata that is emerging and defining itself are minor characters who show other aspects of southern life. Though Sherwood Bonner uses most of the Negro characters in The Valcours strictly for broad comedy, here too she dramatizes well the social confusion of those accustomed to total subservience who now see the possibility of a new role and are hard-put to reconcile the two. The scene in which Garry confronts a former Valcour's slave who has just hurled a fish to protest the General's speech is a master touch: "The negro turned angrily. In a second his hat was off. 'Lor', Mars' Garry, I axes yo pardon. My blood wus up, an' I kinder forgot it wus de general a-speakin'." Sherwood Bonner also gives us in The Valcours the most delightful of her black duennas, Mammy Lucy. Note the flavor of her speech protesting the plan to summon Eva's father: "When he forsook you, your grandma took you up, jes' like de Lord. And on'y think of what old mis' would say at de thought of dat man a-comin' under her own vine, an' fig-tree, an' a-drinkin' outen her cup, an' a-sleepin' in her linen sheets." Rounding out the social scene are poor whites and the city men who are members of Garry's club in Hot Springs.

Against this cleverly sketched social background, Sherwood Bonner spins her romantic tale, all the while satirizing the conventional machinery that she employs. Garry fills his role well as the handsome, noble young lover, as does David Church as the loyal friend also in love with the girl. But Buena Vista smarts at hers, protesting when Eva withholds confidences, "I am not even the confidante in white muslin to whom the heroine in white satin reveals her soul." Mrs. Charenton is an even more consistent iconoclast, especially as regards the opposite sex: "Men, my dear, men—they're a wild lot, with their wine and their cards and their betting books—and worse!—and women are their victims." But much of Sherwood Bonner's satirizing of the genre comes through her handling of the romantic heroine Eva, the figure at the heart of literary romance in the era. She has Eva think of *A Tale of Two Cities* when contemplating the reunion with her father. "How blessed Lucie was, after all," Eva tells Buena Vista, "to find her father, in his madness and loneliness, making shoes on his little bench . . . and by her faithful love to win him back to reason and happiness." The old rake Leacock, however, is a far cry from Dr. Manette, and Eva is bitterly disappointed when he fails to match her ideal. She even shows a great deal of spirit for a Peri when she is willing to lose her entire inheritance just to be rid of her evil father forever. But as he lies dying, Eva reverts to the conventional role and rhetoric of the heroine of periodical romance: "We have been harsh and cruel,—I most of all. But forgive us, and think of your soul. Pray, pray, pray, dear father, while there is still breath for prayer! It is not too late. Father, father, for my mother's sake, for her love's sake! Remember how she loved you! Think how she weeps in heaven for you! Oh, pray, pray!" A few minutes later when the dying man confesses that he is an imposter, Eva flings herself into the arms of Garry Valcour: "Oh, my love! my love! my love! I knew he was not my father!" With the dazzlingly inconsistent and rhetorically repetitive Eva, Sherwood Bonner gently pokes fun at a whole literary era.

Literary romance is, in fact, satirized all through Leacock's deathbed scene. All gather attentively around Leacock; women pray and then swoon; and then, lacking all propriety, the old duffer does not die. And as his rally is announced with the words, "Well, I feel uncommonly peckish," all are outraged. His confession, however, ends various intrigues and problems in *The Valcours*; and Sherwood Bonner concludes her tale by disposing of the characters in a spreading chronological and geographic tableau. Eva and Garry have wed and, with the Charenton fortune, restored the fading beauty of the Valcour plantation. Having come into a small inheritance of her own, Madame Valcour and the General have taken Buena Vista, whose treachery has never been exposed, to Paris to study painting. The talented schemer has forgotten her failure in love and found greater happiness in her art, in whose "cold joys there is no satiety." The author then pauses on David Church. "The Valcours are his staunch friends," we are informed. "He worships Eva as much as ever, but with less sentiment, as it is not to be denied that the Peri has grown a little fat." Sherwood Bonner continues to hold him in view, as if to tell us that her romantic hero and heroine and her Becky Sharp, upon whom she has expended many more words, are not nearly so decent or so real:

> Dear, honest, David Church! Simple loving soul! His face lingers last, as all the others recede slowly from sight. . . . As if loath to go, still it hesitates in air, little by little growing dimmer and more pale, until only its cheery smile is left to hold the gaze, like the pleasant Grin without the Cat which Alice saw in Wonderland.

Thus Sherwood Bonner, an artist thoroughly in control of her medium, ends *The Valcours*.

One reason for this delicately achieved control throughout the novella may well be that *The Valcours* is Sherwood Bonner's most deeply imagined work. General Valcour is probably drawn in some degree from Colton Greene, for the character is much like the members of the chivalric, hot-blooded Grandeis family in "Mars' Colton's Lesson," and the same tiger imagery is employed. Old Leacock's scheme to mine bat guano points to the husband that Sherwood Bonner was in the process of divorcing. Eva's intense desire to sever all connection with Leacock no doubt owes something to the author's own feeling about Edward McDowell; and one can also see more than a little of the author in the vivid, sardonic, scheming Buena Vista. But Sherwood Bonner shows great skill in coolly selecting these elements from her own experience and blending them smoothly into a delicately balanced and compulsively readable whole that is primarily a work of the imagination.

The Valcours stands out amid the work of Sherwood Bonner's last years and provides the capstone of her literary career. The structure beneath is remarkably varied, and within its mixture of hackwork and more serious and ambitious writing, one can discern the gradual, though halting, development of both vision and artistry. During the last five years of her life, as fate dealt her one blow after another, Sherwood Bonner's works reveal a dramatic widening of her sympathies. No longer did the aristocrat show the old disdain for her humbler characters. Instead, in the Cumberland and Illinois stories, she often displayed great empathy as she presented them oppressed and often trapped by their circumstances and environment. Clearly, despite reversions, she was also rejecting the sentimental glow that continued through the century to suffuse the local color movement. As *The Valcours* proves, she was at the same time achieving a perspective on her own work and developing artistic control. Her maturation as an artist can, in fact, be judged by her growing skill with narrative form. The gulf between the fledgling and the master separates the prolix and disturbingly inconsistent omniscient narrator of "Miss Willard's Two Rings" from the subtly revealing first person narrators of the Illinois stories. That line of technical development culminates in the return to omniscience with the sophisticated narrator of *The Valcours*.

After one has separated wheat from chaff in Sherwood Bonner's canon, he is left with only a small gathering of works on which her reputation must rest—*Like unto Like*, a handful of stories, and

The Valcours. The evidence that they give of her vitality and artistry, however, also tantalize us with hints of what Sherwood Bonner might have written had she lived past her meager thirty-four years.

Chapter Eight

The Legacy of Sherwood Bonner

THE DRAMA THAT had surrounded Kate McDowell for the past decade did not end with her death. Hers was a force felt by many of her intimates throughout their lives, and her history and personality had their effects also upon her literary legacy. A best seller based on her life so embarrassed proper Boston that efforts were made there to erase all traces of her from collective memory. Sherwood Bonner, however, continued to be read through the turn of the century; and in the following decades, while her fiction was being forgotten, she emerged as a hauntingly enigmatic and possibly scandalous figure in literary New England's Indian summer.

Three days after her death, Kate McDowell was buried beside her brother and at her father's feet in the family plot in Holly Springs. Shortly afterward, the Nahum Capens received the news in a letter from Ruth. Mourning Kate but feeling relief that her "agony is over," Mrs. Capen dispatched a letter to Dr. Flower and a notice to the Boston *Evening Transcript*; and she and her husband drove into Boston to tell Nellie Willard, while at the Capen house Sophie Shepard began an obituary to be sent to S. S. Conant of *Harper's Weekly*.[1]

Friends in the South were also composing eulogies, and these were remarkably personal. Helen Craft Anderson, writing in the Holly Springs *Reporter*, concluded her tribute to a lifelong friend: "To literature she was 'Sherwood Bonner,' the young author full of genius and promise; to society she was the beautiful, fascinating woman, always the central attraction in every room she entered;

1. [Helen Craft Anderson], "In Memoriam," Holly Springs *Reporter*, August 16, 1883, p. 2; Elizabeth Capen to Ruth McDowell, July 31, 1883, in the collection of George R. Stephenson, Jackson, Mississippi (hereinafter cited as Stephenson Collection).

209

but to the companions of her youth she was only 'Kate,' the loyal, brave, trusted friend, whose untimely death has taken so much from life that it can never look the same again." Within the moving eulogy, however, Helen's sense of puzzlement was apparent. Her memories of Kate included "the strange child, never like any other" and the woman, "prone to 'erring which is human,'" but "full of the 'forgiveness which is divine.'" The notice in the *South*, the other Holly Springs paper, was also obviously written by an intimate. "The theatre of her life had its limits, but within that scope she was always the heroine, the central figure of strength and force," the writer observed, and added, "To those who knew her well, she will never die, for she individualized friendship." But this eulogist was moved also to defend her from criticism. Though admitting that "to describe her were to solve psychological puzzles," the writer argued that "her life was as open as a printed page; her very faults sprang from the soil of a generous soul; subterfuge had no place with her." The local tributes reflect that mixture of responses that would attend the dead woman's memory in Holly Springs for decades: affection and puzzlement, criticism and loyal defense.[2]

The Memphis obituaries gave more attention to her literary career, but the personal note was struck here too, not only in appreciation of her life, but also in its defense. Surprisingly, Margaret Chambers Kellar spoke of Dr. Bonner as a "stern old gentleman of the conventionalities of half a century ago," who had failed to understand Kate's wisdom in going to Boston. Elizabeth Meriwether wrote of her friend's gaining literary fame only "after much needless opposition from relatives and friends." Mrs. Meriwether's eulogy gave a feminist view of Kate McDowell's achievement. "The day has gone by when helplessness in women is regarded as a crown jewel," she wrote. "Now when a woman succeeds in standing alone by merit of her own gifts, aided by patient industry, it is but right that the world should give its mite of commendation. 'Sherwood Bonner' is a loss, not only to the South, but to the country." And the old woman ended her tribute with characteris-

2. [Anderson], "In Memoriam"; "In Memoriam: Sherwood Bonner," Holly Springs *South*, n.d., in the collection of Mrs. John Craft and Mrs. James Driver, Holly Springs (hereinafter cited as Craft Collection).

tic austerity and dignity: "Brave in life, no less brave in dying, her memory will be honored."[3]

Later came Shirley Carter's powerful memoir in the New Orleans *Times-Democrat* of the "enchantress" who stood beside his desk on the day that she had received her death warrant. *The Continent*, the Philadelphia magazine edited by Albion Tourgée to which Kate had contributed occasionally, called her death "a genuine loss to American literature." But the most important national tribute was the obituary in *Harper's Weekly*. Samuel Stillman Conant absorbed the death notice sent by Sophie Shepard in a long eulogy of his own that covered half a page of the journal. "To American literature the loss can be best estimated by those who were acquainted with 'Sherwood Bonner' herself," he commented. "To them the promise of her life had only begun to be fulfilled."[4]

Even as friends were composing these eulogies, however, the private life of the dead woman was being aired in a bitter public confrontation. On the day of Kate's funeral, Addison Craft had filed her will for probate; and three days later, Edward McDowell came to Holly Springs and brought suit for the custody of Lilian. The trial was held before a packed courtroom on August 2, 1883. Holly Springs had never been treated to such drama in a chancery suit, and the proceedings were covered on the front page of the Memphis *Daily Appeal*.[5]

Both the absence of some witnesses and the presence of others reveal a tangle of allegiances. Edward, represented by his old friend James H. Watson, had found only one witness to speak in his behalf, his sister Mary, recently returned from Europe. The co-executors of Kate McDowell's estate, Addison Craft and Aunt Martha Bonner, called twelve people, including Judge J. W. C.

3. Margaret Chambers Kellar, "Sherwood Bonner," Memphis *Public Ledger*. August 11, 1883, p. 2; [Elizabeth Avery Meriwether], "A Southern Authoress," *Meriwether's Weekly*, August 11, 1883, p. 2.

4. Shirley Carter, "Sherwood Bonner," New Orleans *Times-Democrat*, September 2, 1883, p. 3; Review of *Dialect Tales*, in *The Continent*, IV (September 12, 1883), 349; "Sherwood Bonner," *Harper's Weekly*, August 11, 1883, p. 503.

5. Estate Papers of Katharine McDowell, File 1656, Chancery Clerk's Office, Marshall County Courthouse, Holly Springs (hereinafter cited as Estate Papers); *McDowell* v. *Craft and Bonner* (Custody Suit over Lilian K. McDowell), File 1657, Chancery Clerk's Office (hereinafter cited as Custody Suit); "Holly Springs News," Memphis *Daily Appeal*, August 7, 1883, p. 1.

Watson, who offered eloquent testimony opposing his son's client. Aunt Martha was called first. She reviewed the course of the ten-year marriage of Edward and Kate, citing his failure to contribute to the support of either wife or daughter, and detailing the few occasions that he had even seen Lilian since she was twenty months old. She was followed by Sophia Kirk, Ella Topp, various other of Kate's childhood friends and Salem Street neighbors, and finally by Judge Watson, who spoke of Aunt Martha's character and her suitability as guardian of the child.

Edward then took the stand. Describing himself as "what might be termed a speculator," he reported that after the period in 1879–1880 spent in the Colorado gold fields, he had lived a year in North Carolina and another year in Spartanburg, South Carolina. A month previously, he informed the court, he had settled in Georgia, where he was engaged in gold mining near Marietta. Though he had not in the past maintained a permanent or fixed abode, he planned to establish a household there with his mother and his sister Lilly, when she returned from Europe. Arguing that he could well support his daughter, Edward boasted that he was now worth ten thousand dollars. After alluding to his English education, his worthy moral character, and his present wealth, he cast a supercilious glance at his interlocutor, who asked why he had never replied to Kate's letters from Boston in the winter of 1879–1880 or to Lilian's request of money for her schooling. "I did not answer these letters," he replied, "for reasons sufficient to myself."

Kate's will was then read as evidence of her wishes for the disposition of her child, as was a transcript of the divorce proceedings, in which Edward had been described as "of a roving, wandering disposition." The grounds for the divorce were revealed to be abandonment and nonsupport. Next came the climax of the trial, the testimony of twelve-year-old Lilian. The child said simply that she would "greatly prefer" living with her aunt, to whom she was "deeply attached," and that her father was a stranger to her, someone whom she would not even have recognized. The full day of testimony was ended, the judge took the case under advisement, and the crowded courtroom emptied. When the verdict was announced some days later, Kate's wishes had been honored: Aunt Martha was made the sole guardian of Lilian.

Surely Edward could have foreseen the result, but both his actions in bringing the suit and his behavior in court were inevitable, given his character. There is no evidence that after the first years of his marriage Edward felt deep affection for either his wife or his daughter. But such was his pride that he wished to stand before the world in possession of that which was supposed to be his. He could rove as he pleased, but he wished at the same time to appear at the head, and in control, of his own family. Eventually he took his case to the state supreme court, which also found against him in 1885. Aside from exposing his own weaknesses publicly, the suits did nothing to endear him to his daughter, who avoided him for the rest of her life.

A month after the trial, the local eulogies both having appeared in print, Holly Springs paid another kind of tribute to Kate. At the meeting of the Literary and Musical Circle, a relative newcomer to the town, George Reimensnyder, began reading his essay on "the life and literary character of Sherwood Bonner." Reimensnyder's treatise proved so lengthy that he was forced to conclude it at a subsequent meeting, held at the home of Mrs. Kate Freeman. Following his reading, a unanimous resolution was passed ordering the printing of his tribute to "the most distinguished member of our society," and the presentation of a copy to the local library. Reimensnyder's essay (of which no copy appears to survive) was, however, necessarily incomplete; for some of Sherwood Bonner's works were still to be published. Sophia Kirk testified in the custody suit that her friend had left not only a finished short story but "a book nearly complete—it being so far advanced that another party can complete it." Elsewhere in her testimony she referred to this work as "a book to come on the market at Christmas." This was Kate's long-planned "Christmas juvenile," the collection of her stories that she had been gathering and revising. When Sophia left Bonner House after the trial, she took the manuscripts written in Kate's last months back with her to Boston, where she would serve as her friend's literary executrix.[6]

Sophia Kirk did her job faithfully and well. She sold not one but three new Sherwood Bonner short stories—"Christmas Eve at Tuckeyhoe" appeared in her father's own *Lippincott's* (January,

6. "Holly Springs News," Memphis *Daily Appeal*, September 6, 1883, p. 2, and September 12, 1883, p. 2; conversation with the Reverend Dr. George R. Stephenson, Jackson, Miss., August 29, 1978.

1884), "The Tender Conscience of Mr. Bobberts," in *Harper's Weekly* (March 22, 1884), and "Coming Home to Roost" also in the *Weekly* (May 17, 1884). Though the collection for juveniles did not appear for the Christmas market in 1883, Sophia Kirk had placed it with Roberts Brothers in Boston, the country's leading publisher of children's books, and the volume appeared for Christmas of 1884. Miss Kirk no doubt added finishing touches to two of the three short stories, as well as to the collection, which appeared under the name *Suwanee River Tales*. To that volume she also contributed an excellent preface discussing the life and work of her late friend. Devoted though her stewardship proved, it had one result that would cause controversy and hard feelings for some years.

In 1886, Ticknor and Company of Boston published under the pseudonym Henry Hayes a novel named *The Story of Margaret Kent*. The book, which tells the story of a beautiful young southern writer separated for years from her wastrel husband, became an immediate best seller, going through thirty-four editions in its first four years. Within months of its publication, the author revealed herself to be Ellen Olney Kirk, who had married John Foster Kirk in 1879 and thus was the stepmother of Sophia Kirk.[7]

Much of Boston and a great deal of the literary world knew immediately the basis for *The Story of Margaret Kent*, but no revelation appeared in print until 1901, when biographical sketches of Kate McDowell in both the *Dictionary of American Authors* and the *National Cyclopedia of American Biography* noted that "in Mrs. Kirk's novel of 'Margaret Kent' she figures as the heroine." Over a decade earlier, however, Ellen Kirk had tried to deny this apparent resemblance. In an 1889 issue of *Book Buyer*, an interviewer had recorded her explanation in the following tortured sentences:

> The premature and painful death of a richly endowed woman, of whom Mrs. Kirk had heard a great deal, but whom she barely knew, and whom she had never seen in health, brought vividly before her

7. "Mrs. Ellen Olney Kirk," *A Woman of the Century*, eds. Frances E. Willard and Mary A. Livermore (Buffalo: Charles Wells Moulton, 1893), 439; "Mrs. Ellen Warner (Olney) Kirk," *A Supplement to Allibone's Critical Dictionary of English Literature and British and American Authors*, ed. John F. Kirk (Philadelphia: J. B. Lippincott Co., 1897), 956.

mind the possible aspects of a life such as this which had been cut off. And with this conception before her Mrs. Kirk wrote the first half dozen chapters of "Margaret Kent." Then, as the impulse was exhausted, and as another piece of work was pressing, she put the novel by, and did not work on it again until the following year. By that time she had altogether lost what had been at first a powerful imaginative impression of a particular person with whom she had no real acquaintance. Mrs. Kirk thus went on to finish the novel without the least idea that any reader would ever suppose she was treating a real person and real incidents.

In conclusion, Mrs. Kirk had noted that "the novel was finished on the general lines" of one of her earlier short stories, "Better Times." Despite the muddled prose of the interviewer and the obvious smokescreen that Ellen Kirk was attempting to throw over the question of her debt to Kate McDowell's life, it is possible that she revealed a great debt, not to Kate McDowell, but to Sherwood Bonner.[8]

The first half dozen chapters of *The Story of Margaret Kent*, which introduce the major characters and suggest the central situation of the novel, are fascinating. The title character, who must earn her living by her pen because her wastrel husband contributes nothing to her support, is surrounded by a varied and interesting group of people. Living with her in an apartment of four rooms overlooking New York's Gramercy Park are her charming eight-year-old daughter and her close companion Sarah Longstaffe, a spinster artist. The apartment has become a salon for a captivated group of gentlemen, who include Herbert Bell, a world renowned poet of seventy; young Charlton, whose acquaintance with Mrs. Kent began when both were touring Europe; and Dr. Walton, the serious and handsome nephew of Bell. Another frequent visitor is

---

8. "Mrs. Katherine Sherwood (Bonner) MacDowell," *A Dictionary of American Authors*, ed. Oscar Fay Adams (Boston: Houghton, Mifflin and Company, 1901), 241–42; "Katherine Sherwood (Bonner) McDowell," *National Cyclopedia of American Biography* (New York: James T. White and Co., 1901), II, 496; "The Author of 'Margaret Kent,'" *Book Buyer*, n.s. VI (May, 1889), 140–41.

According to David McDowell III, of Batesville, Miss., the theory that Sherwood Bonner had written part of *Margaret Kent* was first advanced by Professor George W. Polhemus in the 1950s. In his Twayne study of Sherwood Bonner, William L. Frank also speculates on the matter, but the only evidence that he offers in support is plot summary and a confused conflation of references from the Custody Suit. See Frank, *Sherwood Bonner (Catherine McDowell)* (Boston: Twayne Publishers, 1976), 129–34.

the grand literary lady Mrs. Townsend, who (despite her own strange marital arrangement) has the wealth and position that Margaret cannot help envying. Through her malicious gossip and innuendo, this patronizing friend becomes finally Margaret's worst enemy.

Margaret Kent's peculiar position as a married woman receiving the attentions of many men makes her of course open to such gossip, as do her dazzling wit and her coquetry. Feeling that her situation is intolerable, several friends entreat her to go west and divorce her husband, the strongest voice being that of the poet Herbert Bell, who wishes to protect Margaret afterward by making her his wife. By the end of chapter six, it is clear that Charlton and Walton are also in love with Mrs. Kent, and even one of Margaret's aunts urges her to gain her freedom and the chance for a new life. By this point in the novel, the plot seems set on an unswerving course.

That, however, is not the case at all. After roughly the first half dozen chapters, the novel instead becomes a retelling of Mrs. Kirk's short story "Better Times." The whole idea of divorce is dropped. Margaret, like the heroine of the short story, begins to feel that she must find herself through her duty as a wife. When her husband appears after his absence of six years, he is a drunkard; and Margaret spends two hundred pages suffering in the bonds of her marriage. All ends happily, however, when Kent finally dies; and Margaret falls into the arms of Dr. Walton, who wishes to marry her and give her a new, happy existence.

In the *Book Buyer* interview, Mrs. Kirk did provide an explanation for the swerving plot of the novel. But there are other strange things about *Margaret Kent*. The vividness of both character and place conveyed in the opening chapters is absent from the rest of the work. The noble Margaret of the conclusion, in fact, bears little resemblance to the proud, capricious, vital woman of the beginning. And there is almost no sense of place in the final half of the book. When Margaret returns south to nurse her husband during a yellow fever epidemic in their native town, the characters seem set in midair. Such vagueness stands in dramatic contrast to the sharply conveyed impressions of both the Gramercy Park apartment and the home of the old poet. All of these flaws seem to point toward another explanation for *The Story of Margaret Kent*: that the early chapters are essentially the work of Sherwood Bonner herself.

Using the outlines of Kate McDowell's history, many people could have produced a fictionalized version of her experience; but it is difficult to believe that anyone else—much less someone unacquainted with Kate McDowell at the time—could have rendered so vividly the very texture of her Boston life in the winter of 1879–1880. Sophia Kirk had written in the preface to *Suwanee River Tales* that her "singularly close and complete" friendship with the author "has helped make even those parts of her life in which I had no share hardly less vivid to me than my own recollections." It is certainly probable that Sophia had discussed that life with her stepmother. But even Sophia's intimate knowledge, transmitted to Mrs. Kirk, cannot account for the descriptions of Kate's Hotel Boylston quarters nor the library at Longfellow House, rooms that neither of the Kirks had ever seen.[9]

The reading of character, moreover, is even more strikingly reminiscent of Sherwood Bonner than is the rendering of place. Of the minor characters, one wonders whether anyone other than Kate McDowell could have drawn the detailed and devastating portrait of Louise Chandler Moulton. But the major characters of the early chapters present the strongest evidence, for in the treatment of them one sees Kate's sharp awareness of her own situation. Consider the narrator's assessment of the old poet's feelings toward Margaret Kent:

> Her beauty, her southern spontaneity and swiftness of gleeful apprehension in her manner and utterance, delighted him. All she said was to his perception both bright and original. As he was an old man, probably what he set most store by was her finely rounded mental and physical development; she had a grand physique, health, strength, high spirits, and was so absolutely free from grovelling wishes and ideas that she could be thoroughly frank in action and speech, without displeasing his rather over-fastidious taste. Perhaps if she had possessed all this beauty and original force, and had at the same time been able to master the world and direct all it contained into channels towards herself, he might have admired her without loving her. Her

9. Sophia Kirk, preface to *Suwanee River Tales*, iii.

manifold endowments might then have steeled his heart against her.
He liked her as Esther rather than as Vashti. She was poor: she was
compelled to gain the very bread she ate by her own will and energy;
she needed his tender encouragements, his patronage, the kindly shut-
ting of his eyes to her pretty feminine follies.[10]

The style is not always Sherwood Bonner's, but the reading of
character unquestionably is, just as it is in this passage:

> In her quiet moments [Margaret] suffered from the knowledge that she
> was always tiding herself over present difficulties by doing work which
> was only half worthy of her. She loved the best; but the grand things of
> life stood afar off, and though it seemed to her she longed to tread the
> difficult paths and scale the heights to reach them, some preemptory
> need compelled her to put off her great effort; rather, perhaps, some
> eloquently-soliciting self-indulgence consumed her energies instead. It
> was so hard for Margaret to remember that life has cares and respon-
> sibilities, cruel anxieties even, as well as pleasures. She hated to feel
> herself dull and discouraged; what she longed for was a permanent
> state of emotion and exhilaration which should lift her above all
> thoughts of everyday necessities.

Here is the same kind of self-knowledge that Sherwood Bonner
had earlier displayed when she had taken a hard look at herself in
the character Blythe Herndon.

Adding to the evidence provided by these passages are the presence of scenes constructed and realized much like those in Sherwood Bonner's fiction. The chapter devoted to Mrs. Townsend's
dinner party, for example, is strikingly similar to the one devoted
to Mrs. Oglethorpe's in *Like unto Like*. But perhaps the whole
matter of Ellen Kirk's debts to Sherwood Bonner is given away
most clearly by one small touch. In the first pages of the novel, we
are told of Margaret Kent: "Had she possessed no other fascination, her voice would have charmed anyone. It was a southern
voice, rich and sweet, just touched with the accent acquired from
mammies and maids in early life." In this, the reader hears echoes
of Sherwood Bonner's countless paens to the southern voice. But
halfway through the novel, one is startled to find the narrator saying that Margaret Kent "recited poetry very well, having a good

10. I have quoted from the thirty-fourth edition of *The Story of Margaret Kent* (Boston:
Houghton, Mifflin and Company, 1890).

enunciation in spite of her southern accent." Can anyone really believe that the paen and the patronage come from the same pen?

If the opening chapters of *Margaret Kent* are indeed the conception of Sherwood Bonner, then one can suddenly find a coherent pattern in a group of hitherto mysterious references. In July of 1880, Kate McDowell had written Longfellow from Illinois: "My life I fear is a failure—and I plan sometimes how I might leave it— with a bare bodkin—or something less violent. But I should write my memoirs first. In fact this summer I have amused myself with writing something of the kind." Longfellow had of course long wanted her to "throw upon a broad canvas some of her more recent experience." Though her subsequent letters contain no further reference to this project, two accounts written after her death suggest that Sherwood Bonner left an ambitious work unfinished. One of her early biographers, B. M. Drake, observes that though the dying woman was "unable to write [does he mean "complete"?] the book she had projected, she worked on to the very last." And in her eulogy, Helen Craft Anderson thus describes her friend's last days: "Within a week of the end, between the stupor of pain and the moans of agony, she dictated chapter after chapter, brilliant in description and witty in expression." One final and tantalizing bit of evidence is furnished by Kate McDowell's notes regarding *Romances by Sherwood Bonner*, the final collection that she wished to have published. Of the fiction to be included, only one romance has never been located, "A Chance in Life"—an appropriate title for the work that *The Story of Margaret Kent* starts out to be.[11]

After almost a century and with all conclusive evidence destroyed, no one will ever be able to answer with complete authority the questions raised by *The Story of Margaret Kent*; and one can argue only for the plausibility of his explanation. It seems most likely that Sophia Kirk showed her stepmother the unfin-

11. Kate McDowell to Henry Wadsworth Longfellow, July 7, 1880, in Longfellow Collection, Houghton Library, Harvard University; Sophia Kirk, preface to *Suwanee River Tales*, vi; B. M. Drake, "Sherwood Bonner," in *Southern Writers: Biographical and Critical Studies*, ed. William Malone Baskerville (Nashville and Dallas: Publishing House of the M. E. Church, South, 1903), I, 109; [Anderson], "In Memoriam"; Dorothy L. Gilligan, "Life and Works of Sherwood Bonner" (M.A. thesis, George Washington University, 1930), 58.

ished manuscript of "A Chance in Life" and that Mrs. Kirk was inspired to complete the work. Since the finished product was not completely hers (though she had no doubt rewritten much of Sherwood Bonner's material), she chose the strange course of bringing the novel out under a pseudonym—an unusual measure since she had already published five novels under her own name. It is possible that both Aunt Martha and Sophia Kirk approved the plan, for it was a way of using Sherwood Bonner's unfinished work and perhaps of contributing a little money to the estate. No one, however, had probably expected the novel to be such a phenomenal success. That, it seems, changed everything. Ellen Kirk quickly acknowledged that she was the author, and her reputation was made. At least one of her later works, in fact, bore on the title page and cover the information that it was written "by the author of *The Story of Margaret Kent*." Apparently no record survives of Sophia Kirk's view of her stepmother's novel, but Sophia's role in the project was clearly unexceptionable, for both Aunt Martha and Lilian remained close to her throughout their lives. Lilian, however, always felt a deep animosity toward Ellen Kirk. If my explanation offers the correct solution to the puzzle presented by *The Story of Margaret Kent*, it brings to light one of the central ironies of Sherwood Bonner's career: that after her death she had a hand in producing a best seller, something that she had never been able to do in life.[12]

But even putting the question of authorship aside, *The Story of Margaret Kent* contributes significantly to the final story of Sherwood Bonner. In the last half of the novel, while Mrs. Kirk explored the effects of wifely duty, she also exploited the McDowell-Longfellow relationship in a way that Sherwood Bonner probably never would have done. The opening chapters had provided an honest and penetrating assessment of the friendship, but Mrs. Kirk wrote later scenes in which the old poet, now confined to his bed, speaks at length of his love for the young Mrs. Kent. To Ellen Kirk's making capital from a revered figure, Boston replied, not

12. The collection of Mrs. Kirk's stories entitled *Better Times* (Boston: Ticknor and Company, 1889) appeared without the author's name, designated simply "By the author of 'The Story of Margaret Kent.'" Lilian McDowell Hammond's attitude toward Ellen Kirk was revealed to me by David McDowell III.

with outrage, but with a profound silence. That silence in regard to the McDowell-Longfellow relationship has lasted virtually unbroken until this day, and the almost complete obliteration of Kate McDowell's memory there began immediately after the great success of *Margaret Kent.*

In the following year, 1887, the Reverend Samuel Longfellow edited his brother's letters and journals for a volume entitled *Final Memorials of Henry Wadsworth Longfellow*, published (interestingly enough) by Ticknor and Company, the publisher of *Margaret Kent.* Samuel Longfellow has since been recognized as a notorious censor of his quite blameless brother's papers, correcting solecisms, deleting any unpleasant comments, and not even allowing the poet to comment that his children had misbehaved. One matter to which the Reverend Longfellow gave his particular attention was the excising of references to Kate McDowell. In his volume, he permitted this one allusion (from an 1878 letter from Longfellow to George Washington Greene) to stand: "Mrs. McD has gone back to Holly Springs to face and fight the pestilence. It is very noble in her to do so. She could not resist the maternal instinct to protect her child, and her desire to share the fate of the family. She will be a great support and comfort to them with her courage and cheerfulness." Although the Reverend Longfellow shortened her name to initials, the reference is still surprising. Perhaps the "maternal instinct" was more than even he could resist. In a later entry from the poet's journal written after Longfellow had gone to Kate McDowell's lodgings to meet her when she returned from the epidemic in Holly Springs, the Reverend Longfellow would allow only: "Went to town to see Mrs. ———." Samuel Longfellow's usual procedure, however, was simply to delete Kate McDowell. Thus the journal entry for March 6, 1875, reads in the original (now in Houghton Library): "Mrs. Sargent, Mrs. McDowell and Whittier the poet came to see me." The Reverend Longfellow's version reads: "Mrs. Sargent and Whittier, the poet, came to see me." Other entries from which Kate McDowell would have been more difficult to remove were simply left out altogether.[13]

13. Edward Wagenknecht, *Longfellow: A Full Length Portrait* (New York: Longmans, Green & Co., 1955), 321–23; Samuel Longfellow (ed.), *Final Memorials of Henry Wadsworth Longfellow* (Boston: Ticknor and Company, 1887), 273–75, 233.

In his attempt to erase Kate McDowell's memory, the Reverend Samuel Longfellow had the support of the female literary establishment of Boston. That group, traditionally a closed shop, had not been kind to Kate in her last years. After *The Story of Margaret Kent* not only revealed publicly Longfellow's infatuation but also presented Louise Chandler Moulton in an unfavorable light, the ladies closed ranks completely; and Kate McDowell was never mentioned in any of their reminiscences of the Boston literary world. So effective were these various protectors of the public good that in the summer of 1978 the staff at Longfellow House had never heard of anyone known as either Kate McDowell or Sherwood Bonner.

But despite all efforts, there was one thing that all who wanted her forgotten were powerless to obliterate from memory. She had written "The Radical Club"; thus she was a part, albeit a minor one, of Boston cultural history. And when she is remembered at all in Boston today, it is as the author of that satire. Every major Boston library has the pamphlet among its holdings, and in the 1950s, Mrs. Ward Thoron, born a Hooper and the niece of Mrs. Henry Adams, made sure that the copies in both the Massachusetts Historical Society and Widener Library were fully annotated for the benefit of posterity.

While Kate McDowell was being consciously forgotten in Boston primarily because of her relationship with one man, other men who had figured in her life were still proving loyal to her memory. After his nervous collapse, his disappearance from New York, and his reappearance in San Francisco, James Redpath had recovered his health through fanatical devotion to a new cause, this time the woeful conditions in Ireland. He spent much of the next few years in that country, and in 1881 he published a book, *Talks About Ireland*. Shortly after he became an editor of the *North American Review* in 1886, he found the last of the causes to which his ardent nature would be drawn. The old abolitionist, the publicist of John Brown, the Radical Republican of Reconstruction days now became an impassioned champion of Jefferson Davis, writing in *Commonwealth Magazine*: "There are two Jefferson Davises in American history—one is a conspirator, a rebel, a traitor and the 'Fiend of Andersonville'—he is a myth evolved from the hell-smoke of cruel war . . . the other was a statesman . . . a man of whom all his countrymen who knew him personally, without distinction of political creed, are proud that he was their countryman." During his campaign to rehabilitate Davis' reputation, Redpath became the close friend of the Confederate president and spent months at Beauvoir assisting Davis in writing his short history of the Confederacy and his autobiography. During a final visit there after Davis' death, Redpath showed that for all his impassioned involvement with various causes, and his recent marriage to a widow of his age, he had still not forgotten Kate; for he planned when he left Beauvoir to come to Holly Springs. Redpath never made his sentimental journey. But on August 20, 1890, he wrote Ruth McDowell to explain his necessary change of plan and to inquire about all of Kate's connections. The inquiry was comprehensive, for at the end Redpath revealed an interest even in Edward McDowell. "I heard from him just before I started to Ireland last," Redpath commented, "& I wrote to a friend of mine in N. Carolina to serve him if he could do so. He was then engaged in gold-mine hunting." Redpath's interest and generosity are characteristic, though this glimpse of the relationship between the two men is surprising. One only wishes that somehow Harriet Waters Preston and her venomous sisters could have read the letter.[14]

Of the men in Kate McDowell's life, however, the most dramatic evidence of her personal legacy is shown in Colton Greene. Two weeks before she died, Colton Greene had removed himself to New York, where he remained for six weeks. What his feelings and motivations had been, no one will ever know; and they become even more perplexing in light of his subsequent actions. One cannot be sure of his even taking definite action, however, until almost six years after Kate McDowell's death. Aunt Martha and Lilian had been living the kind of genteel poverty that was not unusual and not particularly uncomfortable in late-nineteenth-century Holly Springs. Lilian was receiving a sound education at Bethlehem Academy, a Catholic girls' school housed in the old Pointer mansion next door to Bonner House; and the two received some income from renters, from the old Bonner plantation, and

14. Charles F. Horner, *The Life of James Redpath* (New York: Barse & Hopkins, 1926), 289–90; James Redpath to Ruth McDowell, August 20, 1890, in Stephenson Collection.

from meager royalties on Sherwood Bonner's fiction. But they had fallen behind in meeting the interest payments on the mortgage, and on March 2, 1889, Bonner House was put up at public auction. Colton Greene acted at once, buying the house and then deeding it back to them. Evidently at this point he began regularly contributing to their support, and upon Lilian's graduation from Bethlehem Academy, he sent her to Paris to study.

Lilian returned from Europe a beautiful and accomplished young woman, and although Aunt Martha's health had now begun to fail, through Colton Greene's generosity there were now trips to resorts in the Tennessee mountains and on the shores of Lake Michigan. Lilian remained very much a part of her mother's old circle—Mrs. Freeman, the Watsons, the Crafts—and of the life of the town in general. For a time she offered a select group of children weekly Shakespeare classes at Bonner House, and, in 1896, when a ladies literary club was organized at a meeting presided over by Mrs. Cora Carey and held at the home of Helen Craft Anderson, Lilian suggested the name the Thursday Club—drawing on her memories of Boston and its famed Saturday Club. This kind of uneventful small town existence was brought to an end in the year 1900 by two deaths. The first was that of Aunt Martha, after which Lilian began dividing her time between Memphis, where she was now regarded as the adopted daughter of Colton Greene, and Bryn Mawr, Pennsylvania, where Sophia Kirk and her sister Abby had the Misses Kirks' School for Girls. Then, on September 31, Colton Greene died of cancer of the throat. When his will was read, excluding minor bequests of money to institutions and a few rare editions and art objects to close friends, he had left his great fortune to Lilian. The man of mystery, who in life had acted so inscrutably in regard to Kate McDowell, had honored her memory in the way she had most desired: he had insured the future of her daughter.[15]

At thirty, Lilian was an heiress; and one of her first actions was

15. Memphis *Avalanche*, July 5, 1883, p. 4, and August 31, 1883, p. 4; Estate Papers; Deed Book 54, p. 201, and Deed Book 64, p. 555, Chancery Clerk's Office, Marshall County Courthouse; Margaret Chambers Kellar to Martha Bonner, March 24, 1893, in possession of Mrs. Fred Belk, Holly Springs; Lilian McDowell to Mrs. Charnock, September 8, 1899, in the collection of David McDowell III, Batesville, Miss. (hereinafter cited as McDowell Collection). In her last years, Mrs. Netty Fant Thompson (1878–1960), who

to sell Bonner House. Putting behind her the years of duty to her aunt and the years of genteel poverty in a small provincial town, she went again to Europe, and upon her return her engagement was announced to Orlando Davis Hammond, a Memphis cotton broker and the grandson of Judge Orlando Davis of Holly Springs. Married in 1901 at Sophia Kirk's home in Bryn Mawr, they settled in Memphis, where a daughter was born in 1903. Shortly thereafter, they removed to New York, where they lived grandly on East 82nd Street. In 1911 and 1912, Lilian achieved a triumph that would have pleased her mother enormously: she published three delightful satiric sketches of Holly Springs, all showing her mother's influence, in the *Atlantic Monthly*—the journal to which Sherwood Bonner had never gained entrance. On November 20, 1922, Lilian Kirk Hammond (for she had sloughed the name McDowell much as her mother had) died in New York of lobar pneumonia. Her body was cremated, and on Christmas Day Orlando Hammond brought the ashes to Holly Springs. After receiving Lilian's circle at the Addison Craft residence, Mr. Hammond and a few old friends went to the Bonner plot in the cemetery, where Lilian's remains were buried in the grave of her mother—the figure who had been always the guiding force in her life. Even as an adult, Lilian had described Kate to a friend as the person "whom I wish to resemble in every way." [16]

---

had attended the Shakespeare classes, recalled them vividly for me. John Mickle, "Dramatic Club Here in Early Seventies," Holly Springs *South Reporter*, December 10, 1931, p. 10; copy of the will of General Colton Greene, in Colton Greene File, Memphis Room, Memphis/Shelby County Public Library.

16. Conversation with David McDowell III, September 10, 1978; Horace Howard Furness to Lilian K. McDowell, February 12, 1901; Furness to Mrs. Orlando D. Hammond, August 24 and December 27, 1903—all in McDowell Collection; Lilian Kirk Hammond, "The Young Women of Tippah," *Atlantic Monthly*, CVIII (December, 1911), 843–47, "The Tippah Philharmonic," *Atlantic Monthly*, CIX (January, 1912), 80–83, "Sunday in Tippah," *Atlantic Monthly*, CIX (February, 1912), 206–10; Obituary of Mrs. Orlando Davis Hammond, New York *Times*, November 21, 1922, p. 19. Information about Lilian Hammond's burial comes from David McDowell III, and Bessie Craft Driver of Holly Springs. Lilian McDowell to Mrs. Charnock, September 8, 1899, in McDowell Collection.

Lilian Hammond never marked the graves of either her mother or her aunt Martha Bonner; thus a number of people who have sought Sherwood Bonner's resting place in vain. A recent essayist concluded from the unmarked grave that Sherwood Bonner "obviously had been of a different spirit from her fellow townsmen." In a sense that is true, but the essayist of course did not know of the epitaph that Sherwood Bonner's Holly Springs friends had suggested and that she had chosen—"She was much loved." See William D. Miller, "The Cemetery at Holly Springs," *America*, October 1, 1977, pp. 194–95.

Lilian's daughter Martha never married, and thus ends the direct line and, in a sense, the personal legacy of Kate McDowell. But Sherwood Bonner's legacy remains, and it too is not untouched by drama. Sherwood Bonner's fiction was read more widely when it appeared first in periodicals than when later collected between hard covers. But though her books never had large sales, she continued to be enjoyed through the nineteenth century by people of some discernment. Among her admirers, one of the most surprising is a bluff man who was to become president of the United States. When the house at his Elkhorn Ranch was completed, Theodore Roosevelt wrote that the sturdy bookshelves were filled with the works of Irving, Hawthorne, Cooper, and Lowell, as well as his favorite light reading—"dreamy Ike Marvel, Burrough's breezy pages, and the quaint, pathetic character-sketches of the Southern writers—Cable, Craddock, Macon, Joel Chandler Harris, and sweet Sherwood Bonner." Roosevelt's characterization of her as a writer of quaint southern sketches reflects accurately the way that Sherwood Bonner was viewed for fifty years after her death. Increasingly, in fact, she was remembered primarily as an author of Negro dialect sketches. These were the only stories to be reprinted and anthologized from the time of her death until 1947. (The detailed history of the reappearance of these works in print is given in Chapter Seven.) And after 1927, all of Sherwood Bonner's works were out of print for twenty years. In the 1930s, however, her life and works were the subject of two valuable master's theses that preserved valuable personal information and probably saved some of her stories from being lost forever in the files of old periodicals. Working at George Washington University, Dorothy Gilligan received aid from Sophia Kirk both in reconstructing Sherwood Bonner's life and in locating her fiction. A University of Virginia student and a native Mississippian, Nash Kerr Burger, had the cooperation of Sherwood Bonner's niece and great-nephew, Mrs. Ruth McDowell Stephenson and George Royster Stephenson. In 1935, Burger was the first of the Bonner biographers to admit (and perhaps to know) that Sherwood Bonner had gotten a divorce. These students, however, had produced studies of a writer whom few people then read.[17]

17. Edmund Morris, *The Rise of Theodore Roosevelt* (New York: Coward, McCann & Geoghegan, Inc., 1979), 300–301.

The real turning point for Sherwood Bonner in the twentieth century came in 1955 with the publication of Edward Wagen-knecht's *Longfellow: A Full-Length Portrait*. For the first time in a study of Longfellow, Sherwood Bonner was mentioned. Wagen-knecht, in fact, devoted four pages to her, though he explained that he had given more space than she deserved "partly because she is an interesting, neglected minor figure in American letters and partly to guard against misunderstandings." The misunder-standings of course regarded her relationship with Longfellow. "People who really know nothing about the matter," Wagen-knecht wrote, "have sometimes expressed the opinion that Long-fellow was enamoured of her." Wagenknecht discounted this view, but he divulged that there were certain relevant materials evidently still extant that he had not seen. He mentioned specifically Sher-wood Bonner's diary and the letters from Longfellow to Sherwood Bonner that Sophia Kirk had alluded to and even quoted brief pas-sages from in the 1884 preface to *Suwanee River Tales*. Within two years the search began for the Longfellow letters. There were frustrations, one being that Sophia Kirk herself had lived until 1950, dying just in time to thwart the seekers. Miss Kirk's longev-ity is not the only touch in the situation that brings to mind Henry James's "The Aspern Papers," for there was also family resistance to the sudden interest in the personal papers of Sherwood Bonner.[18]

At the same time that Sherwood Bonner was engaging interest as a fascinating and possibly scandalous figure in old literary Bos-ton, her fiction was being reprinted for the first time in decades. In 1947, Gregory Paine selected two of her mountain stories for his *Southern Prose Writers*. "A Volcanic Interlude" was included in anthologies of her period published in 1960 and 1970. In 1972, both *Dialect Tales* and *Suwanee River Tales* were brought out as part of the Black Heritage series by the Books for Libraries Press. The hopelessly dated Negro dialect sketches had become valuable as historical and sociological evidence. Through the 1960s and 1970s, Sherwood Bonner was again the subject of theses and dis-sertations, one of the latter published in 1976 as a very general study of her career. And there appeared also occasional notes and

18. Wagenknecht, *Longfellow*, 283. The McDowell Collection contains scores of docu-ments that chronicle the search for the Longfellow letters and reflect the changing patterns of scholarly interest in Sherwood Bonner.

essays in scholarly journals. Through most of these studies a central interest is the Longfellow relationship, and it is treated inconclusively, most often with what one must characterize as genteel prurience.[19]

To this date, Sherwood Bonner has not been given the kind of careful, detailed, intelligent treatment that she deserves. As the late nineteenth century in American letters becomes increasingly the subject of scrutiny, however, she will receive more attention; and literary historians will see her in a new light. She is not merely the author of creaking period pieces like the Negro dialect sketches, and she is more than just a pioneer in the local color movement. Of all her contemporaries, she is the most varied. Within the group where she is most often placed—George Washington Cable, Joel Chandler Harris, Thomas Nelson Page, Mary Noailles Murfree, Kate Chopin—perhaps only Cable and Chopin are truly more interesting writers. Historians, however, must do more than read the works of Sherwood Bonner now in print (such a great portion being hackwork); they must also look at those works that have lain on musty shelves for a century now. When they do, they will acknowledge the merit of *Like unto Like*, *The Valcours*, and a handful of short stories; and they will give Sherwood Bonner her rightful place in literary history. Twenty years before Kate Chopin wrote so powerfully of a woman's search for her self, in *Like unto Like* Sherwood Bonner had explored another southern woman's awakening. Decades before Ellen Glasgow declared that what southern literature needed above all was "blood and irony," in her best work Sherwood Bonner had given it just that.

For all the undeserved neglect of her fiction, however, it is significant that what has kept her name even so faintly alive is her life and personality. Despite the suppression of facts and evidence, despite the often lifeless academic treatment accorded Sherwood Bonner, the outlines of her life have retained haunting suggestions of the force of personality that drew so many to her in life. And even when her true literary achievement has been acknowledged, it

19. The most valuable study of Sherwood Bonner published in recent years is Louis J. Budd's informed biographical and critical sketch in *Notable American Women, 1607–1950: A Biographical Dictionary* (Cambridge, Mass.: Harvard University Press, 1971), II, 461–62. Many of the other studies are filled with errors.

will still be her life that has the greater fascination. To borrow an image from *The Valcours*: the face peering out through time will always be essentially that of the woman, not the writer. One can only hope that for the readers of this biography that face will seem less enigmatic than it has for almost a century.

The Works of Katharine Sherwood Bonner McDowell

IN ASSEMBLING THIS bibliography, I was grateful for the work of two earlier scholars. In her thesis "Life and Works of Sherwood Bonner" (George Washington University, 1930), Dorothy L. Gilligan made the first effort to compile a comprehensive list of the author's publications. In the essay "Sherwood Bonner: A Bibliography of Primary and Secondary Materials," *American Literary Realism, 1870–1910*, V (Winter, 1972), 39–60, Jean Nosser Biglane expanded considerably Gilligan's list. I have corrected occasional errors and added a number of entries to the Biglane bibliography.

Though Katharine Sherwood Bonner McDowell published most of her work under the name Sherwood Bonner, some of her writings appeared under other names, and some appeared anonymously. For the signature "Sherwood Bonner," I use simply a dash. In the other cases, I give full information.

BOOKS

————. *Like unto Like*. New York: Harper & Brothers, 1878. Published in England as *Blythe Herndon* (London: Ward, Lock, & Co., 1882), appearing in the same volume with *Janetta* by Julia Chandler. Excerpts from *Like unto Like* have appeared in anthologies under the following titles: "Yariba" in *Library of Southern Literature*, ed. Edwin Anderson Alderman and Joel Chandler Harris (Atlanta: Martin & Hoyt, 1907), I, 461–62; and "Decoration Day" in *In Dixie Land: Stories of the Reconstruction Era by Southern Writers*, ed. Henrietta Raymer Palmer (New York: Purdy Press, 1926), 27–33.

————. *Dialect Tales*. New York: Harper & Brothers, 1883. Reissued by the Books for Libraries Press (Freeport, New York), 1972.

————. *Suwanee River Tales*. Boston: Roberts Brothers, 1884. Reissued by the Books for Libraries Press (Freeport, New York), 1972.

————. *Gran'mammy: Little Classics of the South, Mississippi*. New

York: Purdy Press, 1927. Published with *A Trip Through the Piney Woods* by J. F. H. Claiborne. Reissued by Harbor Press (New York), n.d.

PAMPHLETS

————. *The Radical Club: A Poem, Respectfully Dedicated to "The Infinite" by "An Atom."* Boston: The Times Publishing Company, 1876.
————. *A Chapter in the History of the Epidemic of 1878.* McComb City, Miss.: Press of the McComb City *Weekly Intelligencer,* 1879.

PERIODICAL CONTRIBUTIONS

Clayton Vaughn. "Laura Capello: A Leaf from a Traveller's Note Book," *Massachusetts Ploughman and New England Journal of Agriculture,* February 20, 1869, p. 4.
Anonymous. "The Heir of Delmont," *Massachusetts Ploughman and New England Journal of Agriculture,* August 28, 1869, p. 4, and September 4, 1869, p. 4.
Anonymous. "Saved," *Massachusetts Ploughman and New England Journal of Agriculture,* October 9, 1869, p. 4.
Katharine McDowell. "From the 'Hub': A Southern Girl's Experience of Life in New England," Memphis *Avalanche,* March 15, 1874, p. 2.
Katharine McDowell. "The Hub's Good Side: Ralph Waldo Emerson Interviewed by a Fair Southron," Memphis *Avalanche,* April 12, 1874, p. 2.
Kate McDowell. "From the 'Hub': A Personal Chapter on Sumner, Schurz, Wendell Phillips, Garrison, Oliver Wendell Holmes and Others," Memphis *Avalanche,* May 17, 1874, p. 2.
————. "Dr. J. G. Holland," *Cottage Hearth,* II (January, 1875), 1–2.
————. "Mary Clemmer," *Cottage Hearth,* II (February, 1875), 29–30.
————. "Julia Ward Howe," *Cottage Hearth,* II (April, 1875), 85–86.
————. "The Big Celebration: An Avalanche Correspondent's Impressions of the Lexington-Concord Centennial," Memphis *Avalanche,* May 4, 1875, p. 2.
Anonymous. "The Radical Club: A Poem, Respectfully Dedicated to 'The Infinite' by 'An Atom,'" Boston *Times,* May 8, 1875. Published as a pamphlet by Sherwood Bonner in 1876 (see Pamphlets). Excerpts have appeared in Kate Sanborn, *The Wit of Women* (New York: Funk & Wagnalls, 1885), 97–100; and in Wade Hall, *The Smiling Phoenix: Southern Humor from 1865 to 1914* (Gainesville: University of Florida Press, 1965), 342.
————. "Wendell Phillips: Interviewed by a Southern Girl," Memphis *Avalanche,* May 30, 1875, p. 2.

————. "Boston's Centennial: A Southern Woman's Description of the Celebration at Bunker Hill," Memphis *Avalanche*, June 30, 1875, p. 2.

————. "Gran'mammy's Last Gift," *Youth's Companion*, XLVIII (July 29, 1875), 237–38. Revised and reprinted as "Gran'mammy's Last Gifts" in *Suwanee River Tales*. An excerpt from the latter version appears in *Library of Southern Literature* (1907), I, 450–52.

————. "Miss Willard's Two Rings," *Lippincott's*, XVI (December, 1875), 754–61.

————. "Sherwood Bonner's Letter: Longfellow's Home—Its History," Memphis *Avalanche*, December 26, 1875, p. 2. Excerpts appear in *Poets' Homes*, ed. R. H. Stoddard, *et al.* (Boston: D. Lothrop, 1877).

————. "Gran'mammy's Story," *Youth's Companion*, XLIX (January 6, 1876), 1–2. Revised and reprinted in *Suwanee River Tales* and in *Gran'mammy* as "The Night the Stars Fell."

————. "Which Was the Heroine?" *Cottage Hearth*, III (January, 1876), 24–25, (February, 1876), 52–53, (March, 1876), 80–81.

————. "Journey Across the Atlantic," Boston *Times*, February 27, 1876, and as "'Sherwood Bonner': An Avalanche Correspondent's Voyage Across the Atlantic," Memphis *Avalanche*, February 27, 1876, p. 2.

————. "First Impressions of Life in London," Boston *Times*, March 12, 1876, and as "'Sherwood Bonner': A Southern Woman's Impressions of England and the English," Memphis *Avalanche*, March 15, 1876, p. 2.

————. "From London to Rome," Boston *Times*, March 26, 1876, and as "'Sherwood Bonner': A Southern Woman's Trip from London to Rome," Memphis *Avalanche*, March 26, 1876, p. 1.

————. "Rome's Carnival," Boston *Times*, April 9, 1876, and as "Rome's Carnival: 'Sherwood Bonner's' Description of Carnival Week in the Eternal City," Memphis *Avalanche*, April 9, 1876, p. 2.

————. "Interview with the Pope," Boston *Times*, April 30, 1876, and as "'Sherwood Bonner': An Avalanche Correspondent's Visit to the Pope," Memphis *Avalanche*, April 30, 1876, p. 2.

————. "Social Life in Rome," Boston *Times*, May 14, 1876, and as "'Sherwood Bonner': A Picture of Social Life in the Eternal City," Memphis *Avalanche*, May 14, 1876, p. 2.

————. "Visit to Garibaldi," Boston *Times*, May 28, 1876, and as "'Sherwood Bonner': A Charming Web of Italian Gossip," Memphis *Avalanche*, May 28, 1876, p. 2.

————. "Farewell Notes on the Sacred City," Boston *Times*, June 11, 1876, and as "Our Letter from Rome: Peculiarities of Sight Seers—Farewell Visits," Memphis *Avalanche*, June 18, 1876, p. 2.

————. "Florence and the Florentines," Boston *Times*, June 16, 1876, and as "Beautiful Florence: The Art Galleries of the Birthplace of Michael Angelo," Memphis *Avalanche*, July 9, 1876, p. 2.

————. "Romance of Life in Venice," Boston *Times*, August 6, 1876, and as "At Venice: Sherwood Bonner Visits the 'Bride of the Sea,' and Is Happy," Memphis *Avalanche*, August 6, 1876, p. 2.

————. "Leading Theatres of the World," Boston *Times*, September 24, 1876.

————. "Sherwood Bonner: How She Is Seeing Paris," Boston *Times*, September 27, 1876.

————. "From '60 to '65," *Lippincott's*, XVIII (October, 1876), 500–509.

————. "After Thoughts," Boston *Times*, October 29, 1876.

————. "Rosine's Story," *Youth's Companion*, XLIX (December 14, 1876), 421–22. Reprinted in *Suwanee River Tales*.

————. "Louise Chandler Moulton," *Cottage Hearth*, IV (January, 1877), 1–2.

————. "Léonie," *Youth's Companion*, L (February 8, 1877), 42–43. Reprinted in *Suwanee River Tales*.

A Citizen of Holly Springs. "Mrs. Meriwether's Lecture at Holly Springs," Memphis *Avalanche*, March 18, 1877, p. 2.

————. "Breaking the News," *Youth's Companion*, L (December 27, 1877), 441–42. Revised and reprinted as "How Gran'mammy Broke the News" in *Suwanee River Tales*.

————. "In Aunt Mely's Cabin," *Lippincott's*, XXI (February, 1878), 245–50. Reprinted in *Dialect Tales*.

————. "Dear Eyelashes," *Youth's Companion*, LI (March 7, 1878), 74–75. Reprinted in *Suwanee River Tales*.

————. "C. G.; or, Lilly's Earrings," *Lippincott's*, XXII (September, 1878), 362–73. Reprinted in *Suwanee River Tales*.

————. "The Modjeska: Sherwood Bonner's Impressions of the Great Artist," Memphis *Avalanche*, February 9, 1879, p. 4.

————. "Modjeska" [poem], Memphis *Avalanche*, February 14, 1879, p. 4. Reprinted as "To Modjeska in the South," *Harper's Weekly*, March 23, 1879, p. 230.

————. "The Yellow Plague of '78: A Record of Horror and Heroism," *Youth's Companion*, LII (April 3, 1879), 117–19. This is a revision of *A Chapter in the History of the Epidemic of 1878* (see Pamphlets).

————. "The Terrible Adventures of Ourselves and the Marshall," *St. Nicholas*, VI (May, 1879), 456–59.

————. "Maddy Gascar and the Professor," *Harper's Weekly*, October 18, 1879, pp. 831–32. Reprinted in *Suwanee River Tales*.

————. "The Revolution in the Life of Mr. Balingall," *Harper's*, LIX (October, 1879), 753–63.

————. "Lost and Found," *Youth's Companion*, LII (November 6, 1879), 389–90. Reprinted in *Hours at Home: A Journal of Literature, Ro-*

mance, and Information, III (July, 1894), 1–2. Reprinted as "The Finding of Absalom" in *Suwanee River Tales*.

———. "Mars' Colton's Lesson," *Youth's Companion*, LIII (March 11, 1880), 81–82. Reprinted in *Suwanee River Tales*.

———. "A Volcanic Interlude," *Lippincott's*, XXV (April, 1880), 452–59. Reprinted in *The Local Colorists: American Short Stories, 1857–1900*, ed. Claude M. Simpson (New York: Harper & Brothers, 1960), 290–303; and in *Nineteenth-Century American Short Fiction*, ed. William Holmes and Edward Mitchell (Glenview, Ill.: Scott, Foresman, & Co., 1970), 287–96.

———. "Hieronymus Pop and the Baby," *Harper's*, LXI (June, 1880), 20–24. Reprinted in *Dialect Tales*; in *Humorous Masterpieces from American Literature*, ed. Edward T. Mason (New York: Putnam's, 1886), III, 268–79; and in *Library of Southern Literature* (1907), I, 452–57.

———. A Page of Poems, *Harper's Young People*, September 7, 1880, p. 661.

———. "Why Gran'mammy Didn't Like Pound-Cake," *Wide Awake Pleasure Book*, II (September, 1880), 171–73. Reprinted in *Suwanee River Tales* and in *Gran'mammy*.

———. A Page of Poems, *Harper's Young People*, October 12, 1880, p. 741.

———. "The Angel in the Lilly Family," *Harper's Young People*, October 19, 1880, pp. 756–57.

———. "Dr. Jex's Predicament," *Harper's Weekly*, December 18, 1880, pp. 816–17. Reprinted in *Dialect Tales*.

———. "Jack and the Mountain Pink," *Harper's Weekly*, January 29, 1881, pp. 75–76. Reprinted in *Dialect Tales* and in *Southern Prose Writers*, ed. Gregory Paine (New York: American Book Company, 1947), 282–92.

———. "The Case of Eliza Bleylock," *Harper's Weekly*, March 5, 1881, pp. 155–56. Reprinted in *Dialect Tales*.

———. "Sister Weeden's Prayer," *Lippincott's*, n.s., I (April, 1881), 399–404. Reprinted in *Dialect Tales*.

———. "Two Storms," *Harper's*, LXII (April, 1881), 728–48. An excerpt is reprinted as "The Hoodoo Dance" in *Library of Southern Literature* (1907), I, 458–61.

———. "Lame Jerry," *Harper's Weekly*, May 28, 1881, p. 346. Reprinted in *Dialect Tales*.

Bohemian. "In Memoriam: Howard Falconer" [poem], Holly Springs *Reporter*, July 7, 1881, p. 3.

———. *The Valcours*, in *Lippincott's*, n.s., II (September, 1881), 243–58; (October, 1881), 345–61; (November, 1881), 444–62; (December, 1881), 555–70.

———. "The Bran Dance at the Apple Settlement," *Harper's Weekly*, November 19, 1881, pp. 779–80. Reprinted in *Dialect Tales* and in *Southern Prose Writers* (1947), 276–282.

———. "With Her Picture" [poem], *Our Continent*, I (April 12, 1882), 138.

———. "Peacock Feathers," *Harper's Weekly*, April 29, 1882, pp. 266–67. Reprinted in *Suwanee River Tales*.

———. "On the Nine-Mile," *Harper's*, LXIV (May, 1882), 918–28. Reprinted in *Dialect Tales*.

———. "Aunt Anniky's Teeth," *Harper's Weekly*, June 3, 1882, pp. 347–48. Reprinted in *Dialect Tales* and in *The Wit of Women* (1885), 85–96.

———. "Tobey's Fortune," *Our Continent*, II (August 9, 1882), 134–36. Reprinted in *Suwanee River Tales*.

———. "A Shorn Lamb," *Harper's Weekly*, August 26, 1882, pp. 539–40. Reprinted in *Suwanee River Tales*.

———. "The Gentlemen of Sarsar," *Harper's Weekly*, December 16, 1882, pp. 802–804. Reprinted in *Dialect Tales*.

———. "Two Smiles" [poem], *Harper's Weekly*, July 21, 1883, p. 458.

———. "Despondency" [poem], *Harper's Weekly*, August 18, 1883, p. 518.

———. "Christmas Eve at Tuckeyhoe," *Lippincott's*, n.s., VII (January, 1884), 51–65.

———. "The Tender Conscience of Mr. Bobberts," *Harper's Weekly*, March 22, 1884, pp. 190–92.

———. "Coming Home to Roost," *Harper's Weekly*, May 17, 1884, pp. 318–19. Reprinted in *Suwanee River Tales*. An excerpt is reprinted as "Aunt Becky Kunjured" in *A Library of American Literature: From the Earliest Settlement to the Present Time*, ed. Edmund Clarence Stedman and Ellen Mackay Hutchinson (New York: C. L. Webster, 1891), X, 523–28.

———. "A Longed For Valentine" [poem], *Publications of the Mississippi Historical Society*, II (1899), 54. Reprinted in *Library of Southern Literature* (1907), I, 443; in *Southern Writers: Biographical and Critical Studies*, ed. William Malone Baskerville (Nashville and Dallas: Publishing House of the Methodist Episcopal Church, South, 1911), 109–110; and in *The Mississippi Poets*, ed. Ernestine Clayton Deavours (Memphis: E. H. Clarke, 1922), 36.

OTHER POSSIBLE PUBLICATIONS

"Maniac" and two poems may have appeared in the Mobile *Times* in the early months of 1869. "An Exposition on One of the Commandments" was perhaps published in one of the Frank Leslie journals during the period 1869–1875. "A Flower of the South" evidently appeared in a musical journal during that time. Two short stories that were included in the collection *Suwanee River Tales* (1884)—"The Crest of the White Hat" and "The End of the Dancing School at Danville"—had no doubt been published earlier in periodicals.

Index